❀ ❀ ❀ BLACK ROBES AND BUCKSKIN

BLACK ROBES & BUCKSKIN

A Selection from
the Jesuit *Relations*

CATHARINE RANDALL

FORDHAM UNIVERSITY PRESS
NEW YORK   2011

Images from *Indian Good Book* by Eugene Vetromile S.J., 1856 (Plates 6a, 6b, 7a, 7b, 7c, 10, 16, and 17) courtesy of Archives & Special Collections, Walsh Library, Bronx, New York.

Images from *Vita beati P. Ignatii Loiolae Societatis Iesu fundatoris* engravings by Cornelis Galle, 1609 (Plates 1, 2a, 2b, 4, 8, 9, 14, 15, 18) courtesy of Archives & Special Collections, Walsh Library, Bronx, New York.

Plates 3, 5, 11, 12, and 13 are from James Douglas, LL.D., *New England New France: Contrasts and Parallels in Colonial History* (Toronto: William Briggs/ New York: G. P. Putnam's Sons, 1913).

Fordham University Press has no responsibility for the persistence or accuracy of URLs for external or third-party Internet websites referred to in this publication and does not guarantee that any content on such websites is, or will remain, accurate or appropriate.

Fordham University Press also publishes its books in a variety of electronic formats. Some content that appears in print may not be available in electronic books.

Library of Congress Cataloging-in-Publication Data

Black robes and buckskin : a selection from the Jesuit relations / [compiled by] Catharine Randall.
    p.   cm.
  Includes bibliographical references (p.).
  ISBN 978-0-8232-3262-8 (cloth : alk. paper)
    1. Jesuits—Missions—New France—History.   2. Indians of North America—Missions—New France—History.   3. Canada—History—To 1763 (New France)   I. Randall, Catharine, 1957–
F1030.8.B57 2010
971.01′1—dc22

2010044383

Printed in the United States of America

13 12 11 5 4 3 2 1

First edition

CONTENTS

Preface   vii

In spiritu sanctu: Inculturation and the Aboriginal
Relations   1

Cura personalis: Recognizing Christ in the Other   19

Imago Dei: "Finding God in All Things"   37

"We [Engage Them] in Devout Conversations"   57

"The World Is Our Church"   73

"Friends in the Lord"   95

Ad Maiorem Dei Gloriam: To the Greater Glory
of God   117

Familiariter: The Theological Sense of Daily Life   131

Spiritu, Corde: Practice, Heart, Soul, and Worship   159

Conclusion: Inculturation Assessed   181

Appendix. Cathedrals of Ice: Translating
the Jesuit Vocabulary of Conversion   185

Bibliography   209

Illustrations follow page 116

Several years ago, on the occasion of the 200th anniversary of the founding of Fordham University, Father Joseph McShane, S.J., president of
the university, suggested to the Board of Directors of Fordham University Press that a special selection of some of the letters composing the
Jesuit *Relations* be printed. This document is a foundational text for
French Canada—indeed, for North America—and an extremely important source of ethnographic, anthropological, and theological information concerning both the Society of Jesus in the New World and the
indigenous peoples whom the Jesuits sought to convert to Christianity.
Although many editions of the Jesuit *Relations* exist, and although
various selections of some of the letters have been issued, the intent of
this project is to provide modern, contemporary-feeling translations—
or, rather, paraphrases—that would be readable, and, perhaps, to some
readers, inspiring. The goal was to reinstate correspondence in its ver-
nacular, natural, conversationally compelling tenor.

Basing the paraphrases on Reuben Gold Thwaites's compendious
collection of the *Relations*—*The Jesuit Relations and Allied Documents:
Travels and Explorations of the Jesuit Missionaries in New France, 1610–
1791* (originally published in Cleveland in 1898 and now available in CD
form and online as *Jesuit Relations, volumes 1–73*)—we brought together

a sampling of well-known letters along with some that have only rarely, or not at all, been translated.

Hoping to avoid the occasionally off-putting (for a general audience) scholarly weight of footnotes, we simply began each paraphrase with a brief description of the letter and the context in which it was penned. The paraphrases taken together compose a prose narrative representing the dialogue of inculturation that took place among Jesuit missionaries, their helpers (such as women religious, lay workers, and so on), and Native American peoples in French Canada. This inculturation demonstrates an adaptive departure from Jesuit practice and an extreme flexibility and sensitivity in their re-fitting of Ignatian principles to the dramatically new climate in which they found themselves.

As Ignatius said, "*multiplex est modus tradendi Exercitia*"—and never were the *Spiritual Exercises*, that manual penned for the formation of young Jesuits by Ignatius himself, put to such effect! The "*eloquentia perfecta*" of Jesuit training in rhetoric, so as to be effective in saving souls, was sorely tested in the New World, for example, as the Jesuit fathers did not initially speak a word of the native tongues. How were they to render abstract theological concepts or religious doctrine and liturgy into terms understandable to their interlocutors? We see the Jesuits striving to make sense of native belief in witchcraft and sorcery, dealing with a very non-European model of how women should be treated, struggling to convince Indians that a settlement was more beneficial than their traditional nomadic life . . . and all these daily-life factors were then framed within the drama of sin and salvation. A tall order to fill, but the Jesuits fit the bill.

Always mindful to discern and preserve the "*imago dei*" in every Native American, seeking to initiate "devout conversations," as Ignatius had prescribed, with those whom they met, "prepared to die for Christ," these "soldiers of God" sought to "find God in all things." A Society rather than an order, they consequently had no "mother house," no fixed dwelling, but rather viewed the entire "world [a]s our house." They communicated "*pietas*," ultimately, most effectively through "the language of the heart": by living among and helping—nursing, feeding, tending, teaching—the various tribes in the New World; "going in by their door," as they put it, "to come out by ours," they succeeded in converting many to their faith and in placing their indelible mark on North America.

I owe a great deal to Father McShane, who proposed this project and who, it is my sincere hope, will be pleased with what we have brought to fruition; to Patrice Kane, the helpful archivist of Walsh Library, Fordham University, for helping to find images for this volume (most of which are owned by Special Collections at Walsh Library); to Dr. Fred Harris, colleague and ever-stimulating interlocutor, who first proposed me as the one best suited to pursue this endeavor; and to Helen Tartar, editorial director of Fordham University Press, for her time and thoughtful care in superintending this book.

Catharine Randall
(the Reverend Dr.)
Professor of French
Woodbury, CT
October 2010

BLACK ROBES AND BUCKSKIN

IN SPIRITU SANCTU: INCULTURATION AND THE ABORIGINAL *RELATIONS*

> He who only sees New France through the eyes of flesh and
> of nature, will only see woods and crosses; but if he then looks
> at this through the eyes of faith and a strong calling, he will
> see only God, virtue and grace; he will perceive such consola-
> tions, that, were I able to give all of Paradise in exchange for
> New France, I would do it.[1]

In the late sixteenth century, the essayist and political functionary Michel de Montaigne wrote an essay about a French exploration party to the New World, and the people they encountered. The essay, entitled *"Des cannibales"* ("Concerning Cannibals"), earned him recognition and praise as one of the first cultural or moral relativists of the Early Modern era. In his essay Montaigne argued that many of the practices of this reportedly cannibalistic society into which purportedly cultured Frenchmen had stepped were in fact much more civilized and humane than some European customs. At the end of the essay, Montaigne feigned overhearing a European observer (and by extension the reader) who, in response to Montaigne's argument, would raise an eyebrow and exclaim, "Not at all bad, that.—Ah! But they wear no breeches . . ."[2] This ironic

---

1. *"Qui ne void la Nouvelle France que par les yeux de chair et de nature, il n'y void que des bois et des croix; mais qui les considère avec les yeux de la grace et d'une bonne vocation, il n'y void que Dieu, les vertus et les graces, et on y trouve tant et de si solides consolations, que si je pouvois acheter la Nouvelle France, en donnant tout le Paradis Terrestre, certainement je l'acheterois."* (*Relation*, 1635)

2. Michel de Montaigne, "On the Cannibals," *Essays*, trans. Michael Screech (London: Penguin, 1991), 92. The original reads, *"Mais quoy! Ils ne portent point de hauts de chausses!"* (But, hold on here! They don't wear pants!)

twist at the end of the essay indicts the European observer as more concerned with appearances than reality, with façade than inner being, with ornamentation than with right behavior.

Discerning the Barbarian's Breeches

A half century after the publication of "*Des cannibales*," when the first Jesuits arrived in New France (*la nouvelle France* as French Canada was known at the time), they came with the usual European mind-set: to bring Christ to the natives, shape them up, and provide them with the benefits of civilization. Only a few years later, in the letters they wrote home (called *relations*), these Jesuits were admitting that the Native Americans possessed virtues of which they had been unaware, and that the two cultures shared some similarities in their worldviews that might allow for the translation of concepts necessary to the success of the Jesuits' spiritual enterprise in New France. The Jesuits learned to respect the natives, rather than condescend to them, and they wanted to convince other Europeans of the merits of their encounters. The Jesuits had begun to discern that these "barbarians" might just wear their own sort of breeches.

The voices of these "barbarians" have been silenced by historical circumstances. Most of them were illiterate, and therefore unable to leave written accounts of themselves. Yet we are not reduced to reasoning from absences, because of field letters the Jesuits wrote home which were publicized as the Jesuit *Relations*. The *Relations*—and other, lesser known, writings—are filled with references to natives, their helpful and heroic acts, how they responded to Christianity, how they assisted the Jesuits, and what characterized their piety before and after baptism. These references assist us in creating a composite portrait of native responses to, and a retrieval of their experiences with, the Jesuits in the New World. Although this way of listening is, of necessity, limited, we sometimes hear a call-and-response: the native stance spurs a change, or reaction, on the part of their European interlocutor as well. In a lovely historical irony, the Jesuits, who relied on natives, especially native women, to be their interpreters, in the *Relations* themselves become the translators for those otherwise silenced native voices. We hear the voices of aboriginal people as these are translated from one language to another and then written down by the Jesuits. The natives are not present in any immediate way, but rather are mediated to us. But that's better than nothing, and often the Jesuits' recollections of the natives' statements are, as best as we can discern, faithfully and compellingly articulated. The Jesuits become the medium through which native voices can speak again. And the collection that the present-day reader holds offers a new version that is accessible to lay people and scholars alike who wish to hear those voices. We experience the native mind-set, as it were, in a form of palimpsest: like a watermark on fine paper, their perspective lies beneath the surface of the Jesuits' words. Yet those words are usually sympathetic, and do observe contemporary standards for exactitude in transcription. As we read, we hold the two in creative tension (much as missionaries read the Christian Word in a context alien to it, and hope to find points of contact and acceptance).

The Jesuits were not moral or cultural relativists (and neither was Montaigne). They were people of their day and age, and, even more significant, they were the spiritual progeny of Ignatius Loyola and his ideology. They continued to operate out of that set of assumptions. But they adapted their attitude and approach to their new environment and became more flexible, epitomizing a form of inculturation in which they lived alongside and, at times, even in the same dwelling with their potential converts; and, while teaching them, they also learned from them. Inculturation is the adaptation or transformation of Christian liturgical expressions and the gospel message under new or changing cultural conditions. Inculturation implements a *modus operandi* that operates from the good-will assumption that local forms of approaching God may all be acceptable, and even necessary, so long as the presence of a transcendent God operating within these local forms and their interpretation and adaptation is acknowledged.[3]

The Ignatian *mentalité* in some respects facilitated this more congenial approach of inculturation. Ignatius was fond of calling the members of the Society of Jesus "vicars of the mild Christ,"[4] coaching them to

3. Jeffers Engelhardt, "Inculturation: Genealogies, Meanings and Musical Dynamics," *Yale Institute of Sacred Music*, vol. 3 (autumn 2006): 1.
4. John O'Malley, *The First Jesuits* (Cambridge, Mass.: Harvard University Press, 1991), 142.

"find God in all things,"[5] and encouraging them to be, with every person, "friends in the Lord."[6] Since the story of Ignatius was intended to be the prototype for the life of every Jesuit, Ignatian spirituality had a significant influence on how Jesuits preached, witnessed, cared for the sick, catechized, baptized, performed last rites, and dedicated their lives to Christ and to the Christ they sought to discern in the *other*.

The Ninth Part of the *Constitutions* (1559) of the Society of Jesus contains a list that expresses the vision that Ignatius and Jerome Nadal and the early members of the Society hoped would be incarnated in subsequent members of the Society of Jesus.

> The list can be taken as an idealized profile of what Ignatius hoped every Jesuit would be—prayerful, virtuous, compassionate but firm, magnanimous and courageous, not without learning, unswervingly committed to the Society and its goals, a person of sound judgment. This last quality . . . conformed to what was required by one of the principal characteristics of Jesuit ministry: that it accommodate to circumstances and to the particular needs and situation of the persons to whom the Jesuits ministered.[7]

"The World Is Our Church": Ignatius, the Jesuits, and Mission

When a young Spanish nobleman, wounded in battle, was laid up for months recuperating, he set his mind and his will to coming into closer relationship with Christ. Out of that sickbed conversion and disciplined series of contemplations came the classic known as *The Spiritual Exercises,* as well as the influential, at times controversial, and highly effective missionary Society of Jesus, the Jesuits. Ignatius Loyola (1491–1556) structured the Society on a military hierarchy, requiring deep commitment and obedience, a chain of command that reached all the way up to Christ, and a passionate life-long involvement of those who became members. He did not create an order, but rather a society, the difference being that orders had set places to house them and specific churches in which to preach and celebrate. At its inception, the Society of Jesus was

5.   Ibid., 46.
6.   Ibid., 32.
7.   Ibid., 81.

formed as a mobile corps fighting for Christ in mission fields far-flung around the globe; it was only later in its history that, under pressure from the Pope, it gradually became more institutionalized, beginning with the establishment of colleges and seminaries and later with designated churches. Ignatius pronounced, "the world is our church," and he intended that Jesuits be ready at any time and in any place to defend Christ and the Pope.

The Jesuits became the most effective proselytizing arm of the Catholic Reformation. They gained the confidence of many high-placed nobles, including Louis XIV, and set the tone for baroque Catholic piety through the seventeenth century. The Jesuit mission to French Canada took place during the heyday of the Society of Jesus. However, the mission posed challenges and setbacks not foreseen by the founder and without parallel in the history of prior Jesuit missions, such as the highly successful mission of Matteo Ricci to China. French Canada, with its austere climate and vast and forbidding countryside, housed a native people that possessed a cultural integrity all its own, and this people, even though often grateful and welcoming, also frequently resisted missionary attempts. Jesuits like Jean de Brébeuf soon came to conceive of New France not solely as a mission field, but also as an arena for likely martyrdom. Self-sacrifice on a heroic scale was the hallmark of the Jesuit project in French Canada. In this awareness and willingness to persist despite great obstacles, the Jesuits were following the model that Ignatius had established for them:

> I must have as my aim the end for which I am created, which is the praise of God our Lord and the salvation of my soul. At the same time I must remain . . . free from any inordinate attachments . . . ready to follow the course which . . . is more for the glory and praise of God our Lord . . . I should make my choice in conformity with His good pleasure and His most holy will [and I also] will use my reason [to His glory].[8]

Because of the peculiar character of French Canada and its indigenous inhabitants, the Jesuits were obliged to be creative. Sometimes,

8. Ignatius Loyola, *The Spiritual Exercises of St. Ignatius,* trans. Anthony Mottola (New York: Doubleday, 1964), 85.

they had to give up a little of what they wanted, in order to coax the Native Americans along. They used the technique known as *syncretism*—the combining of an aspect of native belief with an aspect of the Christian faith, a form of translating in which a symbol or a metaphor makes a concept understandable to another culture. In this, they were following another of Ignatius's pronouncements; he was fond of a Spanish proverb that stated, "We go in by their door . . . so as to come out by *ours*." Such flexibility, a pragmatic strategy in which the end justified the means, and the willingness to accommodate another culture was unprecedented in European civilization at the time. Jesuits realistically rolled up the literal and figurative sleeves of their habits, acknowledging that "everything, of course, had to be adapted to the needs of time, place, and other circumstances."[9]

Sometimes this strategy of accommodation had a visual component. When Jesuits created pictures that Native Americans could understand and relate to, in order to describe saints' lives or to offer a model for an exemplary convert or to communicate a Bible story, they were also following in the footsteps of their founder. Ignatius's *Spiritual Exercises* were an intentional effort of focus and imagination, requiring the reader to visualize in highly personalized and dramatic, detailed ways, key episodes from the life of Christ, a sort of "you are there" approach. His technique consisted of seeing certain spiritual realities "with the mind's eye" and with "the entire being, both body and soul."[10] Such meditations produced "a mental picture of the place [where] we see in our imagination,"[11] "a mental representation [where we] will see"[12] spiritual realities projected onto the exotic landscape of French Canada.

The images accompanying this volume come from Jesuits who applied Ignatius's technique of creative and prayerful visualization of spiritual truths to their artistic endeavors. The excerpts from the *Relations* are illustrated with images drawn from a book of woodcuts that display similar themes or emphases, from a Native American prayer book produced for the Abenaki tribes (published in 1856, it is somewhat later

9. O'Malley, 85.
10. Loyola, 55.
11. Ibid., 68.
12. Ibid., 69.

than the texts we are referring to here, but it is similar to, and illustrative of, other such translation endeavors to foster piety), from period maps or renderings of mission sites, or from engravings that depict scenes from the life of Saint Ignatius possessing relevance to the events described in the letter.

These beautifully detailed and sensitively rendered drawings encourage the viewer to feel present at the scene, just as the evocative prose and dramatic stories contained in the *Relations* invite the reader to feel a part of the Jesuit mission. Their rich overlay of worldly data and visual documentation parallels the muscular, at times lyrical, prose of the Jesuit Fathers, appealing to the hearts and intellects of their readers to engage them in contributing to the Jesuit project.

The images from *The Indian Good Book* show side-by-side phonetic transcriptions of the Penobscot language along with its translation. They also include finely drawn miniatures, many of which feature Native American children worshiping, assisting a priest at the celebration of the Eucharist, telling the beads of their rosaries, or saying their evening prayers. The prayer book was used in personal devotions as well as in Native American group worship.

The majority of the illustrations in this volume come from the pictorial biography of Ignatius, *The Life of St. Ignatius Loyola* (1609) by Peter Pazmany (1570–1637). This Hungarian Jesuit, a convert from Protestantism, renowned as the founder of the first Hungarian university (a Jesuit university), a writer and preacher of note and eventually named Cardinal by Pope Paul V, commissioned the famous artist Peter Paul Rubens, a good friend and supporter of the Society of Jesus, to draft eighty illustrations to accompany the biography. Rubens agreed to help in this project, hoping that the volume would play a significant role in influencing Rome to canonize Ignatius. His illustrations illuminate certain aspects of Ignatian spirituality and its praxis as well as key episodes from the life of St. Ignatius. In this volume, they convey emphases typical of the Jesuit approach to missionary work in New France, such as the exorcizing of demons or aid given to suffering women. The images display visually the deep conviction and straightforward approach to proselytizing characteristic of the Society of Jesus.

The Indian Good Book, Life of Saint Ignatius, and the Dutch map that illustrates the front of this book (from the Bert Twaalfhoven Collection) are owned by the Fordham University Library and are features in its collection of Jesuit artifacts. Father Joseph McShane, president of Fordham University, conceived this project highlighting the Jesuit and Native American experience of inculturation in French Canada, and paved the way for these wonderful and rare images from the Archives and Special Collections to become part of this book.

In the present study, paraphrased excerpts from the *Relations* are grouped in clusters that orient the reader's attention to issues important to the Jesuits or to significant episodes in the history of the Jesuit mission in French Canada. The clusters exemplify such themes as "the world is our church," "spirituality, heart and practice," "*familiariter,* or the things of the world," the role of women, the differences between Protestant and Catholic proselytizing, and the self-giving martyrdom of Father Isaac Jogues. For example, Jesuits practiced the *cura personalis,* in which each person and each soul was recognized as distinct and different, responding to different messages, because Ignatius had recommended that:

> first one approach individuals with love and a desire for their well-being, while carefully observing each person's temperament and character. One began the conversation with subjects of interest to the other . . . exemplifying the cardinal rule of Jesuit ministry: that it be accommodated to the circumstances of the persons concerned.[13]

These clusters create a narrative that supports the actual historical facts with a spiritual orientation, that of Ignatius Loyola. In that way, the reader reads on several levels or with diverse perspectives, listening with her current presence to the reanimated voices of the past. The action of the Jesuits and the response of the natives, the reaction of the Jesuits to that response and the effect this interaction had on the historical audience and continues to have on today's reader, intertwine in the *Relations.* In this way, the clusters of excerpted *Relations* produce a religious, cultural, and literary multidimensionality.

Many of the thematic clusters derive their concentration or even their designation from phrases often heard from Ignatius Loyola's lips. Loyola spoke often of other foci that are implicitly present in the clusters,

13. O'Malley, 111–112.

such as *militare deo*, or being soldiers for Christ; the "language of the heart" which persuades more effectively than coercion; the *imago dei*, or the image of God, found in every living creature; *ad majorem Dei gloriam*, or to the greater glory of God, the animating force behind every Jesuit mission; the *cura personalis*, or the care for the individual soul, which is such a distinctive concern of the Society of Jesus; the "discernment of spirits," so crucial in assessing whether certain native practices were benign or hostile to the Christian faith; and *noster modus procedendi*, or the Jesuits' way of functioning, which Ignatius famously summed up in the statement, "*multiplex est modus tradendi Exercitia*"—"manifold are the ways to apply the *Exercises*."[14]

Relating the Relations: *A New Sort of Narrative, a New Kind of Mission*

The *Jesuit Relations*—a compendious corpus comprising seventy-three volumes of epistolary reports penned by various Jesuit *missionaires* in French Canada, which were then edited prior to publication under the imprimatur of their Superiors in Paris during the years 1632 to 1673—have made (and continue to make) a monumental contribution. During the years of their immediate influence, the *Relations* attested to the Jesuits' unparalleled eye for observation and detail, due to the Jesuits' near-total immersion in Native American cultures. The *Relations* also manifested the Jesuits' exceptional ability to communicate with their European audiences, and they were enormously effective in fund-raising propaganda campaigns intended to secure the success of the missions to Canada by eliciting contributions and support from well-heeled European sponsors of tender conscience. The letters also, on occasion, prompted new vocations, as was the case with the young Joseph Marie Chaumonot, who, shortly after being admitted to the novitiate, received Père Brébeuf's volumes about the mission in Quebec as a gift from a fellow Jesuit, and soon after left for Canada.

The *Relations* have proved to be a seminal influence not only on the history of French Canada (in this respect they are widely acknowledged

14. O'Malley, 127.

as reliable and trustworthy documents; they are deemed *textes fonda-teurs*) and its ethnography and anthropology (because of the Jesuits' systematic descriptions of lifestyles and lifeways throughout; Father Biard's narratives of Abenaki customs and Father De Quen's description of Iroquois customs are fine examples), but also on the fields of literature and of travel narratives. The *Relations* have evoked creative responses from a wide variety of authors such as the Native American novelist Louise Erdrich (*The Last Reports on the Miracles at Little No Horse*), Princeton academic Natalie Zemon Davis (*Women on the Margins*), many Canadian authors enumerated in Aurélien Boivin's encyclopedic compilation of French Canadian *contes* and *nouvelles*, as well as film makers such as Bruce Beresford (*Black Robe*) and Roland Joffe (*The Mission*). Both scholarly works and works of fiction generated by reference to the Jesuit *Relations* continue to magnify current popular understanding of the epic drama of colonization and "soul saving" during the early years of the settlement of *la nouvelle France*.

French Canada was occupied by numerous Amerindian tribes when Jacques Cartier took possession of the land in the name of François I of France in 1534. It is no coincidence that the Society of Jesus was founded by Ignatius of Loyola in 1534 and was established in France in 1540, roughly contemporary with the first French incursions into Canada; the Jesuits quickly grasped their moment—and it proved to be a historic moment of great scope indeed.

Cartier traversed the St. Lawrence River during the next two years, and then in 1605 Samuel de Champlain began to colonize Acadia with the establishment of a settlement at Port Royal. Interestingly, Samuel de Champlain may have had Protestant sympathies; although himself a Catholic, his wife was Huguenot (French Protestant). In 1608, the town of Quebec was founded, and one of the primary reasons for its establishment, other than to profit from fur trade, was to build a missionary outpost for the propagation of the Catholic faith. Subsequent patrons and charter-subscribers to the endeavor would prove to be ardent Catholics. The Cent-Associés, an organization created by Richelieu in 1627 to help populate Quebec, certainly understood their charge in light of a specifically Catholic initiative. Richelieu hoped to reverse some of the success of the Protestant "heresy" in France. In addition, the Compagnie of the Jesuits explicitly excluded Protestants and *Récollets*, a rival order to the Society of Jesus.

For several decades Jesuit rule prevailed in Quebec; the Society of Jesus effectively constituted the standard and arbiter for cases of law and order. In 1625, Quebec became the Jesuit headquarters in North America. The British expelled the Jesuits from Quebec during the years 1627 to 1629, but the Jesuits had firmly reestablished their sway by 1634. Although in 1663 Louis XIV reintegrated the colony into continental France proper by assuming legal jurisdiction, the Jesuit influence remained strong. In terms of his personal piety, Louis XIV was a staunch supporter of the Jesuits.

Although the first Jesuit fathers arrived essentially ignorant of the conditions and challenges awaiting them in this New World of forbidding climate and illiterate, unchurched people, they did not arrive without tools with which to commence their trade. As already mentioned, it seems more than likely that the well-crafted and rhetorically elegant manual of their founder, *The Spiritual Exercises*, had an impact on how the Jesuit missionaries shaped their rhetoric for their European audience. Following the lead of Ignatius Loyola, who stressed meditative contemplation in (often agonizing) detail on the wounds of Christ, for example, to visualize a way of actively glorifying God in one's own life, the writers of the *Relations* thus conformed to a classical—although stylistically at times somewhat baroque—model in their own epistles.

Another tool was what had been learned from previous Jesuit missionary experiences. For example, Matteo Ricci in China, and the Jesuit missionaries to Latin America established a pattern for action that included learning the indigenous languages so as to build interpretive bridges between the European and the native cultures and to forge apt terms for communicating abstract notions of doctrine (such as sin, salvation, or grace) in a new and alien context.

Further, the French model for colonization in general was one that favored *cohabitation*—unlike the English, rather than seek programmatically to impose Eurocentric cultural norms, the French concentrated on *living among* and coming to understand the idiom and lifeways of the native people. They did not seek to alter conditions through military domination or coercion. Rather, the Jesuits sought to woo minds and hearts. Allan Greer, in *The Jesuit Relations: Natives and Missionaries in*

Seventeenth-Century North America, has termed this approach a program of "directed assimilation" in which the Jesuits elected to recast native thinking and attitudes along the lines of Christian principles, which they sought to inculcate, often by example more than by precept. In this latter regard, the heroic deaths of the Jesuit martyrs did much to shape native opinion and favorable reception of Christian doctrine. Such "martyrdoms" also understandably became an important feature of the epistolary accounts sent back to Europe: Anne of Austria, for example, professed to find the report of Father Isaac Jogues's torture more compelling than any romance novel (at the time, a wildly popular genre). The accounts of the Jesuit martyrs in Canada became a literary subgenre; different from their models, European saints' lives such as the hagiographic *Légende dorée* of Jacob de Voragine, they illustrated the hardships and trials peculiar to the New World and Amerindian context and made the European audience aware of them.

When the first Jesuit father, Père Paul Lejeune, accompanied by some thirty lay workers (or *donnés*) arrived in Quebec in 1634, he began a school for the purposes of Christianizing the natives whom he found there in profusion. The tribes present in the area were numerous. They can be categorized into two groups. The first group, the Algonquian, tended to give the French a favorable reception. The Algonquian peoples, including subtribes such as the Montagnais and the Neutral Nation (or Tobacco People), were less established than the other group, and were primarily nomadic hunters and gatherers. The other group, the Iroquois, including the Five Nations of Mohawk, Oneida, Onandaga, Cayuga, and Seneca, were populous, well-settled with a stable agricultural economy, and very warlike. The Iroquois had an evolved system of government, a council of fifty sachems, which met regularly in the Onondaga valley to adjudicate issues for the nations.

The Jesuit Fathers adopted a two-pronged approach toward their missionary project. Some remained in the Quebec area, or around Trois-Rivières or Montreal, and attempted to preach to and live among the Algonquian and Montagnais peoples. Associated with the Montreal mission were the names of Jesuit Fathers Dauversière, D'Ailleboust, and Maisonneuve; the Abbé Olier; and two women important in the life of the mission—Mademoiselle Mance and Marguerite Bourgeoys—among others. In Tadoussac, another trading outpost, Jesuit Fathers De

Quen and Druillete labored among the Montagnais and the Abenaquis who frequented that region. Father Daniel was active around Trois-Rivières, while Garnier, Chabanel, Garreau, and Grelon worked in the St. Jean area. Other Jesuits voyaged deep into the wilderness areas of interior North America, working to convert the Hurons, who were important partners in the French fur-trading business, as well as potential new converts. Fathers Masse, Brébeuf and Lalemant initiated the mission to the Hurons. Fathers Jogues and Goupil led two missions to the Iroquois, and Fathers Bressani and Anne de Noüe were also active during the Iroquois-Algonquin War (1642). Beyond the scope of this volume, there were also mission bands sent to the Great Lakes region and, later, out into the American West.

A Spiritual Syncretism: Accepting the "Other" While Remaining the "Same"

The first Jesuit *relation* was penned in 1632. The first target of missionary activity was the Huron tribe in the area and then—due to the tribe's small size, location and relative lack of importance for the larger world of native politics becoming apparent—the Hurons farther out to the east of Lake Huron. Father Lejeune resolved to inhabit Native American camps with the goal of learning the native tongue. The Hurons helped the Jesuits by returning during subsequent years to Quebec to trade, taking the Jesuits with them to other trading outposts where new mission camps could be planted, and leading them from Trois-Rivières as far as Thunder Bay to establish a mission.

Huron acceptance of the Jesuit Fathers greatly abetted the mission project. Conversely, the Jesuits helped their plans to prosper by accommodating their aims to native standards: when the Fathers built a Huron mission house, they had it constructed entirely according to local building customs; however, although entirely native in appearance on the exterior, it was engineered inside according to the desiderata of the Fathers when they celebrated mass. In their attempt to win Native American souls, the Jesuit fathers also resorted to tactics typical of the baroque era in European worship—high drama and a reliance on imagery and statuary designed to appeal to the senses and elicit conversions.

This recourse to evocative imagery is not only characteristic of the directed piety of Ignatius Loyola, but of Catholic Reformation piety in general. Father Garnier, to this effect, commissioned an artist in France to paint for him a beardless Christ looking full-face with open eyes at the viewer, and rendered in the brightest possible colors—all criteria that, the Jesuits had learned, would appeal to their prospective native converts. The most telling detail of this painting is that Christ was depicted beardless, since Native Americans themselves were beardless and mocked the Europeans for their facial hair. Thus, the audience's receptivity was a primary factor in stipulating the sort of religious art to be produced.

Such a strategy of selective syncretism fostered cooperation while maintaining the *culte*'s integrity. During the late 1630s, Jesuit fathers built five chapels in Huron country and reaped a healthy harvest of converts due to their basically benign presence among them. By 1640, a significant Jesuit presence and concrete achievements could be witnessed, among them a *collège* in Quebec (begun as an attempt to teach three native boys to pray in Latin), the chapel of Notre-Dame des Anges, a mission house, a hospital, an Ursuline convent, and a coherent program of missionary activity.

However, tensions with the Iroquois were ever increasing. In 1642, the Iroquois launched a series of "mourning wars": implementing a plan to augment dwindling numbers, they either captured and adopted or captured and then killed members of other tribes. Missionary activity initially increased during times of terror, especially those caused by smallpox and other epidemics, when fearful natives requested the sacrament of baptism in a sort of "if . . . then" bet with perceived cosmic powers mediated by the Black Robes (the Native American term for the Jesuits); however, during the Iroquois wars conversions waned, and in the early 1650s, the Iroquois forced the Jesuit fathers to abandon their missions to the Huron for the time being. In 1640, Tadoussac was abandoned as a base of operations. Eventually, Sainte Marie was chosen as a central and neutral location from which to gain access to all Huron lands.

The Jesuits were joined in their missionary endeavors by other Europeans. Marie-Madeleine de la Peltrie, née Chauvigny (1603–71), heard Father Lejeune's call in his *relation* for someone to come to Canada to "teach God's Word to the little Indian children." Around the same time, Marie de l'Incarnation, née Guyard (1599–1672), had a dream in which an unknown lady came to her, accompanied by the apostles, and embraced her in a misty, mountainous landscape. Marie's Jesuit confessor interpreted the location as being that of Canada, and in 1639 she set sail with Madame de la Peltrie and some other Ursuline sisters and hospital nuns, intending to found a Hôtel-Dieu in Quebec. Next, a devout tax collector in Anjou, France, Jérôme le Royer de la Dauversière, heard an inner voice telling him to found an order of hospital nuns in Montreal. His initiative was original in that not only did he hope to minister to ailing natives, but he also twinned this goal with a program to convert their souls. Dauversière met up with Jean-Jacques Olier, a young priest in Paris who had received instructions from a similar voice in a dream to establish a society of priests at Montreal. It is surely no coincidence that both men had recently read copies of the Jesuit *Relations* (which, at the time, were written annually and appeared in print beginning in 1632). They joined forces and formed the Society of Notre-Dame de Montréal. Jeanne Mance, also inspired by her reading of the *Relations* and by the example of Madame de la Peltrie, took a vow of perpetual chastity in order to accompany them to Canada and be their housekeeper. She eventually took charge of the hospital at Ville Marie.

In the 1640s, renewed energies were directed toward Huron conversions. While heading for the Hurons at Trois-Rivières, however, Father Jogues, Goupil, and Couture were attacked by Iroquois. All three were tortured, and although Couture was subsequently adopted, Goupil was killed. (Couture was finally returned to the Jesuits after three years, during an amicable conference held among Jesuits, Montagnais, and Iroquois at Quebec.) Jogues remained among the Iroquois, baptizing and converting them, until he was eventually smuggled out to New York by Dutch fur traders. He returned to his native Brittany, where he wrote a lengthy account of his captivity published in the *Relations* of 1643. Like the written account of the trials of Mary Rowlandson analyzed in John Demos's *The Unredeemed Captive*, such narrations sponsored another literary subgenre, one recounting an experience of the forced adoption yet also of affection and nostalgia for one's captors. Such tales tinged with ambivalence helped European audiences to identify and, to some extent, empathize with the Amerinidan culture.

Along with the "captivity" genre, accounts circulated such as the tale of the extraordinary survival of an Algonquian woman called Marie who was captured by, but escaped from, hostile Mohawks in a grueling wilderness ordeal culminating in a near-death experience over rapids and her rescue, at which time she was found utterly naked and starving. This story was recounted by Marie de l'Incarnation in her contribution to the *Relations* of 1647. This was another note-worthy innovation of the *Relations*; the Jesuits allowed for an occasional female voice, were often collaborative with women, and actively solicited women writers for the *Relations*. Such narratives assisted European audiences in discerning "good" from "bad" natives and in adding nuance and complexity to the literature. For example, in *Women on the Margins*, Natalie Zemon Davis asserts that Marie de l'Incarnation tended to emphasize similarities between natives and Europeans rather than underscore differences.

The *Relations* abound with examples of the Jesuits thoughtfully trying to make sense of native—and of female—difference, rather than to elide it; often, they express admiration for how the natives act and then criticize European culture accordingly, and their inclusion of women is nearly always positive within the cultural and theological categories available to them. Further, it is not insignificant that Christianized Native Americans were granted the same rights and privileges as French citizens.[15]

Women, including native women, formerly marginalized in many respects by European mores, learned significant strategies for how to appropriate the Christian faith for themselves, and then how to apply and live that faith. It is even possible that the Jesuit attitude toward those women—both European and native, secular and religious—involved in the mission to French Canada shadowed forth a form of pre-Enlightenment parity between the sexes in terms of their ability to receive and know Christ, to embody Him to others, to serve Him in the world by preaching, praying, catechizing, teaching, nursing and converting. All these roles were essential to the New World endeavor; to neglect or devalue any one of them would be to prejudice the possible success of the entire venture.

15. Reuben Gold Thwaites, ed. *The Jesuit Relations and Allied Documents* (Cleveland: Burrows Bros. Co., 1896–1901), 4: 257–8.

By the late 1640s and early 1650s, the Jesuits could take stock, and have pride in their establishments at Quebec, Sillery, Trois-Rivières, Lake Huron, the St. Lawrence near the Baie des Chaleurs, and Tadoussac. Father Druillete headed down the Kennebec River to present-day Augusta, Maine, at the time an English trading post: the Jesuits had their eyes on Puritan New England as a potential mission field, and also hoped for reciprocal trade agreements and some military assistance with hostile tribes. Druillete's meeting with John Winslow and Governor Bradford, however, proved unsuccessful. A European-directed reorganization of the governing policies of French Canada culminated in 1645 with the Jesuits being placed in the somewhat surprising role of directors of a fur-trading concern, surely an unexpected part for a religious society to play.

During the late 1640s, the Huron nation began wasting away with a series of epidemics. This decimation, coupled with the effects of starvation and warfare, and all exacerbated by the complexity of political alliances and trade network between northeast natives and Europeans, created a climate ultimately unfavorable to Huron survival.

Father Ragueneau's writing on Huron attitudes toward disease is extensive and well documented. Although many Huron had been Christianized, in some places (such as the Mission of Ossossané, renamed La Conception by the Jesuits) with Christian converts outnumbering those who remained unchurched, Jesuits began frequently to complain of recidivism as the native culture exerted pressures against conversion. (It was Jesuit custom to rename native settlements with saints' names after the majority of the town had been converted. This custom made it easy to trace, even today, the Jesuits' itinerary of conversions across French Canada on a map.)

Numbers also dwindled drastically because of disease. By 1649, the Huron nation had effectively ceased to exist, with remnants being absorbed into other Native American groups such as the Wyandots (which remained Catholic), and approximately 300 being taken by the Jesuits to live at Quebec. With no nation remaining to which to proselytize, the Jesuits abandoned the mission at Sainte Marie along with some fifteen other towns.

A combination of factors ultimately resulted in the destruction of Huronia and the termination of the Jesuit mission there. The Iroquois waged a campaign aimed at exterminating the Huron so as to be able to take over their "middleman" function facilitating trade between First Nations to the north (the best quality furs were supplied by them) and Europeans. Prior to this time, the Huron people had been devastated by diseases brought over from Europe. After the war with the Iroquois routed the Huron from their villages, many died of starvation because they had no crops to harvest for food. Those Huron who survived joined other groups in the region or retreated with the Jesuits to a small settlement near Quebec. The mission to the Huron ended in this way.

The Jesuits next turned their efforts toward the Tobacco (Neutral) Nation, sending Grelon and Garneau to establish two missions at St. Jean and St. Matthias. During the 1650s, however, Iroquois ambitions became more pronounced and a series of wars ensued, hindering missionary activity. With the Huron now decimated, the Iroquois turned on the Neutral Nations, ultimately destroying them. With the fall of the Huron, the most propitious group from which Jesuits had been able to hope for conversions had disappeared. French Canada ceased to be a missionfield and became increasingly identified with its commercial interests. The next chapter in the Jesuit initiative would shift to the American West, the valleys of the Mississippi, and the Great Lakes—but that is another story.

CURA PERSONALIS: RECOGNIZING
CHRIST IN THE OTHER

The very first document published in the compilation of the Jesuit *Relations* was written by Marc Lescarbot, a lawyer, poet, and historian from Paris who some historians have identified as a French Protestant, or Huguenot. Lescarbot arrived at Port Royal in Acadia in 1606 aboard the ship *Jonas*. He had been invited to join two noblemen known to be sympathetic to the Protestant cause, Sieur de Monts and Baron de Poutrincourt. These two men had been granted a monopoly on the local fur trade, and they were hoping to found an agricultural colony in the New World.

De Monts and Poutrincourt were in charge of a considerable portion of Quebec. The King and Queen were concerned that conversion of the natives was not taking place, so de Monts and Poutrincourt tried to find a priest who could facilitate such conversions. They wanted a non-Jesuit priest, since French Protestants and the Jesuits were rivals and sharply opposed to each other's religious stances and methods. French Protestants, as well as the liberal *politiques* who sympathized with them and who favored *gallicain*, or home rule, government for France, suspected the Jesuits of *ultramontanisme*, or excessive political deference to the Pope. However, the political and religious climate in France was changing very much in favor of Catholicism. Jesuit influence over the King was growing and Protestantism was increasingly unpopular, to the point that the Governor of Quebec eventually began to expel all Protestants from the area and forbade them to trade in his province.

At the time Lescarbot wrote his letter, the Protestants were still trying to convince the King and Queen (to whom the first part of the letter is addressed) that a fair number of "Indians" had been converted to the Christian faith. Although Protestants were not allowed to proselytize the natives, they were permitted to minister to Huguenot colonists. Lescarbot's letter was an attempt to keep Jesuits out of French Canada by demonstrating that the process of converting the natives to Christianity was already underway through the ministry of secular priests, who were of neither the Jesuit nor Protestant faith. Lescarbot talks about how a secular priest named Messire Jessé Fléché converted a chief named Membertou and twenty other Micmac Indians.

Lescarbot was ultimately unsuccessful in his attempt—the Jesuits came to French Canada in large numbers and were well organized. The ways in which the Jesuit Fathers convinced Native Americans to convert to Christianity were very different from the ways in which Protestant ministers handled their ministry, or the ways in which they would have attempted to convert the natives, had they been allowed to do so. Lescarbot's letter helps us infer the model that Protestants employed for conversions and how it compares to the Jesuit model as it is revealed in the rest of the *Relations*.

Briefly put, the Jesuit model was one of *inculturation*, of living among the natives, getting to know them, teaching them but also learning from them—especially their languages—and not attempting to impose Catholic or French norms (or, in cases where they did, first weighing the pros and cons, the effects that changes—such as persuading nomadic tribes to live in settlements—might bring, and preparing for those needs). Instead, the Jesuits hoped to persuade by example and by the compassionate witness of self-sacrifice. The Protestant approach was more directive, and more verbal: they relied on lots of preaching from Scripture, citing chapter and verse, and they believed that the natives were "creatures of the Fall" who needed to be saved willy-nilly and, perhaps, despite themselves. One reason why the Protestant model was not as successful was the failure of the French Protestant colonists to commit themselves fully to the project and to a life in French Canada:

they never really came to see the place as their home, but instead worked as employees of a profit-oriented fur-trading concern. Although the first contract of the French Jesuits in America has to do with the fur trade, it is clear that commerce was not their first concern, and never would be. The Jesuit *cura personalis*, the attention and respect given to the care of an individual person and that person's soul, proved much more persuasive and compelling to the natives of New France than did the Protestant tactics and brow-beating rhetoric.

To the Queen

My Lady, God having created me a lover of my country and of His glory, the very least I can do is to share with you—and, hopefully, touch your heart with—the news that the name of Jesus is being spoken in this land claimed for France across the sea. This will be of special interest to Your Majesty, who has already said how much she hoped for such news. Instead of lazily enjoying every benefit that the King, your husband, has given to him, the Lord of Poutrincourt has done much for Christianity here. But, Madame, if you want to see more results, you have to help us. Give wings to our endeavor, so that it may fly from east to west, far and wide, so that every place may resound with the name of France. I know that everyone will glorify you, the King, and also God. And I know from personal experience that God, you, and the King have always rewarded my hard work. If I get any royalties from what I have written, I will dedicate them to this project of yours and to your service. So, Madame, please receive favorably this gospel narrative, this good news from across the sea, and publish in France what I am sending you.

I am your most faithful and humble and obedient servant,

Marc Lescarbot

The Conversion of the Indians baptized in New France in 1610

The Gospel of Matthew quotes to us Jesus' unchanging word that "the good news of the kingdom of heaven shall be preached throughout the world, as testimony to all nations, before the Last Days come." History tells us that the apostles' voices have resounded throughout the whole world for centuries now, even though today there are fewer Christian nations. But as for the New World, discovered about 26 years ago, there is no evidence that God's Word was ever spoken there until very recently, unless we believe what Jean de Léry [a French Protestant explorer] tells us. He reports that, one day while he was telling some natives of Brazil about God's mighty acts, how He created the world and how Christ died for our sins, an old man told him that he had heard his grandfather speak of meeting a bearded man (and no one in Brazil wears a beard) who had told them similar things. But they did not want to believe the old man, and they just kept on killing and cannibalizing each other.

As for other nations around here, some of them seem to have a notion of the Flood, or to believe in the immortality of the soul or in the eternal life of saints, but it is possible that these beliefs were just passed along by word of mouth after the universal destruction in Noah's time. All we can do is lament the miserable and pathetic state of these people who inhabit such a vast part of the world that we can't even grasp how big it is unless we include the land from the Straits of Magellan (Terra del Fuego), the land stretching to China and Japan toward New Guinea, and the land beyond the St. Lawrence River in Canada which reaches to the east all the way to the Pacific Ocean.

All these lands are wretchedly ignorant of the Gospel, except for the little bits that cruel Spanish explorers have recently forced on them. But that small amount doesn't add up, especially since the historians of those forced conversions admit that most of the natives were killed anyway; one historian estimates that more than twenty million have been slaughtered over a seventy-year period. Twenty-five years ago, the British claimed some land between Florida and the Armouchiquois territories; they named it Virginia, after Elizabeth I, the Virgin Queen. But the English do things so secretively, that no one can say for sure what they have done there. Only a little while after I had published my *Histoire de la Nouvelle France*, eight hundred men were rounded up and shipped to New France. There is no doubt that they, too, killed many natives. We can neither praise nor blame them for doing this, though there is no law, no excuse, that allows such killing, nor to steal the possessions belonging to others. But if such men are showing the path to salvation to the natives, the route that our true and unadulterated Gospel lays out for them, then they should be praised.

As for our Frenchmen, I've complained enough already in my *Histoire* about our countrymen's cowardice in this matter of saving souls: we don't have nearly enough zeal for conversions, and we should be doing more to ensure that God's name is proclaimed to the ends of the earth, and especially where it has not been heard before. And we want these lands to be French, just as we would not be proud of a non-Christian France.

I know that there are well-intentioned people willing to go to New France to do this job. But why doesn't the Church, which is so wealthy, and why don't the nobles, who spend so much money needlessly for frivolous purposes, provide the funding for such a holy task? Recently, two courageous gentlemen, Monsieur de Monts and Monsieur de Poutrincourt, have spent nearly all their money trying to fulfill this mission. They have nearly worn themselves out! Both have continued traveling up until now, but one of them has been let down by his backers, and now—having unwisely trusted some unreliable lenders—owes an enormous amount of interest on money he had borrowed for the endeavor.

Now, the most up-to-date news that we've heard about New France comes to us from Monsieur de Poutrincourt, so let me tell you what I've heard: We have good reason to admire him, for he is very different from the rest of us lazy men; seeing that France wasn't doing anything for the [Christian] cause, after having given proof of his own courage over and over during the past twenty years, he wanted to top his already amazing efforts by forwarding God's cause. So he has spent all his money and has done everything he could, even risking his own life, to bring the Gospel to the natives and thereby increase the number of souls in heaven, leading many lost sheep to Jesus Christ the Good Shepherd (lost sheep that pastors and priests should really be saving, since they have the money and the means to do so. Or at least they could contribute to the cause!).

This is the third time that Monsieur de Poutrincourt has crossed the ocean to accomplish this mission. The first year in New France, he and Monsieur de Monts looked for suitable housing and a safe port for ships and men to dock. They didn't have much success. He spent the second year still working on this, then he went back to France. During the third year, we (the French) tried to farm the earth of New France, and we had a good harvest: but, that year, de Poutrincourt found out that some evil men had deceived him and that he would have to rely on his own resources.

He set sail for France on February 26. The ocean crossing was stormy and the longest I've ever heard of. When we went to New France three years ago, the crossing was rough, but nothing like his. It took us two and a half months before we arrived in Port Royal (in Acadia). But it took de Poutrincourt and his companions over three months! One man on board threatened to mutiny, and tried to unite the sailors against de Poutrincourt, but the rest had too much respect for de Poutrincourt to get involved in that, which saved his life. De Poutrincourt first disembarked at Port Mouton, but this was a dangerous spot, since during the summer the area is very foggy, and near Cap de Sable, his ship nearly ran aground on a rock. As he was steering for Port Royal, violent winds blew the ship far off course to the Norombega River (that famous river of which I wrote in my *Histoire,* and which many geographers and historians have described). From there, de Poutrincourt came up the St. John River near Port Royal by crossing Frenchman's Bay, and there he found a Breton ship from St. Malo, which was there for the purpose of trading with the natives.

An Indian chief came to him there and complained that his wife had been taken captive on that ship and that she had been raped. De Poutrincourt investigated and took the ship into custody. He found out who the criminal was, imprisoned him, then let the ship go, but the rapist escaped in a sloop and hid himself among the natives, even turning them against de Poutrincourt and his men! Finally, de Poutrincourt got to Port Royal, and you can't believe how glad the Indians were that he and his men had come. Their joy was even greater because they had never dreamed that Frenchmen would come to live near them; they already had a good opinion of most Frenchmen after meeting us three years ago, and had wept when we left them.

De Poutrincourt's dwelling is at Port Royal. The town is one of the most beautiful that God has made on this earth: it is backed by a row of mountains all along the north side, and the sun beats down on them all day long; to the south are little hills, and the coastline can safely harbor up to twenty thousand ships; the harbor is so large that I've seen a medium-sized whale who regularly comes to swim in it around eight o'clock every morning. Also, in the harbor you can fish for enormous amounts of herring, sturgeon, sardines, wolffish, cod, sharks and other fish, and as for shellfish, we've caught many lobster, crabs, and harvested clams, mussels, conch, snails, and sea urchins. And if you go above the harbor, in the river you can catch a lot of sturgeon, salmon; you really have to wrestle to land them!

To get back to what I was talking about, de Poutrincourt came back to his dwelling, and no one had touched or stolen a thing; the Savages (as we used to call them) had left everything just as he had left it. The Indians, eager to hear the news, asked how things had been for those Frenchmen who had returned, calling them all by name, and also inquired about those who had not come back. Their welcome to us shows how good and kind this people is by nature, shows that they saw that we are human beings just like they are, and that they had no need to be afraid of us (unlike their fear of the Spanish). And so, because of their good nature, like our good nature, it is easy to convince them to do whatever we think they ought to do, and especially to teach them about religion.

We had given them a good impression of our religion when we first met them, and they really wanted to become Christians, and we would have already baptized them, if we had had a more solid foundation on which to build here in New France. But, although we wanted to carry on, Monsieur de Monts had run out of money, the King wasn't sending us any help, so de Monts had to send back all the French who had come there, because they had not brought enough supplies with them to live on for any length of time. We would have been crazy to baptize people and then just leave them; they would just go back to their former filthy state. But now, with de Poutrincourt having come back, and after we had the opportunity to teach the natives about the main points of our faith, it would be possible to engrave a Christian character in their hearts and souls. And that's exactly what de Poutrincourt set about doing, remembering what St. Paul said: "he who draws near to God, must believe that God exists."

After making this point to the Indians, we then led them to an understanding of more abstract points, such as believing that God created the world from nothing, that he became man, that Christ was born of a Virgin, that he died for our sins, and so on. And since the priests and ministers who've come over cannot yet speak the native language, de Poutrincourt arranged to have them taught by his eldest son, a young gentleman who understands and speaks the native language; because he is fluent, he can open heaven for the natives!

The men who are at Port Royal and in the neighboring area around Newfoundland, are called Souriquois, and they speak a different language. But once you get beyond Frenchman's Bay, the people there are called the Etechemins, and farther out there are the Armouchiquois, who speak yet another language (they are also very fortunate: in their area beautiful vines and grapes grow, and if they only knew what those grapes could produce, but—like our ancient Gauls—they think that wine is poison). Good hemp also grows there, better and stronger than ours, and also sassafras, many oaks, walnut trees, plum trees, chestnut trees and fruit trees unknown to us French. I have to admit that there is not as much fruit around Port Royal, but the earth is fertile and should be able to produce what we are used to having back in France.

All these people are ruled by chiefs called "Sagamos." This word came from the West Indies and means something very similar to the Hebrew word "sagan": great prince, according to Rabbi David; this prince usually holds the rank immediately below that of the head priest. In the Bible, it also means "magistrate," but the Hebrew commentators often translate it as "prince." We read in Berofe that Noah was called "saga" because he was a great prince, for he was believed to teach theology and to perform a variety of worship services, all very secret, according to Armenian Syrians (whom ancient cosmographers call "wise men" after the example of Noah). For this good father Noah, the restorer of the world, came to Italy, and then sent the Gauls to repopulate France after the Flood, giving them the name of Gaullois because they had escaped from the Flood.

Speaking of Sagamos, the honorific given to the chiefs in New France; the Sagamos at Port Royal is named Membertou and he is at least one hundred years old, and looks as though he could live another fifty. He is the leader of several large families, and he doesn't rule over them as our King does over his subjects, but rather exhorts them, lectures them, advises them, leads them into battle, settles their disputes and things like that. They don't pay taxes to him, but when they go hunting, he gets a part of the kill even if he doesn't go hunting himself. In the past, when he was called on to help cure a sick person, or to predict the future, his people often gave him gifts of beaver pelts and other things. Each village or tribe has an "aoutmoin" or sort of fortune-teller, and Membertou is the man who has told the future for his people for a very long time. He is so good at it that all the other chiefs in the area admire him more than any others; he has been a great chief ever since he was a small boy, a fortune-teller, a doctor—and those three roles are the most helpful to people and the most necessary to human life.

Membertou, by God's grace, has now become a Christian; he and his whole family have been baptized, along with twenty other men from his tribe. They were baptized last June on the day of St. John the Baptist. I have in my possession a letter from de Poutrincourt dated July 11 which talks about what happened. Membertou was given the name of our late King Henri IV and his oldest son took the baptismal name of the former Crown Prince, today our blessed King Louis XIII. Naturally, Membertou's wife was then named Marie, after the Queen Mother, and her daughter received Queen Marguerite's name. His second son, Actaudin, was called Paul after the Holy Father in Rome. Membertou/Louis's daughter was called Christine in honor of the King's elder sister. So each one was given the name of an important person.

Several other Indians who have since left to live in small groups in seasonal cabins elsewhere (this is what they do when summer comes) were also baptized at the same time, and we believe that they, too, are now Christians. But Satan, who never rests, was jealous of these successes and angry to hear God's name proclaimed throughout New France, so the devil provoked a bad Frenchman—I can't even bring myself to call him French; no, he is a Turk; worse, he's an atheist—to tempt and lead astray some of the Indians who had become Christians over three years ago. One of these was a chief named Chkoudun, a very impressive man about whom I've already written in my *Histoire de la Nouvelle-France*. I am impressed by how he prefers the French to any other group, admires what we have to offer and recognizes that the natives can learn from us, and even, when he comes to mass on Sunday, he watches carefully even if he does not understand everything: he wears a cross around his neck, requires that his servants do the same, and, copying what we do, he has planted a large cross outside his village, Oigoudi, which is near the port of St. John's River, near Port Royal.

Now, this man, along with some others, had been led astray from the true faith by the evil and greed of that bad Frenchman I already mentioned. Because I respect his father, I don't want to say his name here, but if he doesn't change his ways, I'll see him in hell. This man, just because he wanted to get a few more beavers from Chief Chkoudun, went to see him last June to make a deal. He left de Poutrincourt, and went right to the Chief, telling him that whatever de Poutrincourt said was false, that he shouldn't believe any of it, and that de Poutrincourt wanted to take advantage of the Indians, and would kill them all to get their beaver pelts. I'm not even including here some of the awful other things that he said. If he were Protestant, I might be able to understand it; but he doesn't seem to espouse any faith. Even so, he has good reason to thank God for having protected him from danger during our travels.

This chief, despite being a Christian, could be influenced and lead others of his tribe astray. But I hope, indeed believe, that the chief will not be deceived for long, and that de Poutrincourt will find a way to bring him, and many other natives, back to the faith and to remind him of what had touched his soul in the first place. For the Holy Spirit has the power to cause a fresh dew to fall and to cause new seedlings to sprout even there where frost has killed them. God grant by His grace that everything in this messy affair will be resolved to His glory, so that He can continue the good work that He has begun, for the glory of His name and the salvation of all His creation.

I should add that here in Quebec there are many religious men who practice proper piety and will do all they can to convert souls. So, we don't need any clever Jesuit doctors here; they are better suited to rooting out heresy than to converting souls. We don't care for their kind: they are always judging others by their own standards and ordering everyone around. As long as you control your own behavior, there's no need for people drawing their own conclusions by spying on your every movement (even on what is in your heart) and tattling about what you're up to—even spying on kings! Besides, what purpose would people like that serve right now, if they're not willing to help us farm the soil? And that's not all. You have to think about what they'd do once they got here. As far as de Poutrincourt is concerned, he has what he needs for his lodgings.

But if some of those people [the Jesuits] decided they wanted to come preach the Gospel over here, they'd come in big groups, on a big ship, and they'd go around starting colonies all over, like in Tadoussac, Gaspé, Campseau, la Heve, Oigoudi, Holy Cross, Pemtegoet, the Kennebec, and other places where Indian tribes gather. In time, those Indians will be converted, and the King alone should get the glory for that, and send over people of his choosing to live in these lands. Because there is no way the [Jesuits] can live over here among the Indians; we certainly can't!

A case in point: the Indians are nomads, wandering from Newfoundland all the way to the Armouchiquois country, over three hundred miles. The men do not farm, because they never stay put more than five or six weeks in any one place. Pliny has talked about people he calls the Ichthyophages, or fish eaters, who live off the fish they catch. Our Indians live in this same way for three quarters of the year. In the spring they divide into small groups and go up river until the winter when, the fish having gone into the salt water depths, they go by the lakes and into the woods to hunt for beaver, on which they live, and to hunt elk, caribou, stag and other smaller animals. Sometimes, even in the summer, they go hunting; there are an amazing amount of birds on some of the nearby islands during the months of May, June, July and August. When they need to sleep, their bed is a skin spread out on the ground for a mattress. And we shouldn't look down on them for this, because our own ancestors, the Gauls, did the same thing, and also used the skins of wolves and dogs for a tablecloth, if we can believe what Diodorus and Strabonius tell us.

But as for the country of the Armouchiquois and the Iroquois, there's a big harvest to be had there for those who have the energy to do this work, because the people there live a more settled lifestyle, do some farming, and live a little better. It's true that they can't figure out how to bake bread, because they don't have mills, yeast, or ovens; instead, they grind their grain with a sort of mortar and turn it into a dough that they cook as best they can between two stones heated in the fire, or else they roast the grain on the coals like Pliny says the ancient Romans used to do. For some time now, they have figured out how to make cakes by baking them under the ashes of the fire, and lately they've figured out how to bake bread in ovens. So these farmers are settled, unlike the nomads, who own virtually nothing, just like the customs of ancient German tribes in Tacitus's time.

Farther into the lands above Armouchiquois territory you'll find the Iroquois who are also sedentary; they farm and harvest buckwheat, beans, root vegetables, and everything that the tribes of the Armouchiquois grow, and they need to do this because they live entirely off the land, being far from the sea. However, they do have a large and beautiful lake in their region, and their cabins cluster along the lakeshore. There are large, beautiful, inhabited islands in this lake. The Iroquois are a large tribe, and the farther out you travel into their territory, the more of them you'll find.

In fact, if the Spanish are to be believed, even in the land of New Mexico, very far from Iroquois country, there are well-built villages to the southwest with houses of three or four floors, even with herds of cattle (which is why they call one of the nearby rivers "cow river"— because so many cows graze along that river). This country is directly to the north of old Mexico and adjoins, I think, the farthest most end of the Great Lake arising from the river in Canada which, according to the Indians, it takes thirty days to cross. I would think that hardy and dedicated men would be able to live among this tribe, and could do much to win souls to Christianity.

But, as for the Souriquois and the Etchemins, small scattered tribes of nomads, what has to happen first is that they be made to farm and to stay in one place. Because, once they have cultivated the ground, they won't want to leave it. They'll fight to keep that land. But I think that the plan to live among the natives and convert them will take a very long time, if we don't really throw ourselves into it and if some King or wealthy prince doesn't help us with. This is certainly a worthy cause for a Christian kingdom to undertake.

In the past, we spent so much money and lost so many lives in the Crusades, and hardly benefited from that; today, for very little expense, we could convert a multitude of people without firing a shot, but we are afflicted with some strange laziness, we are no longer fired up with the zeal to save souls that our ancestors felt. If there were no hope of getting results, I could understand this stupidity. But there's such a certainty that we could succeed, and our success would shut our critics up—they complain about things here even though they don't want to stop fur trading, and, in fact, they live off that and would die of hunger without it.

If only the King and Queen Mother, who I know are very devout, were interested in this mission (as they cared about the Indians whom de Poutrincourt baptized), they'd be saints, the world would always remember them, and what glory they would experience, to have been the first to preach the Gospel throughout this great land which is, in a manner of speaking, limitless. For example, if the Emperor Constantine's mother, Helen, had found such good works to do, she would much rather have raised up to God living temples (believers) than the many marble churches she built in the Holy Land.

And they'd profit in the here-and-now, too, because de Poutrincourt will always be the agent in this land of His Majesty the King and, as a result, Quebec will always be a great harbor in which French ships can dock and they go to and fro across the sea; and we know that such journeys are otherwise hazardous and many goods are lost. In addition, the farther we explore into this land, the more likely it is that we'll find a road to China and the Molucques; the weather will get better, as we travel in stages from the St. Lawrence, down the Great Lakes, the last of which is not far from the Pacific Ocean (and that's how the Spanish got to the Far East); or, alternatively, we could reach the same goal by traveling on the Saguenay River, beyond which (the natives tell us) is the sea—which must be the Northern Passage that everyone's been looking for. That way, we'd get spices and drugs without having to beg them from the Spanish, and all the profit from this commerce would go to the King; he'd also get the proceeds from the sale of leather, furs, pasture and fishing rights, and so forth.

Many young Frenchmen would get involved in these activities (and right now they're either bored, lazy, or poor): here in these strange lands, young people are taught trades that we used to practice, and in the past these trades brought prosperity to France; but even though we've been at peace (after the Wars of Religion) for quite some time, France has not yet gotten back up to speed, probably because we've forgotten what we knew and because there are many who prefer to beg rather than to work. We can add to this list of problems the issue of too many lawsuits, which has always been a big problem in our country. But lots of voyages would help solve that problem, since those who would go exploring would be involved in that, rather than in being litigious; they'd be conquering a new land and obeying their King instead of trying to ruin others by pursuing them in the courts.

And the people who live here are really very lucky that they don't have that sort of problem. They don't seem to suffer from jealousy or covetousness, nor do they say one thing but do another; and they are not scarred by the cruel and calculating nature of men who claim to be pious as a cover for evil and self-serving acts. They may not know God, but at least they don't blaspheme His name as most Christians do. They don't know how to poison someone else or to corrupt another's innocence with diabolic tricks. There are no poor people or beggars among the Indians, however; they are all rich, in that they all work to live. But with us French, it's a lot different; at least half of the people just live off of others' labor, and don't do anything useful. If they were to go to New France, they'd never dare act that way. But here, no one dares be a lumberjack, a worker, a dresser of vineyards, or anything like that, because his father was a lawyer, a surgeon or an apothecary. Over there, they'd stop worrying about prestige, and would enjoy farming, and they'd have a lot of willing helpers to do it, too. And farming is just about the simplest and most worthy endeavor there is; it's what our ancestors did, and also what the brave Roman legionnaires, who knew how to govern and how to be free, also did for a living. But ever since status and envy have corrupted humanity, admirable things are treated without respect, and lazy men are praised.

Let's leave such men alone, and go back to talking about de Poutrincourt. In fact, let us speak of Your Majesty, oh Most Christian Queen, the greatest and the dearest that heaven ever saw on this round globe. You who govern the most noble earthly empire, how can you stand to sit by and watch such a well-intentioned gentleman and not help him? Do you want him to succeed without your aid? Then you'll get none of the glory. No, Madame, you should receive all the glory, just like the stars steal heir light from the sun, so you and the King have sponsored all good and worthy acts for which Frenchmen are recognized. So, then, decide to reap more glory and don't let anyone else do what you yourself can do: although you have a loyal subject like de Poutrincourt, such a good Frenchman who served your late dear husband the King (who didn't always do what he should have done—God forgive him), realize that Poutrincourt doesn't cross the sea at the expense of his Sovereign in order to see foreign lands, but rather stakes all his own possessions and incomes on such ventures. He shows what his intentions are by the actual results he gets, so you know you can trust him and you know that you don't risk losing anything when you help him in his attempts to promote Christianity in the lands to the west across the sea. You can see how determined he is, you yourself are a woman of great resolve, but see, he can do even more with your help!

I praise the princesses and noblewomen who, for the past fifteen years, have given money to fund monasteries and convents. But I believe that this pious giving would be even more effective if they'd be equally charitable to the poor, miserable people in New France who are desperately need for instruction in the Christian faith; those who have the means to help them, but refrain from doing so, should be punished by God! The Queen of Castile was responsible for Christianity being preached to the colonies of Spain: oh my most illustrious Queen, cause the Gospel to be heard everywhere in this new world where it has not yet been heard.

Getting back to the story I was telling, since we were talking about Monsieur de Poutrincourt's trip, it's not off the subject, after having described his lengthy, uncomfortable ocean crossing (which set his plans back over a year), to talk about his return trip. This will be quick, especially since usually such trips from the western lands above the Tropic of Cancer are fairly brief. I explained why this is so in my *Histoire de la Nouvelle France*, so I'll let you consult that; you'll also find out in there why, during the summer, the sea may be calm one day but covered with fog for the next two, and why I've twice experienced fogs that lasted over a week.

In fact, such fog was one of the reasons why, when de Poutrincourt sent his son back to France, it took the son as long to get from Cape Cod to Port Royal, as it did to get back to France from Cape Cod, even though from Cape Cod to France it is much farther: eight hundred nautical miles as opposed to only three hundred nautical miles from

Cape Cod to Port Royal. During the summer along Cape Cod, you'll usually find many boats fishing for cod; they call this fish Newfoundland cod. So de Poutrincourt's son (called the Baron of St. Just), having arrived at Cape Cod, stocked up on fresh fish and meat. While he was doing so, he met up with a boat from La Rochelle and another ship from Havre de Grace. They told him news of the death of our dear late King, but no one knew the circumstances of his death. Soon afterwards, he met up with an English boat, and got the same news from them, except that they accused some men of having killed the King. Two weeks later, de Poutrincourt's son got to France, having had a fair wind all the way from Cape Cod; certainly this was a more pleasant voyage than this one: de Monts's men had left Havre de Grace nine or ten days after February 26 heading for Quebec, forty miles up the Saguenay River, where de Monts had built a fort, but unfavorable winds really slowed them down. Then rumors started to circulate that de Poutrincourt had died at sea, his ship was said to have gone down, and his crew with it. I never believed the rumors, believing that God would help them and guide them through every trial.

We still haven't heard any news from Quebec, and hope to hear some soon. But I can say for sure that if ever anything good comes of Quebec, it will be due to the efforts of de Monts; if the royal privilege for fur trapping hadn't been taken away from him, today we would have many fruit trees, cattle, settlers and buildings in this province. This is because de Monts cared so much that things be well established here, for God's glory and to the glory of France. And even though the royal privilege was taken away from him, he didn't stop caring, and is not discouraged, continuing to do what good he can, building a fort at Quebec and beautiful, comfortable dwellings.

Here in Quebec, the enormous St. Lawrence River narrows and becomes only a young falcon's flight across in breadth, and there are more fish here than in any river anywhere else in the world. The countryside is stunningly beautiful and there is excellent hunting. But it's colder here than at Port Royal, since it is about eighty miles more to the north; as a result, the pelts here are even more beautiful: the fox skins are black, their fur so beautiful that they rival marten and minks for beauty. The Indians at Port Royal can travel ten or twelve days along the rivers; they can paddle almost to the headwaters of the rivers, and then they portage their bark canoes for a ways in the woods, coming to yet another river that empties into the St. Lawrence, and in this way they make a short trip out of what would be a long journey: we wouldn't know how to traverse the country like that. To go by sea to Quebec from Port Royal, it would take more than four hundred nautical miles, going by route of Cape Breton Island.

De Monts sent them some cattle a couple of years ago, but, since there were no village women who knew how to care for the cattle, most of the cows died while birthing their calves. From this we can see how much women are needed here; I don't see how we can do without them! As for me, I'm of the opinion that, without the presence of women, our work will never be as productive as it could be. With no women around, life is sad and boring, you get sick more often, and you die with no one to nurse you. That's why I can't stand misogynists who hate women, and I especially hate whatever so-called "wise man" said that a woman is a necessary evil, because, in my opinion, there is nothing in the world as good as a woman! And that's why God gave woman to man, "to be his help-meet, to help him and to console him," and Proverbs tells us that "a man who is without a wife is unhappy, for he has no one to warm his body, and if he falls, there will be no one to help him up." And if there are crazy women, you've got to admit that there are crazy men, too.

We still haven't gotten over the loss of those cows, because once they got sick they no longer produced milk and then many men died. There was another guy who'd come over with us, who decided to court quick death another way: he started a plot against Captain Champlain. He and his accomplices were condemned to be galley slaves back in France. A year later, when summer came, Champlain wanted to scout Iroquois territory and, not wanting the Indians to take over the fort while he was away, he organized them into war parties. They left, with him and two or three other Frenchmen, up to the lake where the Iroquois live, some two hundred miles from Quebec. There has always been war between these two tribes, just as there is always bad blood between the Souriquois and the Armouchiquois, and at times the Iroquois have gathered to-gether war parties of over eight thousand warriors, who've waged war and wiped out everyone living along the St. Lawrence, as we heard they did at the time that Jacques Cartier explored the land, some eighty years ago.

When Champlain and his troops arrived, they couldn't hide; the Iroquois, who always post watchmen, spotted them; having thrown up some fortifications, the two groups agreed not to fight until the next day. The weather was calm; shortly after daybreak there was great noise in the camp. An Iroquois child, wanting to leave the encampment, had been knocked over backwards, shot with an arrow. The Iroquois were furious and got in formation to attack and to avenge his death. As the Iroquois were advancing, Champlain, who had loaded his musket with two loads of shot, seeing two Iroquois walking in front with feathers on their heads, thought that they were two chieftains and wanted to go get a better look at them. But our Quebec Indians stopped him, saying, "It's not good for them to see you because, when they do, they'll run away, since they're not used to seeing people like you. Get in the back row, and then when we move forward, come with us." So he did, and that way they managed to kill both chiefs with one musket shot. Our side won that battle, because the rest ran away, and all that was left to do was to run them down, which was not difficult; our Indians scalped about fifty of their enemies, and, after their return, feasted and celebrated with dancing and songs, as is their custom.

IMAGO DEI: "FINDING GOD IN ALL THINGS"

Lescarbot's claims that the conversion of Native Americans to Christianity was underway belied the reality that very little missionary work seemed to occur in Acadia during the time when de Poutrincourt and the Calvinist or Calvinist sympathizer de Monts held the royal patent for Port Royal, the first settlement in New France. King Henri IV (a former Calvinist turned Catholic) became concerned, and put pressure on de Poutrincourt who, in 1610, asked a secular priest, Messire Fléché, to come help out in New France. Twenty-four members of the Micmac tribe and their chief were baptized shortly after his arrival. Still, the colony continued to function more as a trading post than as a center of missionary activity. Increasingly frustrated, the King sent two Jesuit priests, Pierre Biard and Ennemond Massé, to Port Royal on June 12, 1611. A little later, he sent the *donné* Gilbert du Thet as well as another Jesuit, Father Quentin, who was killed shortly after his arrival.

Father Biard struggled to learn the Micmac language. He writes extensively in the following letter of his travels among several Indian tribes and the respect he felt for many of their customs while disapproving of others (such as their apparent inability to commit themselves to only one wife).

Father Biard and de Poutrincourt never quite seemed to get along, and those tensions continued with de Poutrincourt's son, Biencourt, who became Father Biard's interpreter with the Indians. In one exchange, de Poutrincourt reportedly said to Father Biard that he wished Biard would leave him and the colony alone; that salvation came from his sword, even if Father Biard wanted to put his confidence in his prayer book.

Despite a less than enthusiastic reception, Father Biard was hopeful about future missionary work among the Indians, and described in his letter several baptisms and conversions that had occurred in the first Jesuit mission in New France. Father Biard's model for missionary activity was notably different from the paradigm that the Protestant sympathizer Lescarbot sketched out in his letter. Lescarbot's approach was more "top down"—an imposition of expected religious affiliation on the Indians. By contrast, Father Biard advocated a "bottom-up" approach to conversion, which manifested itself in the patient dwelling among the Indians to learn their ways so as better to be able to persuade them to convert to Christianity. In his letter, Father Biard noted his own painful struggles to communicate with the Indians, and seemed to agonize over the gulf of comprehension separating him from the natives. He speaks of them in a personal, almost intimate way, seeking to understand and be understood by them, both in terms of language and of lifestyle. Father Biard also provided important details about the different tribes, and he described what may be the first written account ever of the aurora borealis, the northern lights, as well as the first record ever of hosts for the Eucharist being baked from Canadian wheat.

The tensions between Biard and Monsieur de Biencourt worsened when Madame de Guercheville, a wealthy noblewoman much influenced by her Jesuit confessors, persuaded the young, recently crowned King Louis XIII to cede the royal patent that his father Henri IV had given to de Poutrincourt and de Monts to her. Along with that privilege, Louis XIII also gave her enormous new holdings in the New World, effectively allowing her to claim for France everything from the St. Lawrence River down to Florida. Unfortunately, these land grants included the massive British colony at Virginia. Although England and France were officially at peace, the English very quickly became upset about the cavalier cession of their lands to a Frenchwoman and her Jesuit advisors.

Soon after, Father Biard was captured, along with some fifteen other Frenchmen, off Mount Desert Island by Captain Argall, a Virginian commander aboard an English sailing ship, and taken to Virginia. Some time after Father Biard's capture, the English engaged in a raid on Port Royal—some historians claim that they did so with Father Biard's assistance—and wiped out the French settlement. Biencourt and his men were left fugitives wandering in the woods over the hard winter. The English then returned Father Biard to France. En route, Father Biard recorded an interesting encounter with some Anglican churchmen in Pembroke, Wales, who praised the Jesuits and supported them against the English Puritans.

Biencourt and his men eventually rebuilt Port Royal in 1624. The conflict that would divide France and England on the North American continent—and pit Protestantism against Catholicism in the history not only of New France but also of all of America—had begun. The Indians would take sides, and the more war-like Iroquois tended to support the British. The following letter was sent by Father Biard to the Reverend Father Provincial in Paris.

Letter from Father Biard (Port Royal January 31, 1612)

My dear Reverend Father,
Peace of Christ.

If we had to give an accounting to God and to you about New France and Christianity in New France, this new possession managed and obtained by us as a new possession for Christ, from the time of our arrival to the beginning of this year, I don't doubt that, in totaling up the costs, it might seem that we're in the red rather than in the black. The expenses here have been very heavy; but we have been obedient; we have worked hard; and we've used all our gifts, talents and abilities in the service of God our Creator. Even so, since I have to admit that our failures are hardly uplifting, and the endeavor has been costly, we won't talk about what hasn't worked; instead we'll talk about our successes. We'll imitate that steward in the parable who, told by his master to invest his money wisely, used it to make friends for himself. That's what we have done; we have made friends and converts, teaching some who wouldn't otherwise know of it about Christianity. Even while we make a profit, we do not forget the debt we still owe to God—somewhat like the accountant in another parable who hoped that his debt to his master would be cancelled if he continued to make a profit for him. May it be so!

Today, January 22, 1612, it's been eight or nine months since we arrived in New France. Shortly after our arrival, I wrote to you about the condition of God's church in this new colony. Look at how things have changed!

Monsieur de Poutrincourt left for France last year. He left his son, Monsieur de Biencourt, in charge. This young man is much admired; he has about eighteen servants and the two of us Jesuits are also part of his household. Our responsibilities are to preach and celebrate in his house and in the Jesuit residence as well as to travel to spread the Word. Let me describe what it's like inside, then we'll move outside.

Here we say mass every day, sing a high mass on Sundays and holy days, say vespers and we also process; we offer public prayers mornings and evenings; we preach, hear confessions and give penance; perform the sacraments, bury the dead; and do everything that a parish priest would do, since there is no one here to do the work but us two Jesuits. We really need to be good workers for Christ, especially since our "parishioners," almost all of them sailors, aren't usually very worried about the sate of their souls, and don't know much about religion except for when they swear and blaspheme God's name, and have no knowledge of God beyond what they learned in France (which is hardly helpful, since most people who call themselves Christians nowadays live a corrupt life like heretics). Which just goes to show you how hard it is to witness to men like this. In fact, the first thing the Indians learn, they learn from them: how to swear, obscenities, and even the Indian women (who are normally shy and modest) use these swear words and say horrible things that they've learned in French. They don't know what they're saying, they're just imitating what they hear all around them every day.

How can we fix this, when there are so many men who speak this way and don't care at all whom they offend?

When we say mass here, the Indians sometimes come and watch when they are in town. I say "sometimes," because neither the Indians who are already baptized nor those who have yet to be baptized have set habits or know what they should know, because they haven't been properly taught. That's why we decided, as soon as we arrived, not to baptize any adult who did not first know his catechism by heart. But we can't teach them the rudiments of the faith if we can't speak their language!

Actually, Monsieur de Biencourt, who speaks the Indian language better than anyone else, has tried every day to serve as our interpreter. But as soon as we start talking about God, de Biencourt is like Moses without his mouthpiece Aaron: he feels like he can't talk, can't find the words, he's tongue-tied. Part of the problem is that the Indians have no established religion, no courts, no police, no arts or industry, no commerce, no civic life; they lack the words for all such things, as well as for anything they've never seen or touched.

In addition, because they are uncivilized and rather simple, everything they think or know is drawn from what they can perceive with their senses; nothing abstract or spiritual makes sense to them. *Good, strong, red, black, big, hard*: all these words they can say; *goodness, strength, redness, blackness*: they have no idea of these concepts. It's the same thing when we try to talk to them about qualities or virtues such as *wisdom, faithfulness, justice, mercy, gratitude, piety* and other such ideas; at the most, they might understand sentiments such as *happy, love, kind*. If you use words such as *wolf, fox, squirrel*, or *moose*, they recognize them, and they can tell you every species (all of which, with the exception of dogs, are wild); but the concept of just any animal, or a body, or a substance, and other similar universal terms and types—all this is beyond them.

Add to this, if you will, the enormous difficulty we have in getting them to share with us even those words that they do know. Because we don't know their language and they don't understand our speech (except for a few phrases having to do with trade or daily life), we have to use body language to express ourselves and to get them to share the names of concepts that can't be perceived physically. For example, the idea of *to think, to forget, to remember, to doubt*: to figure out how to say these four words in their language, you're going to look really crazy and they're going to laugh really hard at you for at least an entire evening while you try to pantomime what you mean; and, after doing all this, it's often the case that they don't tell you the correct term anyway, because they like telling you the wrong word and laughing at you when you mis-speak. And we still can't figure out if they have an expression for "I believe." Just imagine how we're going to struggle to communicate other Christian concepts!

All this talk about learning languages should show you not only how hard we're trying—how breathless we are!—but also how lucky Europeans are, since they can communicate with each other, because, one thing is sure: no matter how much we work at it, these Indians are still in some childlike state as far as their language and logic are concerned. I say, their speech and their rational capacities, because it is clear that in situations where words remain poor, confused and unclear, it is impossible for wit or reason to be profuse, polished, and orderly. Nonetheless, these poor childlike creatures have a very positive opinion of themselves, and don't want to change their ways for anything! But that's no surprise since, as I said, they are like children.

Not being able, as result, to baptize any adults, as I've said, we turn our efforts to the children to whom belong the Kingdom of God: and we baptize them with their parents' permission and with the sponsorship of godparents. We've already baptized four, thank God. If there is an adult who is dying, we teach him as much as God enables us to; and it is true that when we're in such dire circumstances God enables us to do more than we thought we could and things work out according to His will! So, for example, there was an old Indian lady who was really sick, and her daughter was baptized. The old lady is still alive. The daughter died.

I saw this girl, who was only eight or nine; she was skin and bones. I asked her parents for permission to baptize her. They told me that, if I wanted her, I could just take her and keep her. To them, there was no difference between her and a dead dog. That's how they talked, and it was their custom to simply abandon anyone who they thought was too sick to get better. So we took them up on their offer, hoping to show them the difference between how Christians act and how unbelievers act. We had her poor bony body carried to a nearby cabin, and we nursed her and fed her as well as possible, and we taught her enough to baptize her. We named her Antoinette de Pons, in memory of and in gratitude to Madame the Marquise de Guercheville, who has done so much for the Society of Jesus; that good lady will be glad to know that her name precedes her in heaven, because this girl died several days after being baptized and her soul flew up into the skies.

This was our "firstborn," and about her we could say the same thing that Joseph did when he met up with his brothers in Egypt: that God caused us to forget all our troubles for her. By the way, although the Indians abandon their invalids, this was a chance to show them how Christian charity works, and it had a happy outcome, one that was instructive for them. There was another opportunity to get this message across.

Chief Membertou's second son, of whom I'll say more shortly, was named Actodin. He had already become Christian, he was married, and then he became very sick. Before setting out for France, Monsieur de Poutrincourt had visited him and, since he cares for his people, had suggested that he be brought to the main settlement where he could get medicine. I was waiting for him to be brought here, but no one came. Realizing that no one was going to bring him, and not wanting his soul to be endangered by his failing health, I went there. It took me several days, for he was several miles from the settlement. When I got there, the sick man was in quite a state. People had gathered, and they were about to have a festive gathering to say their final goodbyes.

Three or four big cauldrons were boiling on the fire. The sick man had a beautiful robe under him (since it was summer), and was getting ready to deliver his death speech. This speech customarily ends in a farewell, and then everyone mourns. The farewell and the mourning end when the dying man's dogs are killed so that they'll go before him into the other world. The dogs are killed and lots of pipe tobacco is smoked, then afterwards there is dancing and chanting. After all this, the dying man no longer eats, nor does he ask for any help; he just lies there as though he's already dead. So this is the state I found my patient in when I arrived.

I gave them a really hard time about what they were doing, more with gestures than through anything I was able to communicate verbally, because my interpreters never translate much of what I say. Even so, old Membertou, the father of the dying man, understood pretty well what I was getting at, and promised me that he'd put a stop to these goings-on. So I told him that, as far as the farewell and the mourning was concerned, and even the pipe smoking, I could put up with that, but that killing the dogs, chanting and singing around a death bed, and especially giving the man up for dead before he actually had died, was unacceptable; I reminded him that they had promised Monsieur de Poutrincourt to take the invalid to the settlement, and that, with God's help, there was still hope that the dying man might recover. They said that they'd do all this, but they still waited another two days to bring him to the settlement.

He really did look about to die right then and there. And one night his wife and children totally abandoned him, leaving him alone and going to sleep in another hut, thinking that he'd already died. But God was pleased to change their despair into hope, for, in only a few days, the man was healthy again, and he still is today (thanks be to God); and Monsieur Hébert, our famed pharmacist from Paris, tells me it is a true miracle. I don't know what to say, except that I don't have enough evidence to say one way or another. But I do know that, while he was lying there dying, we placed on his body some holy relics, the bones of Saint Lawrence, Archbishop of Dublin in Ireland, which Monsieur de la Place, Abbot of Eu, and the Priors of the Abbey of Eu, had given us to protect us on our journey here. So we put these relics on the sick man, making a vow on his behalf, and he got better.

This cure convinced Membertou, the father of the man who was healed, and strengthened his faith even more and, because of this, feeling sick himself (of the illness that was eventually to kill him), Membertou had himself brought to us. Even though our cabin was very small—with three people inside, there was hardly room to turn around—he asked us, showing how much he trusted us, if we would put him in one of our two beds. We kept him there for six days. Then, when his wife, daughter, and daughter-in-law had come to be with him, he knew that he had to leave, and he did, apologizing for all the work he had caused us in nursing him day and night. One thing's for sure: changing his lodgings and treatment didn't help him at all. So, seeing that he was dying, I heard his confession and then afterwards (this is how they make their will) he made his death speech. In this death speech, he said, among other things, that he wanted to be buried with his wives and children but in the foundations of his former dwelling.

I was not happy about this, worrying that both the French and the Indians would think that Membertou did not die as a good Christian should. But others told me that, at the time he was baptized, this had been a promise made to him and, besides, were he to be buried in our cemetery his other children and friends would never come to see us again, because the custom of their tribe was to shun and avoid any memory of death or marker of the dead.

I argued with them about this through Monsieur de Biencourt (the only interpreter I have), but without success; the dying man was determined. Late that evening, we gave him Extreme Unction, and in every other respect he was ready to die. The sacraments had an effect: the next morning, he called Monsieur de Biencourt and me and began his death speech again. In this speech, he declared that he had changed his mind of his own free will; that he wanted to be buried in our cemetery; that he ordered his children to continue to see us, like Christians and not like heretics, so that they could continue to pray for his soul and to lament his sins. He also advised his tribe to remain at peace with Monsieur de Poutrincourt and stated that he had always been friends with the French, and had put an end to several attempted plots against them. A few hours later, he died in my arms; it was a very Christian death.

He was the greatest, most famous and feared Indian anyone could remember: robust in size, taller and more muscular than the average Indian, bearded like a Frenchman while hardly any other Indians have any hair to shave; he was also discrete and serious as suits a commander. God had written on his soul a deep understanding of Christianity, more profound than he could have learned from anyone else, and he often talked to me about this in his mixed French and Indian speech. "Learn how to speak our language soon," he would say to me, "because when you are able to speak it, you will teach me so much that I'll become a preacher like you." Even before his conversion, he never had more than one wife living at a time, which amazed me, especially since the great chiefs of this land always keep a big harem, not because of sexual desire but because of their ambition, prestige, and the need for many children (which is the best indicator of their potency), just like they also have many servants, domestics, slaves—and it is always women who fill these roles; women bear all the burden of tiring and menial work.

He was the first Indian in the area to be baptized; he was also the first to receive Extreme Unction, and the first who, by his own will and order, was given a Christian burial. Monsieur de Biencourt gave the eulogy, conducting the ceremony very similar to the funeral ceremonies that we hold in France for great captains or noblemen.

Now, so that we will all remember to fear God as much as we love his mercy, I'm going to put in writing what happened to a Frenchman who came to a fitting end, just as Membertou deserved to be remembered as he was. This Frenchman had, for many years, successfully avoided death by drowning, most recently on the Feast of Pentecost. He didn't appreciate his good fortune. To make a long story short, on the eve of the Feast Day of Saints Peter and Paul, as we were heading out into a choppy sea and making the customary promises to the saints so that they would protect us from harm, this creep started to laugh at us and to mock us, making fun in particular of those of the group whom he knew were religious. He sure got what was coming to him! The next morning, a big gust of wind blew him overboard, off the sloop into the waves, and he was never seen again.

Enough of my sea adventures. If the ground of New France had any feeling—like some poets claim is the case—it would no doubt have felt an unprecedented feeling of happiness this year because, thanks be to God, we've had a good harvest, and with some of the leftovers we baked Hosts to use in the sacrament of the mass. These are, I believe, the first Hosts ever to be made from the wheat of this land. May Our Lord graciously receive them as our gift to him and, like the Psalmist says, "be good to us, since the earth has given you its fruits."

Now let me report to you what is going on around the countryside.

Monsieur Biencourt and I took two trips, one twelve days long, the other a month and a half, and we went west-southwest all along the coast from Port Royal to the Kennebec. We canoed along the great rivers of St. Jean, Holy Cross, Pentagoet and the Kennebec mentioned above; we visited French winter camps, one near the St. John's River and the other, headed by Captain Plastrier, at Holy Cross.

During these trips, God saved us frequently from many ever-present dangers; but although we should always remember His mercies to us, we don't want to bore you by writing them all down. I'll tell you about the things that you'll find the most interesting.

Along with young Monsieur du Pont and Captain Merveilles (who, as I mentioned, spent the winter at a camp near the St. John's River on an island called Emenenic, about 6 miles back from the river), we went to see the Malouin tribe. We were still about a mile and a half from the island, and it was already nightfall. The stars came out, and, suddenly, to the north a part of the sky became as red and bloody as scarlet, and, this color, gradually extending itself into spikes and rocket-trails, finally came to rest over the Malouin settlement. It was amazingly red and so bright that the whole river took on its color and shone red. This phenomenon lasted about a half an hour, and right after it went away, another similar light show started.

Everyone thought that this meteor was a miracle. Our Indians started to yell, "Gara gara enderquir gara gara," which means, "there's going to be a battle; these signs predict a war!" Even so, our landing was peaceful that evening, and the next day we came into the settlement peacefully. There was nothing but friendliness the next day. But (bad luck) the next night everything changed, I don't know how or why; our people and the men from St. Malo were arguing and quarreling among themselves. I have no doubt that there was a band of crazy men and bloodthirsty spirits flying around that night, looking for the opportunity to massacre the few Christians who were there; but God in His goodness kept these evil men from doing their dirty deed. No blood was shed. The next day, arguments of the previous evening vanished, and everything again became calm and serene.

To tell the truth, Monsieur de Biencourt's kindness and foresight really helped in the midst of this cauldron of high tempers. But I also realized that, if guns and ammunition were to get into the hands of undisciplined men, it would be hard to control them. I don't think anyone slept a wink that night. As for me, I made all sorts of vows and pledges to Our Lord, promising Him that I would never forget the good things He had done for me, if only He'd be sure that there was no bloodshed. And He heard my prayers.

I didn't even have a chance to eat until three o'clock the following afternoon; I'd been so busy running back and forth trying to settle things down. Finally, everything got calm again.

Captain Merveilles and his men showed themselves to be very devout men, because, despite all this trouble and dispute, on the day after they went to confession and set a good example for us all by taking communion. As I was leaving, they all—especially young Monsieur du Pont—very kindly invited me to come and stay with them when it was convenient for me. I promised them I'd do so when I was able, for I truly am fond of them all.

However, putting them out of our mind, let's continue our trip. When we got back from St. John's River, we traveled toward Armouchiquois country. There were two main reasons why Monsieur de Biencourt wanted to go there: the first was to find out what the English were up to, and the second was to trade for Armouchiquois wheat to help us through the winter, so that we would not starve to death in the event that no aid arrived from France.

To understand why he was so concerned about the English, you need to know that, just a little while ago, Captain Plastrier from Honfleur, Normandy, whom I've mentioned above, was taken prisoner by two English ships off the island of Emmetenic, eight miles from Kennebec. He was released on condition that certain "gifts" (as they call them) be handed over to the English, and on the condition that he promise to stop up and down the coast. The English wanted to be masters of the area, and even showed letters from their King saying they were entitled to sole trading rights there (but we think the letters were faked).

When Monsieur de Biencourt heard everything that Captain Plastrier had to tell him, he spoke seriously to us all of how, as an officer of the Crown, the steward of his father's lands, it was incumbent on him—as it was on any good Frenchman—to confront the English about their attempt to steal the rights and possessions of His Majesty the King of France. "Because," he said, "everyone knows (but obviously the English don't care) that great King Henry, God rest his soul, in 1604 gave this entire region (from the fortieth to the forty-sixth degree longitude) to Monsieur de Monts, as was his right since this land had belonged to earlier French kings. Ever since receiving this grant, de Monts, with my father, de Poutrincourt, assisting him, has occupied the land; this all happened three or four years before the English ever came here, or before they ever made any claims on the area.

As for myself, there were two reasons why I wanted to go with them on this trip. The first was that I wanted to provide spiritual guidance to Monsieur de Biencourt and his men, and the second was to preach the Gospel to the Indian nations along the way. So these are the reasons why we set off.

We arrived in Kennebec, eighty miles outside Port Royal on October 28, 1611. It was the feast day of Saints Simon and Jude. Our men disembarked right away, eager to see the English fort; we had learned as we were traveling there, that no one currently occupied the fort. Since anything new provokes interest, our men couldn't stop talking about what a good fort it was, how well situated it was, and how well the English had done to build it there. But that good opinion didn't last long; a few days later, we realized that we could easily build a fortification opposite theirs, and that such a structure would make it possible for us to take them prisoner by cutting them off from both the sea and the river, although they might have been able to get some supplies from some of the river's tributaries farther inland. Even worse, we saw that there was no arable land around for miles; the soil was very rocky. We stayed there until the wind turned, and then Monsieur de Biencourt decided to sail up the river, with a full wind in our sails, in order to reconnoiter the river.

We had sailed about three nautical miles. The current turned against us, so we dropped anchor in the middle of the river. Suddenly, we saw six Armouchiquois canoes heading for us. There were twenty-four braves altogether. They hailed us, then carefully came closer. They looked just like a flock of birds trying to get into a nest of hemp and twigs, but afraid to come in for fear that a squirrel might be lurking. This made us happy, because we had the time to arm ourselves. So they came closer, then darted back; they checked us out, calculating how many of us there were, how many weapons we had, looking at every angle; and when night came, they camped on the far river bank, out of sight—if not out of reach—of our cannon.

All night long they danced, sang, and made angry speeches; that is what they do when they are a war party. We figured their songs and dances were probably curses and calling on the devil, so, to counteract Satan's powers, I ordered our men to sing some hymns like the "Salve" and "Ave Maria stellis" and others. But after a while, they ran out of spiritual songs and began to sing others, and when they ran out of those, they decided (as Frenchmen, natural mimics, will do) to imitate the chanting and dancing of the Armouchiquois braves. They imitated them so effectively that the Armouchiquois stopped what they were doing so they could hear better; when our men stopped, the Armouchiquois started up again. It actually was very funny; it sounded like two well-rehearsed choirs, and it was hard to tell the true Armouchiquois from the counterfeit.

When morning came, we continued our route upstream. Some of the Indians who had come with us told us that if we wanted some of their "piousquemin" (wheat, in their language) that we should steer to the right and continue—with some difficulty—upstream, and, doing so, in a few hours we would get to the land of the great chief named Meteour-mite, who would give us all the wheat we wanted; they said they'd be happy to guide us there, as they wanted to visit the chief.

Now we realize that they only told us this to deceive us, to lead us into an ambush; they figured they'd let Meteourmite finish us off: he was known to hate the English and, they must have thought, would hate any foreigner.

But we believed them, so they split into groups, part of them leading us, some of them in the canoes with us, and another group bringing up the rear. Monsieur de Biencourt was uneasy, and constantly on the alert; he frequently told the sloop (which was carrying a depth-sounding de-vice) to go ahead of us all. We'd only gone about a half a mile when, coming to a large lake, the depth-sounder yelled, "Two arm lengths, one arm length, only one arm length depth everywhere." Immediately he commanded, "drop anchor." Where were the Armouchiquois? Nowhere to be seen. They had suddenly abandoned us. The traitors! May God help us! They had led us into a trap. "Turn around; turn back!" We turned back and headed down river.

But Meteourmite had heard of our arrival, and ran ahead of us, and even though he saw us turning back, he still decided to chase us. Mon-sieur de Biencourt wanted to shoot him, but others in the group con-vinced him that would be foolhardy, because there were more of them than of us, and they were in a frenzy.

Monsieur de Biencourt settled himself down and hailed Meteour-mite. The chief told de Biencourt that there was an easier route we could take; he offered to send some of his men to guide us; then he said we should come to his dwelling and he'd give us what we were looking for. We believed him, and hoped we wouldn't be sorry that we did, because there were such dangerous heights and straits in the river that we thought we'd never get through it. In a couple places, some of our men had already cried out that we were all going to die. But, God be thanked, they worried too early.

When we landed, Monsieur de Biencourt armed himself and prepared to go meet Meteourmite face-to-face. He found the chief bedecked in a magnificent native costume, alone in a well-built cabin, with about forty braves guarding him in a circle around the cabin; each one had his quiver, his bow and arrow on the ground in front of him. These people are not stupid, no matter what we sometimes think.

That day, people were really welcoming to me; since I was carrying no weapons; the strongest braves came over to greet me in a very friendly way. They took me into the biggest cabin of all; more than eighty people were gathered there. Since all the seats were taken, I fell on my knees and, having made the sign of the cross, I began to pray. After a few minutes, my guests, as if they had actually understood what I was doing, began to clap and to praise me, crying, as is their custom, "Ho, ho, ho!" I gave them some crosses and saints' cards, explaining what I could about them. The Indians kissed these objects enthusiastically, making the sign of the Cross, and each of them brought his children to me so that I could bless them and give them each a little gift. That's how the visit went, and I had another similar visit with them later

In the meantime, Meteourmite answered Monsieur de Biencourt that they did not have much wheat to share, but they did have a few furs to trade, if he'd like.

That morning when we were to trade, I went with a boy to a nearby island; we were going to celebrate a mass of reconciliation. Our men from the boat had armed themselves against any attack; they had left space amidships for the Indians, but this plan didn't work because so many Indians crowded on board that they were soon all mixed in with our men. The men began to shout, "Get back, get back!" But it was no use. They just yelled back at us.

Then our men thought they were being attacked, and for some time everything was noise and confusion. Monsieur de Biencourt had often said that he would raise his arm and yell "kill them" as a sign to make the first strike, but because I was outside the boat he was afraid I would be harmed and so he held back from doing this. God used this concern to save not only me, but the whole boatload. Because, as we all realize now, if we had attacked, none of us would have escaped, and the whole country all around would have hated the French forever.

God caused Meteourmite and some of the other chiefs to realize that this was a dangerous situation, and they called off their men. That evening, after they had all left, Meteourmite sent some of his people to apologize for what had happened that morning, claiming that the responsibility for the fracas lay not with him, but with the Armouchiquois; that they had even stolen from us an ax and a big wooden bowl (which he was returning to us); that this theft had made him so angry that, as soon as he had found out about it, he had sent the Armouchiquois away. As for himself, he stated that he was acting in good faith, and knew that we were not the sort to kill or to do battle with the local Indians, but rather we would invite them to dine with us, would smoke peace pipes with them, and would give them nice presents from France—and that was why they liked us. These people, I think, are the best and biggest talkers ever; they don't do anything without a lot of words!

Since I've mentioned the English, you might want to know what they'd been up to, which is something that we also found out while among the Indians. What happened was that in 1608 the English had begun to sail around one of the mouths of the Kennebec River, as I've already said. They had a good man for ship's captain, and they treated the local natives pretty well. But some say that the Armouchiquois were afraid of these new neighbors, and so they killed the captain. The Indian style is to kill by using magic. In 1609, the English, under a new captain, changed their strategy. They pushed the Indians back shamelessly; they beat them, handling them cruelly and aggressively without provocation. Finally, the poor, mistreated Indians, worried about what was going on and even more concerned for the future, decided, as the saying goes, to kill the wolf while it was still a cub and before its teeth and claws got stronger. They were in luck: a few days later, three sloops went off separately from the English fleet to do some fishing. The Indians who were plotting revenge tracked them down and, coming up with friendly gestures (as is their custom: the more they profess kindness, the more likely they are to be contemplating treachery), they got into the boats and, at a certain signal, each one chose his man and cut him to pieces. Eleven Englishmen were killed. The others were terrified and left that same year as soon as they could, and have never come back, preferring instead to go fishing in the summer of the island of Emetenic which, as I said, was about eight miles from their fort.

For this reason, having heard of the Englishmen's hostile treatment of Captain Plastrier on that same island, Monsieur de Biencourt decided to go reconnoiter it, and to leave some mark of our presence there. He erected a large cross bearing the arms of France at the harbor. Some of his people advised him to burn the ships that were still there but, as he is kind and thoughtful, he didn't want to do that, especially since these were fishing boats and not ships used by soldiers.

From there, since it was already November 6 and winter was coming, we set sail for Port Royal, passing by Pentagoet as we had promised the Indians we would. Pentegoet is a great, beautiful river; it's not unlike the Garonne in France. Pentegoet empties into the Bay of Fundy, and there are many islands and large rocks at its mouth, so that, if you don't go up higher, it's possible to think that the river is actually just some big bay or part of the sea. It's about three miles around, and is located at forty-four and a half degrees of the Equator. What else could it be but the mythical Norembegue River that ancient writers talked about? Even though we made a lot of inquiries about this river, we were never able to find out anything else.

As we were going up this great river, and had progressed about three miles or more, we came into another large river called the Chiboctous, which empties from the north-east into the Pentegoet. At the meeting of these two rivers, there was the most impressive Indian settlement I'd ever seen. They had eighty canoes and a sloop, eighteen cabins and about three hundred inhabitants. The head chief was named Betsabés. He was a discrete, mild-mannered person; to tell the truth, I've often noticed that these chiefs display innate virtue and political sense that would make anyone with sense ashamed of how little some of our Frenchmen possess such qualities.

When they had recognized us, they spent the evening showing how happy they were by doing their customary dancing and singing. And we were really happy to feel that we were in a safe land, because, when we were with the Etechemins (the tribe to which these Indians belonged) or with the Souriquois (the tribe that lives at Port Royal), we never had to be on the alert; we could relax, as if we were with our own people, and God knows they did not abuse our trust in them.

The next day, I went to visit the Indians, and did with them what I've described doing at Kennebec. In addition, since some of them were ill, I visited those who were sick and recited the Gospel and the prayers for the sick, giving each of them a cross to wear around their neck.

One of them was lying in front of the fire (as is their habit). His eyes and face were agonized; big drops of sweat were running down his face; he could hardly speak, and was in quite a state. They told me that he had been ill for four months, and, from the way he looked, they didn't think that he had long to live. I don't know what he was sick with, or whether the illness came and went in stages; all I know is that, two days after I prayed for him I saw him hale and healthy; he got into our boat and he was wearing the cross I had given him. He saw me, and grabbed my hand. I didn't have the chance to talk with him, as trading was going on, the midships were crowded with people and all the interpreters were busy elsewhere. But I was very glad that these tribes are beginning to see God's goodness and mercy, and that they are realizing that the sign of the cross has a saving power for them, too.

·Finally, so as not to repeat myself, inasmuch as we were able, in every place where we met up with Indians we tried to imprint on their minds and hearts some notion of the great beauty and worth of Christianity. To sum it all up, this was the fruit of our trip: we began to know them and to be known by them; we took possession of the land in the name of God, His Church, putting all in subjection before the throne of our Sovereign Lord and Savior Jesus Christ. The Indians saw us pray, celebrate the Eucharist, and preach by means of speeches, holy images, and crosses. We instructed them in how to live, and other matters, and they began to perceive the seeds of our holy faith. These seeds began then and there to germinate and to grow abundantly and some day, God willing, they will produce a great harvest.

To tell the truth, that is also the main fruit that we've produced here at Port Royal, and will remain so, until we can learn their language. It does our hearts good to see young and not-yet-baptized Indians, when they are here, volunteer to carry the tapers, the little bells, and the holy water in procession, and walking in orderly fashion in funeral processions or in other processions. That's how they learn to be good Christians, even before becoming Christian.

The only thing more that is required is that we all sin less and that we all try not to hinder—by our own sins and unworthiness—souls from coming to Jesus. As for myself, I have plenty to feel guilty about, as should everyone who cares about the welfare of his soul. May Our Lord, by His holy mercy and through the prayers of His Blessed Mother and of all His Church, have compassion on us!

I especially beg Your Reverence and all our Reverend Fathers and Brothers in Jesus to remember us in your prayers, and also to pray for these poor souls still enslaved by Satan's tyranny. May it please the kind Savior of the world, whose grace no one deserves but whose kindnesses are infinite and more than we ever could merit, to take pity on these poor tribes, and bring them soon into the fellowship and happy freedom of those who are the blessed children of God. Amen.

From Port Royal, January 31, 1612.

As I write this letter, the ship that has been sent to bring us assistance has, God be thanked, arrived safe and sound; Father Gilbert du Thet is on it. He knows how happy we are to welcome him among us, and he can see how great was our need for help. Thanks be to God. Amen.

I am the son and servant of Your Reverence,
humbly in the Lord,

Pierre Biard

"WE [ENGAGE THEM] IN
DEVOUT CONVERSATIONS"

At the request of Samuel de Champlain, who wanted to pacify the native tribes through conversion to Christianity for the purposes of colonial expansion and commercial activity, King Louis XIII sent the Récollets, a very strict branch of the Franciscan order, to missionize New France. However, since the Récollets were an itinerant and mendicant order, they had no funds of their own and very little resources; their mission was not very successful. Six friars established five missions; they went to the principal French outposts of Tadoussac, Quebec, Montreal, and Trois-Rivières, said mass, and tried to preach to the natives. They were not received with much enthusiasm. They also ran into opposition from the Huguenots, or French Protestant, traders, who refused to comply with King Henry's demand not to practice their faith in the New World. The Huguenots were prone to bellowing out psalms or hymns whenever the Récollets offered an open-air mass, drowning out the words of the priests. In 1621, two Huguenot traders were given monopoly over the fur trade in the area: William and Emery, brothers from Caen. Their appointment only caused further harassment of the friars by the Protestants. Further hindering conversions, in the summer of 1622, a war party attacked the Récollets at Quebec. Finally, the Crown sold control of the area to the Duke of Ventadour, a devout man who had entered holy orders and who wanted to purchase the land grant so that he could save the souls of Native Americans in New France. His confessor was a Jesuit.

At this point, the Récollets requested that the Jesuits come help them. However, there was tension right from the beginning between the two orders, which had very different approaches to the job at hand. Some of these differences had to do with the disestablished nature of the Récollet order; wanderers themselves, they did not perceive a need to settle the nomadic tribes so that they could better be taught, cared for, and ministered to. Settlement, however, was a Jesuit priority. Father Charles L'Allemant, the author of the following letter, was one of the first three Jesuits, accompanied by Enemond Masse and Jean de Brébeuf of martyr's fame.

Although Canada had already existed officially for eighteen years, very little had been done in terms of proselytizing the natives. With Cardinal Richelieu having come to power in France, however, things were about to change: he was an autocratic minister whose authority was not to be questioned. Opposed to Protestantism, he quickly revoked the trading rights of all French Protestants, starting with the Caen brothers, and formed a Company of one hundred associates, the Company of New France, which he himself directed and which controlled the monopoly of all trade and any other affairs, secular or spiritual, for the colony of New France. He required the Company to write in its by-laws that by 1643 at least four thousand men and women would have been sent to the colony; each person must be both French and Catholic, and at least three priests must be posted to each new settlement.

Of course, England was infuriated by this move. The British colonists in the New World were Puritans, bitterly opposed to any sort of episcopal (bishop-governed) church polity and even more adamantly set against Rome, the Pope, and the Jesuit order. They, too, wanted the fur trade routes for themselves.

The Indian tribes had not changed much since their initial contact with the white man, and Father L'Allemant records the differences in lifestyle between natives and Frenchmen, their mutual incomprehension, and his objection to some of their qualities (such as their lack of hygiene), and others he admires. Most of all, he describes the struggle to cross cultural boundaries and to translate Christianity into concepts comprehensible to the Indians. Other Jesuit Fathers describe this challenge as well, but Father L'Allemant stresses more heavily the issues of available interpreters, their skill or lack of it, their faithfulness to sense or distortion, and the whole process of interpreting as not only a linguistic skill but also as an exercise in learning about a different culture (and, in the process, reflecting on one's own). Another characteristic of the Jesuits comes out in Father L'Allemant's style: his careful attention to Indian lifeways, his inclusion of meticulously observed detail, and his obvious attempt to describe and, if possible, comprehend but not judge, are evident in his letters. Although Europe would wait at least another century before any notion of cultural relativism was fairly widely accepted, these letters show a first step in the direction of tolerance and *inculturation*—the dwelling within a formerly alien culture so as better to understand it, rather than recoiling from strange practices, labeling them or denigrating them.

This is how the stage was set when the first contingent of Jesuits arrived in New France. The following letter from Father Charles L'Allemant, Society of Jesus and Superior of the Mission to Canada, sent to his brother Father Jerome L'Allemant, also of the Society of Jesus, describes the lifestyle and customs of the natives living in New France, and how they got along with the Christian Frenchmen who came to live among them. The letter was published in Paris in 1627.

Letter from Father Charles L'Allemant

Peace of Christ.

I wrote last year (around mid-July) to Your Reverence about the success of our trip; since then I haven't been able to send word because ships only dock here from France once a year. That's why you shouldn't expect to hear from us except for on a yearly basis, and if, for once, the ship failed to come, it'd amaze me if you heard from us in under two years' time. Besides, each year we have to hope that God will just keep us alive! So, since I last wrote, here's what I've found out about this country, and what has happened.

This country is amazingly large; it stretches for at least a thousand or twelve hundred miles; it is forty degrees wide toward the west; the Atlantic Ocean and the Pacific Ocean circumscribe it. Many tribes live here; I've heard there are at least thirty-eight or forty of them, not including those that we haven't yet had contact with (but which the Indians tell me do exist). The place where the French have settled is called Quebec; it's near the forty-sixth and a half degree of latitude and situated at the edge of one of the most beautiful rivers I've ever seen. The French call this river the St. Lawrence. It is over two hundred miles from the river's mouth, and the river continues for at least another thirty-five or forty miles up river from where we are. The narrowest part of this river faces the settlement, and, even so, it's at least a quarter of a mile across. Now, even though this country is more southerly than Paris (near the forty-sixth and a half degree of latitude), winter, nonetheless, is usually five and a half months long; the snow falls in drifts of three to four feet, and so heavily that it doesn't usually begin to melt until around mid-April; and it begins to fall in November, so during all this time you never see the bare ground. Some of our Frenchmen have even told me of sledding on snow on May 1 the same year that we arrived, and they also used snowshoes to walk on it, as is the custom here. This way, they don't sink too deep in the snow. The Indians taught them this; this is how they go hunting for moose. The mildest winter they've ever had is the one that we just got through (or at least, that's what those colonists who've been here the longest say), and even so the snow began November 16, and began to melt toward the end of March. The length and duration of the snow makes us wonder if we'll be able to grow wheat and rye here; I have seen crops that were just as abundant as you plant in France, and even the crops we planted last year were pretty successful; but, to be on the safe side, we should probably also plant a mixture of wheat, barley, and rice; barley and hay will come along fine here, good for seed, even better than in France. And you should see our big, beautiful peas! So the earth is arable (as Your Reverence can see).

The farther up river you go, the more you see what a good river it is. There are also strong winds prevailing from the northeast, the northwest, and the southwest. The northeaster brings winter snows and rain during the other seasons. The northwest wind is so cold it chills your bones, but the sky is always clear when it's blowing.

From the mouth of this river up to where we are, no land has been cleared; it's all forest. The local Indians don't seem to care about planting crops; there are only three or four families who have cleared two or three acres and have planted buckwheat, and they only did so just a little while ago. I hear that the Récollet Fathers were the ones who persuaded them to plant crops. And whatever the French have grown here doesn't amount to much, maybe eighteen or nineteen acres at the most. Two hundred miles upstream there are more settled Indian tribes than the ones here; they build large villages and fortify them against their enemies, and they are successful farmers, so they have plenty of buckwheat and are not starving like our Indians. But they are wilder and crueler in their ways, and they do all sorts of evil things without shame.

Even though this river is navigable, it's not an easy trip, because there are many falls (and some are so powerful that there's no way you can cross them). This is why, when the Indians get to such falls, they portage their canoes and all their baggage on their shoulders, traversing at times two, three, four, or even eight miles in this way. When Frenchmen go up there, they have to do the same thing. The Récollet Fathers have been up to this territory and took a years' worth of supplies with them or enough to trade for them with, because if you wait for the Indians to give you anything it will take forever, unless they've decided to take you under their wing. If they let you live among them, in their cabins, then they'll feed you along with the rest of the tribe—but who's to say whether they will take care of you or not? And besides, virtuous men would be offended by the sorts of goings-on in this tribe, so the Récollet Fathers felt it better to build cabins away from the rest of the village; as a result, they had to provide their own food.

No missionaries live at present among these tribes. When we arrived here last year, there was one Récollet Father who was returning with an Indian group that had been fur trading thirty-five miles above the village, but at the last waterfall his canoe overturned and he was drowned. The Indians never portage their canoes coming down, only going up the falls. That's why it's so difficult to travel to their territory. Now, even though there weren't any missionaries to these tribes, trading companies continued to send Frenchmen to deal with the Indians and to trade with them every year. As a result, these Frenchmen go an entire year without hearing mass, without confession, without taking communion at Easter, and they are living in circumstances which encourage them to sin. I ask you, should this be allowed to happen? Your Reverence would help me greatly if you would have one of our Jesuits think the matter over and send me his advice to how to proceed.

As for the Indian lifestyle, let's just say that they are totally uncivilized. From morning to night, all they care about is filling their bellies. They never come to see us unless they want food, and if we don't give them any, they complain. They are real beggars, even though they are also surprisingly arrogant. They think that we French have no courage, compared with them; sexual misconduct is common among them; some men marry several women at the same time and then just leave their "spouses" if they feel like it and marry someone else. There are even some here who have married their own daughters, although it's true that the other Indians find this disgusting. They are unhygienic and unclean, their food and cabins are dirty, and they are infested with lice, which they eat if they can catch them.

It's their custom to kill their fathers and mothers when the latter are too weak to walk; they think that by so doing they are making things easier for their parents, because otherwise they'd die of hunger, not being able to follow the rest of the tribe when it changed camp. One day, I asked a young brave how he'd feel if his tribe treated him like that when he was old; he said that was fine with him. They wage war on their enemies in a treacherous way, ambushing them, and if they are not able to take prisoners, they shoot them with arrows and scalp them so they can brag about this to the rest of their tribe; if they take prisoners, they keep them in their cabins and torture them mercilessly, killing them bit by bit; what is really strange is that, during these tortures, the prisoner will never cry out, because that would be cowardly; instead, he sings. After the poor man has been killed, they eat him, and even the smallest children eat a piece; they have a big feast and invite everyone, and they even invite some Frenchmen whom they know, and at this feast they give everyone a piece of flesh on plates or in bowls made of bark. Once you've been served, you have to clean your plate; otherwise, you have to pay a fine and you lose your reputation as a brave man.

When they have a feast when someone dies, they set aside a piece for the dead man just as they serve those who are alive, then they throw that piece in the fire; to make sure the dogs don't eat the remains, they throw all the bones and leftovers into the fire.

They bury their dead with all their earthly possessions, such as candleholders, pelts, knives, and so forth. One day, I asked an old man why they did this. He told me that they buried all this with the corpse so that he would have what he needed in the other world. When I said to him that, if you open the grave, the possessions are still there, proving that the dead man wasn't using them, he answered me that the physical entity of the cauldrons, knives and so forth remained, but that the soul of the cauldrons, knives, and other implements went into the other world with the dead man, and he used them there. So they believe, as Your Reverence sees, in the immortality of the soul. They even say that, after death, they go up to heaven where they eat mushrooms, and that they are able to communicate with each other up there. They call the sun "Jesus." People tell me that there were Basque explorers in this land earlier, and that these explorers taught the Indians this. So, when we pray, the Indians think we are praying to the sun.

The Indians also believe that the earth is pierced with holes and that, when the sun sets, it is actually hiding in a hole in the ground, and comes up the next morning when it comes out through another hole. They have no worship service and they don't have any formal prayers. But they do believe in a Creator who made all things, although they do not do anything to worship this Creator. Among them, there are some people who claim they can talk to the Devil; these people are also the tribe's doctors, and they cure sickness. The Indians are afraid of these people, and always treat them well for fear of retaliation.

Little by little, we are finding out more about other tribes, which are generally more settled than our Indians here, because the ones we know are nomadic and wander about for six months out of the year, depending on how productive their hunting grounds are. They camp in groups of two or three families in one place, two or three in another, and so forth. The other six months of the year, twenty or thirty of them gather on the riverbank near the Jesuit residence, as they also do at Tadoussac, and also about forty miles upstream from us, and they live off of whatever they caught while hunting during the winter months: mostly smoked moose flesh and foodstuffs they got by trading with the French.

I think I wrote you last year about what they wear, and how they never wear hats and only cover their bodies with a moose hide or with a beaver pelt made of five or six beaver sown together, and they wear these skins as though they were churchmen wearing copes, fastening them in the front with a strap. Sometimes they wear a belt, but often they do not wear a belt; nonetheless, they are careful to cover their private parts. In the winter they have leggings and shoes made of moose skins, but these moccasins are supple like a glove both on top and bottom. Most of the time they paint their faces red and brown-gray in various designs, depending on the whim of the women who paint their husbands' and children's faces. They also grease their hair with bear grease or with moose fat. The men are beardless, just like a woman; any hair that grows there they pull out, and the women like them better this way. I've seen three or four of them who let their beard grow a bit to copy the French, but they really don't have enough hair to make a full beard. Their skin color is very dark; none of them is white-skinned, but their teeth are amazingly white.

They travel on the river in little bark canoes, which are very well made. The smallest canoes can hold four or five people, and they put some baggage in, too. The paddles are proportioned to the canoes, and one person paddles in the front while another paddles in the back of the canoe. Usually the women bring up the rear and steer. These poor women are real pack-mules, doing all the work. Two hours after giving birth they go gather wood for the fire. In the winter, when they break camp, the women drag the heaviest loads along the snow; the men only seem interested in hunting, going on war parties, or in trading.

Concerning trading, I haven't really said anything to you about that, but it's really the only thing left to tell about the Indians. Their wealth is all in animal skins, especially beaver pelts. Formerly, the King gave trading rights to a large organization of gentlemen, contingent upon certain stipulations, and there was a lot of trade. One of the elders of the tribe told me that he has seen up to twenty ships at a time in the Tadoussac port. But now that those trading rights have been given to a private association, excluding all others, there are no more than two ships a year, and these usually only come once a year, at the beginning of the month of June. These two boats bring everything that the merchants trade to the Indians (capes, blankets, nightcaps, hats, shirts, sheets, hatchets, arrowheads, bellows, swords, ice cutters to break up ice in winter, knives, cooking pots, plums, grapes, buckwheat, peas, biscuits, cakes, and tobacco), as well as everything that the French who live in the area need to survive. In return, the Indians trade to them moose pelts, lynx, fox, otter, marten (sometimes even black marten), badger, and muskrat, but most of all beaver, which is the pelt most prized by all: I've been told that in one year these ships sailed away with over 22,000 beaver pelts. The average take in any year is 15,000, or 12,000 at one *pistole* per pelt, which is a good deal; it's true that the trading companies do have to go to considerable expense, since the ships have to carry, feed, and pay at least forty merchants, in addition to the costs of the crew for two ships, which can add up to over one hundred and fifty sailors who must be fed and paid. The wages vary: usually, they're paid about 106 pounds, but some get one hundred *sous*. I know an interpreter who got a hundred *pistoles* along with some pelts to keep for himself each year. It is a fact that this trade, as Your Reverence will see in each year's report, really helps us out. Your Reverence will look on this favorably, I'm sure, because the trade allows us to do better work for Our Lord.

Now I just need to tell Your Reverence about what we've done since we got here at the end of June. July and August were spent in writing letters and in scouting out the land. We also looked for an appropriate place to build our dwelling. We didn't want to presume on or inconvenience the Récollet Fathers. So, after having looked carefully at all possible building sites, and having asked the opinion of the Frenchmen who were already there and of the Récollet Fathers, on the first day of September we solemnly erected a cross in the place we had chosen. The Récollet Fathers helped us, and some of the Frenchmen also set to work after lunch. We five Jesuits have been involved with the building project ever since; we've uprooted trees and spaded the ground as long as weather permitted. With snow coming, we had to lay off work until the spring. Even while we were working, we constantly tried to figure out how best to learn the Indian language, because most of the interpreters can't be relied on. Asking God to help us, I decided to talk to the Indian interpreter, expecting he'd refuse to help us (as he had with everyone else). While I spoke with him, I tried to give him a good impression of us, and a better opinion of the trading company than the one they had.

Believe me, Your Reverence, I found the antidote to this negative impression, and worked hard to change it. I asked the Indian interpreter to teach me his language. Oddly, he agreed right away, and said that he'd give me as many lessons as I liked all winter long. We have to recognize God's hand in this, because the General of the company was under firm orders to return immediately to France (or else his wages would be docked), yet the General decided on his own authority not to go back, but rather to stay for the rest of the year. As a result, he stayed as long as we needed to learn the language. The other amazing thing is that this interpreter had never before agreed to teach anyone how to speak the tribe's language, not even to the Récollet Fathers, who had been trying to convince him to do so for over ten years. But at my very first request he promised to do what I wanted, and he kept his promise faithfully all winter. Even so, we weren't quite sure that we could trust him, and we worried that the winter would go by without us having made any progress in speaking the Indian language. So I consulted with the other Jesuits if maybe it would be better if two of us were actually to go live with the Indians for the winter, so that by associating with them constantly we should learn the language faster. The Jesuits thought that it'd be enough to send one; the other could stay to oversee devotions for our French settlers.

So Father Brébeuf was chosen; he left on October 20 and went back on May 27, having never been farther from us than 20 or 25 miles. During his absence, I reminded the Indian interpreter of his promise to me, which he eagerly fulfilled. As soon as I had gotten from him what I needed to know, I decided to go spend the rest of the winter with the first Indian who came to see us. We left on January 8, but I had to come back eleven days later, because, not finding enough for them to eat, the Indians had to come back to the French for help. When I returned, without losing any time, I asked another tribe's interpreter if he could teach me what he knew. I was amazed at how quickly and openly he agreed, since in the past he had always refused to teach the Récollet Fathers. He gave us whatever we asked for; it's true that we didn't ask him to give us what we would have liked the most: seeing that he was somewhat of a brute, we knew we could only get so far with him and then he'd be at a loss for words; nonetheless, we were pleased with what we did learn. Yet again I saw the hand of God at work in this, because this interpreter wanted to go back to France the same year that we'd arrived, and the Récollet Fathers were encouraging him to do so; we, however, feeling it necessary to keep him with us to help us—and for the good of his soul—we went with him to the General of the fleet. The General insisted on sending him back to the tribe for which he was an interpreter, so that's how he came to be among the French traders who were waiting to sail back to France. The ships were about to leave, and on the evening before their departure he came to say goodbye to us at the Récollet Fathers' residence. God set things in motion so that, while he was coming to see us, he got sick with a chest infection and had to be put to bed at the residence; the ships returned without him, and, in this way, he stayed with us although he was now out of danger, and we were happy to have him stay. I'll let you imagine how, during his convalescence, we did everything we could for him; it's enough for me to tell you that as soon as he got over the illness (from which he had expected to die), he assured us that he was grateful and would do whatever he could to help us. He said that, if God would please just restore him to health, he'd spend the whole winter helping us, and he did just that. Thanks be to God!

Maybe I've spent too long telling about this, but I love to talk about how God intervenes to help us; everyone should benefit from these little miracles. If he had gone back to France, we wouldn't be any farther along than the Récollet Fathers were after ten years. This is how, thanks be to God, we spent the better part of the winter. Other than this, I also helped out by celebrating all the festival days and every Sunday mass for the French (and I also always preached). Father Brébeuf did the same. Together, by God's grace, we made a lot of progress and won the hearts of everyone in the Indian camp. We heard general confessions from most of them, and we got along very well with the Chief. Around mid-Lent, I took it upon myself to ask the Captain to give us some carpenters from the settlement so that we could build a little cabin where we had begun to clear the land; he agreed very graciously and the carpenters were more than happy to help us, and, in fact, they had already offered to do so. They worked with such good will that, despite the poor weather and the time of year (there was still at least a foot and a half of snow), they will have finished our cabin on the Monday of Holy Week; to do so, they had sawed more than 250 logs, some for the roof, some for the exterior of the cabin, as well as twenty timbers for rafters, and they had also planed more than twenty-five big beams to use in erecting the cabin. So it's a great beginning; I don't know what progress they've made since, because I haven't been feeling very well, so haven't followed their work.

Besides, while we live among the Indians, we are not entirely safe. If a Frenchman happens to offend them, the Indians avenge themselves by killing the next Frenchman to come along, without thinking how that person might have been able to help them. If they dream during the night that they've killed a Frenchman, they'll kill the first one who wanders along by himself. Some of them will tell you a few days before it happens the time when the next ships are to arrive, and all they'll tell you is that they know this because they saw it in a dream. That sort of person has the reputation among the other Indians of being able to talk with the devil. And their conversion to Christianity doesn't seem to change much of this! Their lazy and amoral life, their vulgarity and, what I really can't understand, their lack of words for anything that could explain our mysteries (since they've never had any religious worship of their own) wear us out when we try to communicate with them. But we keep our faith in God and we take heart from remembering (and this is true) that God will not so much count up how much we've produced, but rather will consider our good will and hard work in this endeavor. The more we doubt our own abilities, the more we are made to trust in God.

If I am able, I will travel to other tribes; if this happens, don't expect to hear anything from me, because I will be very far away and will not be able to write much if at all; if that does happen, I say goodbye to you and to the world, until we are reunited in heaven. Don't forget to pray for our souls from time to time. When you're saying mass, if you think of us, say a mass for a Jesuit, whether he is alive or dead.

Help has been sent to us from France, and we've made a good beginning in this mission, but things still aren't in the kind of shape that they ought to be, so that God can be served faithfully. Heretics have as much power here as ever, and that's why I'm sending Father Noiroit back (with our Superiors' permission): he's the one who can best explain everything here. If the Jesuits want this mission to be strengthened and to succeed, they've got to do everything they can think of to help it. I know it'll be hard for Father Noiroit to come back, since he has such a hard time with seasickness. I sent his partner, along with Father Brébeuf, about 300 miles away from here to one of the more settled tribes; they should have arrived by now, if they were able to meet up with some Indians who could show them the way; otherwise, they'll have to come back to the Jesuit residence: I'm hoping daily to get word from them.

I've just heard that they've left. The devil, whose bad conscience won't let him be put to any test, was involved in this, I am sure: as soon as our Jesuits had gotten into the canoes, the Indians insisted repeatedly that the canoes were too heavily loaded down with pelts and that they should get out, but finally God triumphed over Satan's tricks and the Indians were convinced to take the Jesuits with them, after they'd been given many presents. If God will help this mission succeed, it will truly be an important opening onto an infinity of other nations, tribes that are more stable and settled. I would have liked to go along, but the other Jesuits did not think that was a good idea, believing that they needed me here to help in building our little dwelling and to provide spiritual care for the Frenchmen here. Your Reverence may be surprised that I sent off Father Brébeuf, who was already able to speak a certain amount of the Indian language, but it was in fact that God-given ability that convinced me to send him: we are looking for a very different sort of progress to be made among that tribe than what we experience here. May God bless our labors; we have a great need of more workers. Certainly the Indians seem inclined to listen to our message. The interpreter having asked one of their chieftains, in my presence, if they would like some of us Jesuits to go live with them to teach them about God, the chief wondered why we were even asking, and stated that they'd like nothing better. Looking around at the Récollet residence, he said that he doubted they'd be able to build us a stone house like that. Ask them if they'd be able to find a little wood cabin for us, like the one we're building, when we get there, I said to the interpreter. He was very friendly toward us. Another reason why he was so eager to have us may have been because there were very few births in their tribe this year; they think that's because there aren't any men of God living among them, so we are encouraged that they'll give us a good hearing. I asked if they'd give us their children to teach and they said they would; I asked if they'd come for instruction and they said yes, they wanted to. They'd wait for us to get settled, then it was up to us to earn their friendship and to learn their language.

For those interested in Quebec and in what we are doing here, I'd beg you not to get frustrated if you don't heard of much progress for a while. It takes time to convert the Indians. The first six or seven years may seem pretty unproductive to some. It might not be an exaggeration to say that it'll even take ten or twelve years to get results. But does that mean we should just give up? Doesn't everything have to begin somewhere? Isn't preliminary work necessary, before we can accomplish our goal? As for me, I tell you that if God will look on my efforts favorably, I don't need to see any results for my entire life, as long as God is using those to prepare the way for those who will come after us. I am more than happy to spend my life and my strength and to give my all, even to shed my blood, to this end. But if our Superiors don't think it's worth it, I will obey their orders and do as they command.

Here is a little Huron who has come to visit. He is so enthusiastic about anything French! He really loves us and is very eager to learn about God, but his father and the chief of his tribe want him to return next year to be with them. They say that afterwards they'll let him stay with us for a few years, if he wants to. It's really important that he be happy with us, because once this child has been taught well, that will be an opening for many other tribes to learn from him. The interpreter from his tribe has gone back to France. This child was so close to the interpreter that he even called him his father. I beg Our Lord to care for him on his journey.

And I thank Your Reverence for the encouragement that you've given me. I've read your letters over four or five times, but never without crying, for several reasons, but most of all because they make me so aware of my weaknesses and failings that make me so unfit for this great mission in establishing Christianity in this country. There's nothing I fear other than failure in this. I beg you, by all that you love best in heaven, to never stop praying for divine aid for us; pray that God will give me the grace to succeed, or, should my weakness again come upon me, that it not affect the Indians' desire to learn from us; pray that my inadequacies not get in the way of God's grace; pray that my human frailties may be more than compensated for by His goodness and the good order that He will cause to be established throughout this land.

We continue, even more than before, our good relationship with Father Joseph, the only one of his order in this country, the other having gone with our Jesuits to the Hurons, and the third having returned to France along with two other brothers. Monsieur Champlain is always helpful to us; he has asked me to be his spiritual director, as has Gaumont, and I will take special care of him, as Your Reverence has ordered. The advice that Your Reverence gave me concerning the dedication of our first church is actually exactly how I'd hope to handle that matter, if my Superiors will let me; the name of the church must be Our Lady of the Angels, and that's why I beg Your Reverence to send us a beautiful painting—surrounded by angels—for the church. The Récollet Fathers celebrate the Feast Day of St. Charles, and that's why they've called their chapel after him, and the river along which we live is also called the St. Charles. That's how it was named before we got here.

I don't think I've left anyone out of my letter; I have remembered our benefactors as well as those who have written to me. So now, I have to admit that I'm a bit tired; this is the 68th letter and certainly not the last that I will write! May God use all this to His glory.

Our Reverend Father Assistant has been very enthusiastic about our mission, so I'm sending him this map of the country.

Please know, Your Reverence, that I am always your devoted servant in Our Lord,

Charles L'Allemant
Quebec, 1 August, 1626

"THE WORLD IS OUR CHURCH"

Father Paul Le Jeune wrote the following two letters in 1636 to report back to Old France on what was going on in New France. When Father Le Jeune first arrived in Quebec, he was greeted with great joy and relief by Madame Hébert, widow of Monsieur Hébert, and their children. They had been the first family to settle there. They were devout Catholics and had been frightened and greatly concerned when Quebec had been evacuated by the English in 1634. Le Jeune and Father De Noue reassured them of France's continued concern for her colony, and they reinstated a Catholic presence.

The Catholic settlement was on rocky ground at present, though. Father Le Jeune entered the Jesuit residence at Quebec, called the Residence of Notre-Dame des Anges, and found that rats had been busy and snow and rain had leaked into the small structure. The tiny chapel had no decorations, so Father Le Jeune put up three pictures: one of a dove (the Holy Spirit), one of Ignatius Loyola, and one of the Blessed Mother.

Father Le Jeune also quickly moved to re-establish order at the Jesuit residence, appointing Father De Noue to supervise the crew of workmen employed at the mission. He also arranged with a young native named Pierre to give him lessons in the Algonquian language, and paid him for each lesson with a plug of tobacco. Le Jeune started a school for Native American children with two children whom an Indian gave to him as a present. He began by teaching them Latin, and then he taught them certain prayers and the Creed. Le Jeune then went to spend the winter among the Indians on the Ile d'Orléans. There, he attempted to share the Christian faith with the inhabitants, but was opposed by a man known as the "sorcerer," the tribe's medicine man. The letter communicates his frustration and gives examples of how the "sorcerer" tried to counteract Christianity. From this experience, Father Le Jeune developed two principles that were to guide his ministry and the mission of other Jesuits. He came to believe that proselytizing to nomadic Indians was virtually guaranteed to fail, and that therefore the Indians should be encouraged to live in settled communities. He also felt that any conversions made among the Indians as they currently lived, in scattered and shifting clusters, would probably not prove terribly fruitful in influencing other tribes to convert to Christianity. Eventually, this latter principle would have an important effect in causing the Jesuit mission as a whole to shift its focus farther west.

Finally, in this letter Le Jeune talks about various people with whom he had been, and still was, in contact back in France. He describes their interest in the mission and their concern to make converts. One of the people from whom he quotes excerpts of their correspondence is a Protestant. Others are influential noblemen, and he also mentions the significant role played by several French women. The collaborative construction and maintenance of the mission, in terms of publicity, promotion, fund-raising and on-going conversation about the nature and efficacy of the Jesuit mission, are very evident in these two letters. We hear from many voices—all, in different ways, are part of the Jesuit project.

Concerning the feelings of affection that many people of note in France express toward New France

I have no idea what our work in New France will produce, nor when the door will be opened all the way to receiving the Gospel, but one thing I am sure of: God is in charge of our mission, because Nature alone could not carry us as far as we aim; Nature is too self-interested to encourage so many hearts and minds to persist in our single-minded mission, a goal of which Nature is unaware. To leave family and friends, saying goodbye to acquaintances, leaving beautiful, gentle France; to cross the ocean, braving wind and water; experiencing all manner of suffering daily; to leave all our worldly goods, only to throw ourselves into the pursuit of hopes and dreams; to change earthly concerns into heavenly considerations; choosing to die among an alien people—is the sort of speech you just don't hear and the sort of behavior you simply don't see in the ordinary, natural, run of events. These actions are beyond Nature's comprehension, and yet these are, indeed, the actions and the sort of speech of at least a thousand worthy people. These people express concern—with as much, or more, conviction as they would show for matters in the Old World—about how things are going in New France.

I don't know all the details about everything that goes into the support of our mission; I only hear once a year about such matters and then only in writing; that sort of communication is a lot like that of deaf-mutes, who speak without saying a word. So I can truly say, seeing so much energy and zeal, so many holy emotions expressed by people so different in age, sex, social standing and material wealth, that only God could create such thoughts; only God could set these hearts on fire so that everything they say and do is oriented toward the noble goal of reaching Heaven. And I haven't even mentioned our King's noble desire that these people, for whom he feels such affection, become Christians; in fact, that's exactly why he founded the Company of New France, and continues to encourage and support it in many ways. Neither have I spoken of the efforts of the Cardinal on our behalf; it's enough to say that he made himself the head of the Company of New France so as to be better able to encourage and support this great undertaking, which he protects as his pet project. The Duke of Enghien, the eldest son of the Prince, honored me by writing to me himself last year to assure me of his high regard for us and of his intention to provide material support, God willing, as he gets older and has more influence. In addition, I have thanked God for having inspired this young Prince with such good plans to serve him, and for giving him the means and mind to see those plans through. I know from good sources, and can say without exaggeration, that all those who have seen him at his studies recognize the quality of his intellect and respect him for it. Praise God! Across the skies of our beautiful country, such stars conspire to favor our endeavor, even this new star who has just appeared among those of greater stature.

No one can fail to realize that the Marquis of Gamache is the primary support of our mission. I found out this year that he has received letters authorizing him to establish a school in New France; our Reverend Father General wrote to tell me this, and at present many have prayed for the Marquis. Throughout this land and everywhere the Society of Jesus can be found, we pray for the prosperity of the Marquis's family and for the success of his plans. We began to teach here last year; Father L'Allemant and then Father De Quen taught the French children, and I taught a few Indian children. We are amazed to see that, even though we have only begun to teach, there are already so many children gathered around us.

I have heard that some blessed person wants to establish a seminary for the Huron youth: what a wonderful idea! It's from this sort of seedling that we expect great fruit. Praise God forever for the care that He has taken for our new colony, blessing it with the help of people who care—even more than they care for themselves—for the well-being of these young Indians.

I wasn't even going to talk about the members of the Company of New France, because it's not so surprising that they would take an interest in this country, since the King has given them title over it, but I have to admit that the affection they demonstrate is a very pure and holy zeal, and I constantly marvel at how people who by right should be more attached to the world (because of their wealth and standing) care more for the things of heaven. I'm not just saying this; these men have done me the honor of having their secretary write to me, saying: "The letter that you sent us so pleased the Company of New France that we all agree that we've already been paid back for what we've put into the Company. What we've done for the colony of New France, we have done out of love for God and the care we have for the easing of our people's burdens. But to be assisted in this enterprise by [the Society of Jesus] able ministers of support and consolation, is to be recompensed up front, and to receive overwhelming wages for the little work we have done. You thank us for our help, but your act of thanking us is of greater worth than anything we have done, and inspired us to do even more, when God makes it possible for us to do so."

I have quoted from their letter, and that's not all they said. After they said how they hoped that all their work would be for God's glory, they expressed their joy over having been delivered from the power of a nobleman who had exercised too much influence over the mission. "Even though we lost something, we also gained much, because now no one person can claim to have control of New France. Now, thanks to you, we can dedicate New France entirely to God." I only have one thing to say to them: if they do God's work, God will make their work prosper and they will lose nothing in this trade. They should continue their noble work; they should continue to plant the seeds of blessings that the children of those whom they convert will reap in heaven. This is how the Directors and Associates of the Company of New France feel, too.

I am a bit upset that people who have so much worth in God's eyes and in the eyes of men should require me to keep silent about the good things they are doing here. They tell me not to quote their letters or to speak of their good deeds. In this way, they hide from Frenchmen the strong feelings they have for our holy faith and their hope that it may flourish in this strange land, only letting those from whom it's impossible to hide it see their good works. I'm talking about people employed in the highest offices of the land. One of them cares for France and for Canada; his concern is not only for Frenchmen but also for the Indians, and he does what he can for both. Another states that his interest in the Company of New France has nothing to do with financial gain; his only concern is to expand the Kingdom of God. Here is a quote from one of his letters (which someone gave to me in confidence): "I want to get all the news I can from Canada, because I want to help Catholicism to spread there." That's his only motive, he repeats, and the only reason he's joined up with the Company of New France.

Farther along in the letter, he says that even the best cities began with a group of vagabonds, but in New France we have this advantage: there are many good and noble people who have joined us: "Our chief preoccupation there should be to serve God faithfully. You'll see a big change when the Company of New France takes over, because the

Company has decided to plough all profits back into bettering the country, and also to send over many Frenchmen, and to refrain from taking any profit from the trade with New France." Now that's a selfless person! It's not natural to hold back from wanting to transport to a new land all the comforts that we experience in the Old World, but here we see the secret inclination of this man's heart, prompted by God, to dream grand and noble plans to help this poor native people here. They've been passed by for too long by civilization. Some of the Company's associates have written this to me: "It looks like our Company will continue to trade without making a profit, but your mission will make an ever greater spiritual profit as a result; the intention of most of the members of the Company is this: to help you in your efforts to convert the Indians. You are the ones who suffer and are greatly inconvenienced in this endeavor, sometimes even risking your lives."

I'd never get anything done, if I were to quote to you all the things that many people have written to me on this subject. Their modesty swears me to silence as much as their good example makes me want to speak out about it. But I don't want to offend them, and that's why I don't say anything about the holy desire that several religious have expressed. Many Fathers earnestly desire to come work among us in this new vine of the Lord's vineyard, to clear this wild land for planting; it's true that this desire to live and die for the Cross of Christ is fitting to their vows, but it's still really impressive to see such men, men who are involved in deliberations of the highest sort in the Old World, be willing to leave all that to come and care for New France, so dearly do they love this mission. Even more, there are noblewomen who hope to share in the glory of this endeavor, overcoming the frailty of their sex by the extent of their courage.

Last year, I was looking for some brave soul who could sponsor charitable work in this country, and God was good enough to provide this person. I learned that Madame de Combalet wanted to help out; she hoped to found a hospital in New France. This is how she informed me of her intention: "When I had read the *Relations*, God having granted me the desire to try save these poor Indians, it seemed that what would be the most helpful would be to found a hospital, staffed by a religious order, in New France. So I've decided to send six workmen over this year. They will clear the land, and erect lodging for the hospital nuns. I beg you to help them any way you can. I have asked Father Chastelain to talk to you about this further on my behalf, and to convey my specific wishes to you in this regard. If there is any other way in which I might contribute to the salvation of these poor souls for whom you care so deeply, I would be more than happy to do so." What more can I say about this, except that all of heaven, its angels and saints before God's throne, are singing hymns of praise and thanksgiving for this assistance. We give thanks to this great lady, in the name of all the guardian angels of these poor Indians.

They themselves are incapable of understanding the great honor being done to them and the great love being shown to them. I told them that a great lady was going to put up a big house where they could bring all their sick to be nursed; they'd lie in good beds; they'd be fed good food and given medicines and dressings for their wounds; and all this would be free! Astonished, they replied that was wonderful, but I could see by their smiles that they didn't believe me, and would only accept this miracle as true if they saw it with their own eyes. Basically, they are unable to understand what such charity really is. It's enough that God, the God of all human hearts, has made this holy thought grow in your good heart. God sees this holy work and is pleased. Surely nothing could so powerfully persuade these people of the existence of God than your plan to build a hospital—even the idea of putting up schools for boys and girls doesn't compel them as much! May God be blessed for all time, and for all eternity.

If I let myself start talking about the quality of devotion that an infinite number of holy people have expressed for our mission, and that a good number of religious have shown through their concern that Christianity spread in New France, I will go far over the customary limit for a chapter, but, after all, charity will excuse this fault in me. I've learned that in the Church of Montmartre, in the austere and purifying presence of so many martyrs laid to rest there, nuns pray day and night to beg Heaven to bless the Jesuit project. The Carmelite nuns are on fire to help us; the Ursulines are full of zeal; the Visitation sisters can't say enough about their belief in what we are doing. The nuns from Notre-Dame entreat us to let them share the suffering that we endure among the natives; the Hospital nuns beg to be brought over next year to help out. Nature herself doesn't possess such holy breaths that can ignite such coals; no, these flames are the result of a divine fire, one that will burn forever. "We are more jealous of your suffering than sorry for them," some sisters write us. "We send along with you our prayers to the Blessed Mother, for whom we have a special devotion, and we also pray St. Joseph and St. Theresa, as well as the angels of the far country where you are, so that their strength and power will be with you." What great help this is to us! "If it were as easy a thing," one nun says, "to build a Carmelite convent as to build an Indian cabin, and if we had as much strength as we have weakness and lack of ability, you would find very many sisters ready to assist you."

These are the very words of another nun: "You should know that New France is very much on the minds of many people, and that leads me to believe that God looks with favor on her. Oh, what would you say were I to tell you that, God willing, we will soon have both the will and a way to come and help you. If this is God's will, nothing in the world could keep us from it, even if we are soaked to the bone by waves on the way there."

That is how a true Ursuline speaks, who explains to me how her order may soon come to live among us in the Canadian forest. As I write this, I have before me the names of thirteen Ursuline nuns who, in a letter sent to Father Adam, express their common desire to join us, and their Superior is one of them: "I have let my sisters pour their hearts out in this letter," she says, "I've only indicated my approval by signing my name to it, to show me that I will join them. I feel more envy than pity for you, engaged as you are in this work." Hear what these resolute souls have to say: "No difficulty can frighten us; our Lord will strengthen us and so strongly warm our resolve that we will be bold to say, as St. Paul said, I can do all things through Him who gives me strength; sea and storms do not scare us, because our hearts cannot live without He who has redeemed us by giving up His life, and we want nothing more than to give our lives for the salvation of the Indians." This shows that "perfect love casts out fear." I leave unspoken other equally emotional statements, which a good number of hearts and souls in other religious orders have expressed; even non-cloistered people have made such statements. "If delicate women, for reasons known only to God," some say, "can throw themselves courageously into a dangerous sea crossing, should we let our courage flinch before the same perils? Especially since we only seek to go to this wild land, so as to give honor and glory to God?" The sisters who want to come over first, after they have faced down their fears, are very vocal in stating that, trusting in God, they no longer fear anything—except for having to wait. I tell them, and others like them, to pray without ceasing that God will smile upon our mission; but I also warn them not to rush into things; if they come over before the country can be made ready for them: to "all things there is a season," and God will let us know in His time; they should wait patiently.

That's all I have to say for now; I've certainly said enough to show you that New France has a firm place in God's heart, because New France resides now in the hearts of so many people who hold her dear.

Concerning the natives baptized this year, and several burials

It seems that Our Lord wants to commemorate the Immaculate Conception of Mary, for he gives great honor to those who remain virgins. Last year I sent Your Reverence a written vow that we all took in the Jesuit residence, on your recommendation, last December 8, the Feast of the Immaculate Conception. Although we didn't make this public, Your Reverence published our vow, and we will swear to it again every year on the same day, God granting us the ability to keep it. We are very aware of the blessings that Heaven has showered us with ever since that day, so much so that we might ask that all Jesuits in France, indeed throughout the world, and every good person who values the conversion of these people, unite themselves with us and take a similar vow. Then, every fast, every prayer, all suffering, every good work (even those done in secret) may be presented before God in honor of the Immaculate Conception of the Holy Virgin, so that she might intercede for our natives with the blood of Her Son, his utter devotion and love on the Cross. That way, our natives may all die a truly Christian death, a death that obtains salvation for all those who practice these devotions and make this vow. You can find its written form at the end of the *Relations* for last year.

I wrote in that letter that we baptized twenty-two people last year. This year, we have baptized more than a hundred since we made that vow to God, whereas we didn't have a lot of baptisms before that. Since the ships returned to France, we have made a total of one hundred and fifty native baptisms. In addition, God has given us a way to save these people, helping them to understand two important things, so that faith can indwell their souls. The first is that they are not sad when we baptize their dying children; indeed, they ask us to do it. The second is that the oldest among them begin to want to die as Christians, asking to be baptized on their deathbed, so as not to go to hell. So we have accomplished what we hardly dared dream: they don't think the way that they used to. They've also given us a few little girls to instruct, and I'll talk about that in a little while. All these gifts have come from God through the intercession of the Virgin and her blessed Spouse, who have heard the vows that I mentioned earlier.

Now let me go back over the order in which we did the baptisms. On December 9, in fact on the day after the Feast of the Conception, Monsieur Jean Nicolet, the interpreter for the Algonquians in Trois-Rivières, came to tell the sixteen Jesuit Fathers lodged at the Conception Residence that a young Algonquian was very ill, and that they should visit him as soon as possible. The Jesuits immediately went to this young man's cabin, asking permission from his father to enter. God seems to have prepared their hearts to receive us; we had made our vow the day before. The poor father was so pleased that we were bringing help to his son. Father Buteux taught the young man, but since he only partly understood the Montagnais tongue that Father Buteux spoke, a native woman (able to speak both Montagnais and Algonquian) offered to translate. So much faith and Christian truth flowed from her lips and into the soul of the sick boy; she gave her all: she was like an aqueduct through which water surges full force, with nothing held back. Finally, on December 12, seeing that the young man was dying, they baptized him after having catechized him, and they named him Claude. He died soon after, speaking the holy names of Jesus and of Mary. His family asked the Fathers to bury him in the French graveyard: "This is our desire," they stated. "We will do him this honor, " we told them, "an honor that we would refuse to the greatest leader in the world, if he were not a Christian." "Get whatever is necessary to bury him in your way ready as soon as you can," they told us, "we entrust him to you."

All the French made a great procession, and then the Indians came along two by two, their demeanor more European than native. As soon as the burial was over, the father of the dead man gave a great feast for the natives, during which, as is their custom, he himself ate nothing; but he continually sang and made speeches. "I have lost heart," he declared. "The death of my son has separated me from myself. In the past, I've nearly been in the hands of my enemies, ready to be torn into pieces and eaten alive bit by bit, and I was never afraid; I must not lose courage now. I console myself that my son, had he lived, would surely have brought the wrath of the Iroquois on himself." And, turning to the Jesuits, he said, "You have greatly eased my sorrow by giving these last honors to my son." That is what this Indian said on the occasion of his son's burial, and these thoughts and wishes are now in Heaven with him.

On December 22, the same Jesuits again felt the blessings of the Holy Virgin, when they baptized a young boy of about 10 years old. This child didn't want to hear anything about our faith, imagining that baptism, and death immediately after, were one and the same thing. And, actually, because we are very careful not to use up our holy water frivolously, except for those whom we were sure would not forsake their conversion (because they were about to die), most of the Indians believe that baptism causes death! We did our best to tell them that we, too, were all baptized, and we were still alive, but they responded that "this water is good for you, but not for us." The Jesuits, seeing their resistance, prayed to Our Lady, and asked that she might obtain this young boy's soul for Her Son. A strange thing happened: the child not only did not run away from us any more, but asked to be taken to us. When Father Quentin heard this, he took the child into our residence, embraced him, brought him to his room and baptized him. His godfather, Monsieur de Mala-part, named him André. This poor little boy was of such a sweet nature, so easy to be with, that all of us loved him. That's why Father Buteux asked his mother if we could keep him with us. "I don't want to give him to you," she said, "I love him like my own life." It was an act of God that this mother was nowhere nearby when the boy was taught the faith and baptized, because she might have tried to stop us, acting out of her misconception (that baptism would kill him rather than give him life); we had a hard enough time getting to keep his body after he died, as I will tell shortly.

December 27, Monsieur de Maupertuis gave the name of Marie to a little girl of two years old whom the Fathers baptized. She was the daughter of a deceased Indian chief, the leader of the natives, a brave and very wise man. He had left his wife with three children: a son of about seventeen years old, and two daughters. The youngest of the girls had died, and the son died a miserable death as I'll describe shortly. At the same time as he died, little André died. So, since they were related, they buried them in the same tomb (without telling us Jesuits, since we would have complained to André's grandmother that the little baptized boy had been buried without our permission.) Father Buteux begged that they give back the body to bury it in the French graveyard, but an Indian retorted, "Get out of here, we are not listening to you." This is a response that the Indians make to us from time to time if we ask them to do something that they don't want to do. It's true that we are still only able to express ourselves with small words and phrases, as if we were stuttering; but, just the same, if we say something that suits them, they never give us a hard time. Father Buteux, seeing their stubbornness, called an interpreter. But they told him that it had all been taken care of; the child was buried with the chief's son, and the chief's wife would be very upset if anyone started digging around in her son's grave. Father Buteux went to this woman and asked her permission to have André's body removed from the grave, but she refused to speak to him. A chief who was present spoke instead. "So be it," he said, "take both of the bodies with you and bury them in the French graveyard, but do not separate them, because they loved each other." "But they are actually very far apart," Father Buteux said, "because one was baptized and the other was not; as a result, one is blessed, but the other is burning in hell." "If that's all it takes for them to be together in heaven," the chief said, "then take the other boy's body and throw as much water on it as you like, then bury them in the same grave." Father Buteux smiled, and told him that wouldn't do any good. Finally, the Indian gave up, and the Jesuits took little André out of the unblessed grave and buried him in hallowed ground. *Thus was one kept, and one given over.* After the burial, the mother of the unbaptized boy, seeing that her son had been rejected like a lost soul, cried and cried. "Oh, my son," she wept, "I am so saddened by your death." Father Buteux, who had seen the young man as he suffered in his death throes, said to the mother, "See, here is the cure that those jokers thought they could get for your son: your daughter is near death; don't let them sing over her or follow their native customs." "Never," said she, "will I let them come near her, but instead, if she gets worse, I will call you." Several days later, as she was dying, the Jesuits baptized her with her mother's blessing.

On December 31, a girl about sixteen years old was baptized, and our Frenchmen named her Anne. When Father Buteux was teaching her about the faith, he told her that once she became Christian, when she died her soul would go straight to heaven where she would experience eternal joy. This talk of death frightened her, and she didn't want to talk to him about it any more, so they sent the interpreter Monsieur Nicolet to her (he often got involved in such acts of charity), and she listened to him more calmly. But he had a lot going on and couldn't meet with her regularly, so Father Quentin set about trying to teach this wild girl some of the rudiments of Christianity. This worked so well that, once she was convinced of the faith, she asked to be baptized, which the Father did. Grace has several effects: while this girl was haughty and fierce formerly, she became sweet and amenable after her conversion.

On January 7, 1636, the son of one of the great medicine men of this tribe became a Christian, although his father resisted this mightily for quite some time (since the Jesuits were very critical of him and exposed all his tricks, he couldn't stand them). However, since his son was about to die, the Indians begged Monsieur Nicolet to do what he could to save this soul. So Father Quentin and Monsieur Nicolet went to his bark hut and urged the medicine man to give his consent for his son to be baptized. He refused to listen to them, but then an old native woman said to him, "Do you think that the water that the Black Robes will sprinkle on your son's head will make him die? Can't you see that he's practically dead already? He's barely breathing! If these men are asking for some wampum from you, or for some beaver pelts for what they're offering to do for your son, then you could question their motives, but they want to do this for nothing in return. You know how they care for the sick; let them do their thing, and if the poor boy dies, they will bury him better than you could." So the sick boy was baptized and named

Adrian by Monsieur du Chesne, the doctor of our residence. The boy died shortly after. Father Buteux asked to be allowed to give him a Christian burial. "No, no," said the parents, "you can't have him before we have decorated his body as is our custom; then we will give him to you." They painted his face blue, black, and red; they put a small red hood on his head and then wrapped him in two bear skins and a panther skin, and over all that they put a great white sheet that they had bought, and they wrapped the little body up in this way like a package well tied up on every side, then they gave this to the Father, who gently kissed these holy remains to demonstrate to the Indians his respect for this small baptized angel. We buried him with great solemnity in the French cemetery. This greatly pleased the Indians, and encouraged them to allow more of their children to be baptized.

On January 8, a young girl beloved by her parents, but even more loved by God, died and went to heaven after having been washed in the Blood of the Lamb. Let me note here in passing the crazy lengths her father went to in his attempt to have her cured. His brother-in-law came to tell him that he had dreamed that his niece would get well if she were bedded down on a sheepskin colored with various figures. They found such a sheepskin, painted all sorts of strange pictures on it (canoes, oars, animals, and the like). The Fathers, who had not yet taught this girl about the faith, told them that this would be a useless remedy, but the Indians wanted to try it anyway. So they laid the sick girl on those paintings, and she was not cured. Another charlatan had the idea that if they laid her on a white sheet on which dancing and singing men had been painted, her illness would abate. So right away they painted such figures on a sheet (these actually looked more like monkeys, because they are not very good artists) and this remedy failed, too. The poor girl lay on the sheet, not being able to sleep and not getting any better. What will loving fathers and mothers not do for their children? These good people searched high and low, trying to find a cure for their daughter—but they did not seek out the one thing that was able to save her. They consulted a famous witch. This woman told them that the spirits had told her that they must kill a dog and eat it at a feast. Then, they should make a beautiful robe out of deerskin, decorate it with reddened porcupine quills, give it to the sick girl, and she would then get better. As they were getting the feast ready, another Indian had a dream that, in order to cure the girl, they must feast on twenty elk [moose] heads—but this really troubled the parents because, since it had not yet snowed, there was no way to hunt for elk. In the midst of this consternation, someone consulted an interpreter of dreams, and he said that twenty large loaves of bread (such as we French eat) could be substituted for the twenty elks' heads and that would have the same effect. They at least accomplished this much: the bread, or elk meat, could at least fill the Indians' stomachs—but as for curing illness, neither banquets nor beautiful robes could do anything.

While these great remedies were being tried, the Jesuit Fathers prayed to God for the salvation of this poor soul. They came to visit her, but the parents didn't want us to talk to her about our faith, imagining that baptism could hurt her body and possibly harm her soul. "Let's wait," they said, "until our daughter is beyond hope, and then, after we've tried every other remedy and if those don't work, we'll let you instruct her in the Christian faith." The Jesuits stopped visiting the sick girl for a while, but they continued to pray to God for the healing of her soul. The girl's mother actually wanted them to instruct her daughter, but her husband opposed this plan. Finally, God, who knows the hearts of all humanity, softened the hearts of the Indians for their daughter's good; not only did they no longer hate the Jesuits, but, on the contrary, they invited them to come, promising them that their daughter would be happy to listen to them. The Fathers went there right away. Father Buteux spoke first, explaining as clearly as possible the Christian creed. The parents, trying to help the Father who still did not speak the native language fluently, and hoping thereby to help their child, softly repeated to their daughter what he said, explaining the concepts in ways easier for her to understand. This poor soul was very thirsty for Christian doctrine, like dry earth yearns for dew from Heaven. It took some time to teach her, now always with the parents' approval, and even more eagerly on the sick girl's part. During the night she said to her mother, "when will it be daybreak, when the father shall come?" Then, praying to God, she said, "Missi ka khichitaient chaouerimitou," or, "You who have made all things, have pity on me." "Khiranau, oue ka nipien khita pouetatin khisadkihitin," or, "You who died for us, I believe in You, I love You, help me." When the Father visited her, she said to him, "You make me so happy when you come to see me; I have remembered everything you taught me," and she repeated it all to him word for word.

The night before she died, one of her uncles having come to see the Fathers, as he was eating with them he told them, "My niece is indeed very sick; you should baptize her." They answered him that they needed to finish teaching her. "But nonetheless, " they said to him, "if you see her getting much worse, call us, and we will come right away." About ten or eleven o'clock that night, he returned through the cold, across the snow, shouting with all his might outside the French residence that the Fathers needed to come right away to baptize the sick girl, as she was dying. The Fathers woke at the sound of his cries, astounded that neither the big guard dogs set loose at nighttime, nor the chilling cold, had kept this good man from coming to call them. Monsieur Nicolet and Monsieur de Launay came with the Jesuits; Nicolet was the godfather of the child and named her Marie, and her mother, even though she was a savage, expressed relief at this action and thanked the Jesuits and the rest of the French for having gone to the trouble of coming out (on such a bad night and in such terrible weather that Nicolet even got sick from it). The poor girl wasn't able to speak much, just enough to agree to the baptism (which she had wanted for some time). As soon as she was baptized, her death throes began, and soon after she went to Heaven, where she will be robed forever with a white robe symbolizing her purity. Her uncle, seeing that she was dead, called Father Buteux and said to him: "You show love during life, and you continue to show love even after death. Take my niece and bury her according to your custom. Make a deep grave, because my brother, who is so saddened by her death that he can't even speak, wants to bury her possessions with her." They wanted to bury two dogs with her, and several other things. But, the French would never want such dirty beasts to be buried with them, so the Indians requested, "let us bury them near your cemetery, because the dead girl loved them, and it's our custom to give to the dead that which they had owned or loved while they were alive."

We've fought this superstition as much as we could, but, as we are only beginning to spread the faith, sometimes we have to make accommodations, and hope this sort of belief will disappear with time. If we were to tell these poor people that they couldn't bury their dogs and possessions with them to take into the next life, they would refuse to let us visit their sick, and then many souls would be lost as a result. These are souls that we are harvesting one by one, until the days of great harvest finally come upon us. So they wrapped up the dead body in several robes, adorned it with trinkets and wampum (the diamonds and pearls of this country). They also put two oars in the grave, and two big bags filled with treasures, and various tools and instruments that girls and women use. Finally, the father of this beloved daughter, seeing how her body had been honored, and what a beautiful coffin we had made for her (something that really impresses the Indians), threw his arms around Father Buteux and said to him, "Nikanis, my dear friend, truly I know that you love me, and that all the Jesuits care for our people." Then, addressing his child's corpse, he said, "My daughter, you are happy to be so well lodged; this man is one of the chiefs of his tribe." Then, the wife became a Christian—as it were, as his proxy—and we hope that he, too, will one day become a Christian, along with all of his household. May it be so.

On the twentieth of the same month, God showed his goodness to us: we converted and baptized an Indian we'd been about to give up on. Because this young man was sick, Father Buteux went to call on him. There were a lot of people in the hut, so he invited him to come to our residence, if he was not too sick to come. He had himself brought to us right away. The Father spoke to him about our faith, but without much success, as he was married to the daughter of one of the worst sorcerers in the country, and so was not likely to be easy to convince. But, as we questioned him closely about his hopes for the afterlife, he answered that he didn't believe in it, because his soul, he said, "after my death will have no spirit, and so will not have any need of heavenly joys." "How do you know," asked the Jesuit, "whether souls after death feel things or not?" "Two of our men," he replied, "came back from the dead, and told us." "These souls that came back, were they able to feel anything?" "No," he said. "You are wrong," said the Jesuit, "because that's precisely what 'spirit' is: knowing that one might not have spirit; but let's stop making these subtle distinctions. If one is a good hunter, does one not 'have the spirit'?" Now, the Indians would never deny that statement, for all their best philosophy and theology is not in their head, but in their feet. "Now, is it true," the Father continued, "that there are souls of Indians who bravely hunt for souls that are in beaver and elk? So they have spirit." This reasoning got a bit too complicated for the Indian, so he didn't say anything more, but only observed that, if his fellows were not getting into Heaven, he didn't want to go there either. "You Jesuits say that you will go to Heaven," he said, "so go there; each of us has his own tribe and his own customs, and I will stick with mine." The Jesuit, seeing that he was getting stubborn, changed the subject and asked him how he was feeling. "It's some bad Algonquian who gave me this sickness," he answered, "he has put this sickness in my body because he's mad at me. He was afraid that I would kill him, so he went to the Manitou (Great Spirit) and made a deal with him to kill me." "How do you know that?" "I asked the Manitou, and he told me that I needed to give gifts to Manitou-siouekhi, the magicians, and then he would kill my enemy and I would get better. But I have nothing to give him: I already gave my wampum and my beaver belts, and unless I keep giving him things I will die."

That's what these witch-doctors do: they get everything they can out of these poor sick people, and when they have nothing left to give, they leave them to die. The Japanese believe similar fallacies; they believe that if the poor people have nothing to give to the high priests, then they cannot go to paradise. Christians, on the other hand, are compelled to recognize and adore God's goodness. Let our faith burn brightly, instead of being just a hidden ember, and may our belief—coupled with rational thought—triumph over the forces of nature! Theologians are right when they say that we need a softened heart, so that our will may follow God's purposes. This happens by a special act of the Holy Spirit, who makes it possible for us to have faith. Every day I see people who profess to believe that Christianity is true; they say believe that our faith is good, holy, and reasonable; yet, even admitting all that, they do not convert! I cry out to God, asking Him, what good is it that He has given us faith, if this faith is not welcome in the Indians' hearts?

But, getting back to my subject, the Jesuits had begun to give this young man up for dead, and had lost hope of saving his soul; but, since the conversion of a soul depends on God, who is all-powerful, they still went on visiting him, trying to give him a fear of hell, or some hope of eternal life. Finally, this young man was touched to the heart; his understanding, formerly full of figments of the imagination, opened to admit the light of day; his will became supple and obedient to God's will, just as a well-born child obeys his parents' wishes. When the Jesuits came to his cabin one day, he gave them a piece of elk meat that someone else had brought him. Father Buteux said to him, "We do not come here to get things, but rather to give to you; we do not want your worldly goods, but we would like to give you the treasures of Heaven; if you will only believe in God, we will be so happy!" "Yes," he said, "I do believe, and I want to go to be with God." He said that with his hands joined in prayer, and raising his eyes to heaven, with such devout speech and such a humble posture that the Jesuits were filled with astonishment and joy. They saw that God had done more in one moment than any man could do in a hundred years. That's why He is the Lord of all hearts. Here was this heart of stone changed into a true, feeling heart; he listened avidly; he believed already; he was full of repentance for the resistance he had put up before; he was lost in admiration of the God who had won over his heart. The Jesuits seeing him so well prepared, offered a mass for him, and after teaching him and catechizing him, in Holy Baptism they changed his Indian name to that of Nicolas.

God does what He will, in His own time. As soon as this young man was baptized, he died. Certain mockers and scoffers dwelled in his cabin. They would have done their best to dissuade him from turning to Christianity, but they were out hunting. They came back two hours after his death, astonished at what had happened, but who can resist the will of God? No one can turn away God's goodness; neither can they resist his ire. Even a heart made of bronze becomes molten if God chooses to burn it.

On the twenty-fifth, the day of St. Paul's Conversion, a young Indian named Paul finally gained in his illness what his father would not permit that he receive when he was well: this father had been very angry when we tried to catechize his young son, aged fifteen or sixteen; now he urged his son to listen to the Jesuits, and he even came to listen to them himself sometimes. Having heard them talk of the afterlife, the father then told his children what he had learned. He did not have enough courage, however, to express belief in Christian doctrines, even though he felt their truth in his heart. Human pride causes a lot of problems everywhere.

On the twenty-eighth and twenty-ninth, two sisters joined the rolls of God's children. The youngest, two years old, now sings of God's glory in the heavenly choir of angels. The eldest followed her soon after. She was about sixteen when she was born again in Christ. She had gotten sick, and it was not difficult to persuade her to believe in Him. It seems as though she believed even before the Jesuits talked to her about faith; her brother had often hung around our residence, helping the Jesuits to learn his language, and, since we often spoke about the mysteries of faith, he told his sister what he had heard. The brother was even happier than the Jesuits that he had helped to sow this sacred seed. Although no one knew it at the time, that seed had already taken root in her soul, and was beginning to bear fruit and flowers in his sister's heart. When she was asked, while lying sick, if she wanted to be baptized, she answered that she ardently desired this. The Jesuits, proceeding to catechize her, found that she already knew enough to be baptized. This astounded and relieved them. They named her Jeanne. With this name, she received an abundance of grace, so much so that it seemed the Son of God took particular pride in her, his new bride.

Father Buteux, as he was leaving, seeing that she was going to go off into the woods with her mother and the other Indians, said to her, "Farewell, my daughter, remember that you are now the beloved of God, and, if you die, He will take you to be with Him in his house, which is filled with every good thing." "Farewell, my Father," she replied, "I will not see you again, but it doesn't matter if I die, because I will go to a better place." She said this with such pious emotion that tears came to the eyes of the two Jesuits. They were so thrilled to see this little Indian speak like a heavenly angel. "But what can we give you, Jeanne, since you are leaving us for such a long time?" they asked her. "If you have some wine, give me a little, because this will be the last time you will give me medicine for my sickness, since I am going off into the woods to die. But I know that I will go to Heaven, isn't that right, my Father?" "Yes, my daughter, you will go there, if you continue in the faith." "Believe me, then," she said, "that I believe in God, and I will believe in Him for the rest of my life."

They gave her all the wine they had with them, which wasn't much, since not much had been sent to them and they had already given it out to the sick and needy. When the Indians came to fasten to their sleds and take away into the forest this poor girl, together with her little sister, both of them newly baptized, it seemed to the Jesuits that they were tearing their hearts out: for these poor people had no more food than a little bit of bread that they had given them; their lunch and dinner were in God's hands; their lodging would be snow and trees and a little bark. A strong northeast wind was blowing, the coldest wind in the whole country, and it was blowing directly on these poor sick girls. Nonetheless, they were happy to be on their way, as if they were setting forth to the Promised Land. "I reproach myself," the Jesuit who sent me this relation told me, "this people would reproach me for cowardice, for I did not have as much faith as they, and wept for the girl, forgetting to put my trust in God."

"FRIENDS IN THE LORD"

Women played a small but crucial role in the *Relations*. During the foundational days of the order, such powerful women as Vittoria Colonna gave succor, shelter, and financial support to Ignatius's earliest followers, Fathers Jay and Rodrigues, who also, through her, came into contact with the Italian Evangelicals or *spirituali*. Jesuits heard women's confessions, becoming confessors who could incline the potential patronesses' hearts to give money and material aid to the Jesuit mission. In 1553, the Jesuits were urged to cease from hearing women's confessions so as not to cause scandal, but Ignatius refused, and as late as 1561 Jesuits still heard women's confessions in women's homes, thus bringing them into intimate contact and positions of considerable influence.

Ignatius maintained an extensive correspondence with many (usually noble and well-positioned) women throughout Europe. Indeed, it is a little-known fact (intended to be a well-kept secret) that the Jesuit order actually had one female member. In 1545, Pope Paul III compelled Ignatius Loyola to bend his rules and allow "a few devout women" to live in obedience to him effectively as unofficial members of the Society. In 1554, Infanta Juana of Austria persuaded Ignatius to admit her into the Society under the code name of Matteo Sanchez. She died in 1578, still a member of the Society of Jesus. Juana's is a fascinating and untold story reminiscent of the tale of the medieval Pope Joan. Apparently, Juana proved somewhat difficult, and the Jesuits resolved never again to admit a woman to the order.

However, they continued to encourage—indeed, to expect—women to be touched by the example of the Society of Jesus and to play an ancillary role, as was the case with women in Messina in 1552 who visited hospitals and poorhouses to imitate the Jesuits by performing acts of mercy and service.

Women also occasionally joined the Jesuits as unofficial street preachers, as in Padua in 1556 when three or four women were encouraged by Jesuits to feed, preach, and minister to prostitutes in the area.

Father Polanco's report of 1565 narrated the inspiring tale of a woman, who gave Last Rites to a person who was dying because no priest was available at the time. The Society praised this *donna devota*.

So it is not surprising that the Jesuits continued this pattern, and were more than happy for the sponsorship, support, and service provided by other women in French Canada. Spurred to philanthropic giving by their reading of the *Relations*, some European noblewomen became major donors to the Jesuit endeavor. Henrietta of France read the *Relations* and declared them to be more passionate and inspiring than the romances she so adored; subsequently, she became a major proponent of their cause.

Another category of Frenchwomen supportive of the Jesuit cause was the mystic—women such as Marie de l'Incarnation, who left the security of an Ursuline convent in Tours for French Canada to missionize Indian children, in response to "a spiritual stirring" she felt while reading a Jesuit *relation*. Or the wealthy Madame de la Peltrie, who, inspired by the *Jesuit Relations*, sacrificed her house, money, and influence to realize her dream of establishing an Ursuline house, church, and hospital in Quebec. She traveled with a nobleman named Bernières, living a chaste *mariage blanc* in which their joint passion was dedicated to Christ and the service of others in tandem endeavors with the Society of Jesus.

The Jesuit account of Madame de la Peltrie's work is included in the following *relation*. Also included in this letter is an account of the Duchess d'Aiguillon, who conceived the plan of endowing a house for the religious in the New World; this house became an Ursuline-staffed hospital for Native Americans. The Duchess d'Aiguillon was the niece of

Cardinal Richelieu and the widow of Antoine de Beauvoir de Roure. After her husband's death fighting Huguenots, she devoted her life to philanthropy. She read Father Le Jeune's report of 1635 and was so inspired by it that she devised the project of having a Hôtel-Dieu, or hospital, built; she appealed to her uncle Richelieu for additional funds, and the hospital was established in Quebec in 1639. Another noblewoman, Madame de Guercheville, acquired a land grant from Henri IV for most of colonial America (much to the chagrin of the British, who also claimed the vast Virginia colony); she supplied money, energy, supplies, and encouragement for the early stages of the Jesuit mission.

The reading, interpretation, and personal appropriation of the *Jesuit Relations* prompted these women patrons and Jesuit collaborators—noble and non-noble, rich and poor, secular and religious—to exert agency in novel ways and positions that were often unavailable to them in European society. And their commitment to their work earned them the respect of the Jesuits.

Finally, other women came as *données* to the mission—lay sisters who devoted their lives, with no protection or remuneration, to helping the Jesuits in the New World. In the New World, Jesuits praised the hard work and self-sacrifice of Frenchwomen such as the hospital nuns in Montreal.

Native women, too, contributed to, or commented on, the Jesuit mission. Recent work by anthropologist and ethnographer Allan Greer has turned up archival evidence showing an explicit link between what he calls strong female "spiritual practitioners" and secret native circles of female penitential devotion in Quebec. Such native women, Greer claims, deliberately appropriated the pious practice and language of the European hospital nuns, layering over them traditional Iroquois techniques of soul strengthening and body testing (Greer, *Mohawk Saint*, 36). One such woman was the Indian saint Kateri (1656–1680), whose tale is recounted in several of the *Relations*.

Kateri grew up near the Jesuit mission church of St. Francis Xavier, close by Montreal. As a young, handicapped Mohawk girl, she lived the life of an outcast from her own people. She embraced Catholicism and found in it spiritual fulfillment as a way to possess social value. The accounts that the Jesuit Fathers Chauchetière and Cholenc penned of her pious death created a new genre: a hybrid narrative that melded traditional hagiographic characterizations with an unprecedented valorizing of a native woman. It had formerly been an unthinkable blurring of categories to conflate the words "saint" and "native" in the same phrase; the Mohawk saint Kateri is a true example of inculturation at its most compelling and convincing.

It is important to note that Jesuits were initially troubled by the extent to which Native American women held power. The Jesuit response to these often matriarchal cultures was often to try to reconfigure the roles of men and women, as well as their sexual customs, to more closely resemble those of their European contemporaries. The Jesuits patiently explained to native women that, in France, women were to be obedient to their masters, their husbands. Many native women were concerned about such teachings, fearing that ensuing social reorganization sponsored by the Jesuits would deprive native women of their strength and freedom.

As time went on, Jesuits allowed greater latitude of roles to native women in the missionary project. Most of the first converts to Christianity were women, and, in the zeal and dedication, these native women often surpassed many Frenchwomen in terms of their dedication to Christ and their aid to the Jesuits. Some functioned as interpreters, some were schooled by the Ursulines, others helped to convert other natives. There were even occasions on which Jesuits allowed women to act as confessors to other women. (One Jesuit famously said of a female native confessor: "She's a better confessor than I am."[1]) Overworked Jesuits, ministering to villages of upwards of a thousand Christian Indians, deferred to native women and to women's groups, encouraging them to model and teach the Christian way to men, children, and other women.

So, while women were sparsely spoken of by the Jesuits, they did nonetheless speak of them, when they did speak of them, with admiration, almost with awe. They paid these women the highest compliment available by referring to them as "virile": almost like men in their undaunted courage and strength of purpose and faithfulness of heart. The weight and significance accorded to woman, both native and European,

1. John O'Malley, *The First Jesuits* (Cambridge, Mass.: Harvard University Press, 1993), 152.

by the Jesuit Fathers in terms of their companionship in the cause for Christ is, in fact, startling.

It appears that the Jesuits eventually came to view their female partners in a way that crosses (or disregards) gender categories. This phenomenon might best be viewed as a sort of translation exercise (appropriately enough for a mission so dependent on translating concepts from one language and culture to another in order to proselytize!). Women appear here as strong manipulators of symbolic discourse, complex carriers of social mores, who are able to bridge the gap between two cultures, to cross categories.

Thus, the *Relations* is, in the words of Québecois literary historian Aurélien Boivin, a seminal text, but also an "ovarian" text, one in which we hear what women have to say, and also what the Jesuits have to say about them.

❁ ❁ ❁

Report on what took place in New France in 1639

By Father Paul Le Jeune
My Reverend Father:

The birth of an heir to the French throne; the fondness our King expresses for our Indians and the presents he sends them; the concern that Monseigneur the Cardinal feels for New France and the funding he gives to our Huron mission; the provisions that the members of the Company of New France make for our new catechists and converts; the Chevalier de Montagny's leadership as our Governor; the arrival of the nuns; the financial assistance that you yourself have sent us; the help that many people of all walks of life have given us; the prayers of the pious—this is what we talked about during the ocean crossing. I am even more grateful, since I was able fully to experience all these blessings back in Europe, and now see their results here. Further, I believe, with Your Reverence's decision to send Father Vimont to us, that he will be able to make up for any lack I may have had in the exercise of my duties. Father Vimont tells me that you want me to write this year's report, so I'll begin.

About the joy we felt in New France when we heard that the Crown Prince was born, and about a council that the Indians held

We were worried this year when the fleet from France did not get here by its usual time, but we were relieved when a ship appeared some 40 nautical miles away from Quebec. This ship brought a letter addressed to our Governor. Everyone ran out to hear the news, but, when the letter said nothing about the much-hoped-for birth of an heir, we were a bit sad. We had heard last year that the Queen was pregnant and we were hoping for a child whose birth would be a blessing and a miracle; we all believed that God would give us this good gift, and that the Queen would give birth to a Prince. This ship should have brought us that news but, no, not a word: the letter just told us that other ships were following close behind; a thick fog had separated them from this ship. However, when the winds changed, the news that we had been hoping for finally arrived.

We all shouted the words "Crown Prince" and we began to celebrate. The news spread everywhere; we sang the *Te Deum Laudamus* and lit bonfires and set off all kinds of fireworks! The members of the Company of New France encouraged this display and showed how happy they were over the birth of a Prince; but even before we had heard from them, the Governor had already said we could start celebrating. Fireworks shot up into the skies, then fell back to the ground with sprays of golden sparks and silver stars; torches lit the beautiful night even brighter; booming cannon shots echoed far away in the deep Canadian forest. The Hurons who were there covered their mouths to show how amazed they were; they had never seen anything like this, and thought that such display meant that we ruled not only on earth but over the heavens as well.

Not content just with fireworks, we made a parade that would have impressed even Parisians. Before I tell you about it, I want to say something about the presents that His Majesty had sent us and that we brought out for this festive procession. Last year, a Canadian Indian, the well-known Iwanchou's son, was sent to France where the King received him at court. This Indian gave the King a crown made of porcelain beads as a symbol of his nation's desire to be loyal subjects of the

King. The King and Queen showed him the Prince, were very gracious to him, and gave the Indian six suits of expensive nobleman's clothes, made of gold, velvet, silk, scarlet, and other expensive fabrics.

After this young Indian man returned to his people, he came to Quebec with some of them and went to visit our Governor, bringing him the expensive suits of clothing. There were Hurons, Algonquians, and Montagnais there with the Governor, and they all admired how generous our King had been, and called them *their* King. When the packages with the clothing were opened, the Governor did not want to cause jealousy among the different nations, so he decided that rather than give the clothing to just one group of Indians, he would share them, especially since this young Indian had conveyed his obedience to the King not only on his own behalf but also as the spokesperson for other Indian tribes. So the Governor gave the young man three of the suits of clothes—one for himself, one for his son, and one for his father. Trying to decide to whom to give the other three suits, the Governor decided to choose three Christian Indians from three tribes; he said that His Majesty would like this idea, since he himself had asked the young Indian if he were baptized and if he were from a settled tribe. When I told three of our Christian Indian the presents they would receive, and told them to pray for His Majesty and for the Crown Prince, they were amazed, and then they amazed me with their answer: "Nikanis, tell our Captain to write to our King," they said, "and tell him that we are grateful and we admire him. But, keep these clothes here with you, because we don't need them except if we wear them in a parade thanking God for him, his son, and his wife." (He meant that they would wear them in a procession such as the one we had when we celebrated the birth of the Prince.) "And when we die, if you or the other Jesuits say prayers for the King, tell our children to wear these clothes so that they may always know the love our King showed us when he gave us these presents."

Now let me tell you about that procession in which they wore these beautiful clothes. We decided to have the parade on the Feast of the Assumption. In the early morning, our new Christian converts came to hear mass, to confession, and to take communion. All the other Indians in Quebec got together and we put them in marching order for the procession. The procession began, the Cross and banner leading the way. Monsieur Gand came next, walking in front of the Indians, the first six of whom were wearing the royal clothes. The Indians processed two by two in a very dignified way. Next came the founder of the Ursuline order in Quebec, Madame de la Peltrie, with three or four Indian girls—dressed like French girls—walking next to her; then came the Indians' wives and daughters dressed in their native clothes, perfectly in step with the rest. The clergy came next, and then our Governor, the Frenchmen and Frenchwomen of Quebec in an order appropriate to their social standing.

As soon as the procession began, cannons were shot off, frightening and impressing the Indians. We walked to the hospital and, when we arrived, all the Indians knelt down on one side and all the French facing them, with the clergy in the middle. Then the Indians prayed together for the health of the King, thanking God for having given him a Crown Prince. They also prayed for the Queen, for all the French, and for all of their own people; then they chanted the Creed. Next, the clergy, the Governor, and the chief of the Indians entered the chapel dedicated to the Blood of Jesus Christ, and there they prayed the same prayers as before. When we left the Hospital, we went to the Ursuline convent. As we processed in front of the fort, we heard ceremonial musket shots, and the cannon boomed out again. We did the same thing at the convent, then the nuns sang the *Exaudiat*, much to the Indians' delight, and we French were very proud to hear two choirs of holy virgins praising God's greatness here in the New World.

When we left the Ursulines, we went right to the church, remaining in the same order and maintaining the same humble bearing as when we started to process. At the chapel door, we repeated the prayers in the Indian language, then everyone came inside and the procession ended. Then the Governor came a feast to about a hundred Indians. We brought the six Indians who were dressed in the royal clothes, and fed them in our house. After dinner, they came to Vespers with us, still wearing their clothing. Some didn't even seem at all Indian except for their brown skin, and they carried themselves with grace and dignity.

After Vespers, we were going to dismiss them, but one of them told me that the Indian chiefs were waiting in our hall for me to hold a council. I went there to listen to them, and since they were beginning to make speeches I sent for Father Vimont to let him know. He brought the Governor and Madame de la Peltrie with him. They were both very impressed with the Indians' piety. When everyone was seated, the Indian Captain said to me, "Be smart, Father Le Jeune and don't say anything; pay attention so that you don't miss anything." "Ho, ho," I said, as the Indians do. "I'm not the one speaking," the Captain said, "But I'm speaking for everyone you see sitting here today; they have asked me to tell you that we all want to be Christian, and we all want to live near you and farm the land. You've lead us to believe that many people will come to join you, but so far there are not many. So let's have our Captain write to the King and say, 'All the Indians thank you; they are surprised that you take time to think of them; and they ask you to help us, since we love you. We want to settle here but we can't build houses like yours unless you help us.' Tell your brothers to write, and you write, too, so that the king will know we are sincere." That is how Indians speak.

When the Indian had finished speaking, another one said to me, "Father Le Jeune, I'm not from this area. My home is in the mountains to the south. I've not been in Quebec for a long time. These men came to see me at my home and told me that you were having houses built for the Indians and that you were going to teach them how to farm. They asked me if I would come see you and live near you with them. Here I am, and I see that you've begun work but not made much progress yet for as many people as we are. So, be sure you are telling the truth and do what you have said. I'm going back to my home and when spring comes I'll return here to see if you've made good on your promise. It would be good for us to live in houses and to learn to farm, so that we will no longer live like animals in the forest."

Everyone hearing this understood how he felt. The Governor promised to do everything he could to help. Father Vimont was almost impatient; he felt that, because we don't have enough workers to do this work fast enough, Satan is still in control of the Indians' souls. Madame de la Peltrie exclaimed, "For the price of one dinner in Paris, or for a ticket to a ballet that lasts only two hours, we would have whatever we need to save so many souls here in New France! I have only a few workers with me, but we'll do what we can to help. Father," she said to me, "tell them that if I myself could work beside them, I would." The Indians laughed at this idea, saying that corn planted by such feeble arms would be too weak. We all agreed that we would help the Indians when spring came.

I made them feel a lot better when I told them that the Captain who had begun to build St. Joseph's Residence had provided enough funding for six workers, so that, even after his death, the work could continue. The Indians couldn't understand how this happened; why the workmen wouldn't just leave with the money he'd left for them; how a dead man could make living men keep working; for they don't know what a "rent" or a "revenue" is. If only more wealthy people would follow the Captain's example! It's never a loss to think of heavenly matters instead of earthly needs.

Now the Indians asked the man named Ioanchou, and his son who had been to France, to join with the others. They answered that they would go and see how their people felt about this and, if they wanted to come to Quebec, they would return with their people.

I was happy to talk with an Indian who had been to France about the glories of France. "Tell me if I'm right," I said to them, "ask your friend here; everything I told you about how wonderful France is, isn't it all true? So never doubt me again!"

This Indian told great stories of what he had seen, but what he had to say was according to how he had experienced these things. So, although he had admired many things, like the crowds in Paris, the many restaurants, the enormous statue of Saint Christopher at Notre-Dame Cathedral (which terrified him at first), the coaches, which he called "big rolling moose," he said that nothing had impressed him as much as the King, whom he saw on New Year's Day walking with his guards. He carefully watched all the King's guards as they marched in order; the Swiss guards really impressed him with their uniforms and precision, and he liked the sound of their drums. When he left, he did not speak for the rest of the day—so the Jesuit who was with him told me— because he wanted to think about the marvels he had seen.

He told his people all these things, and they listened to him eagerly. The King's piety promoted our Society of Jesus, because this Indian said that the first time he saw the King was at mass; the Indian prayed to Jesus there as he is doing here. He also said in public that the King had asked him if he was baptized, which helps reinforce our efforts to convince the Indians here of the significance of baptism. As soon as the

Indian saw the King, he said to the Jesuit with him, "Okay, we can go now; I've seen everything I wanted to see now that I've seen the King."

After all this, our Indians, the recipients of the gifts of French clothes, decided to send the Crown Prince a native costume. When they handed it to me, they made a little speech, saying, "We're not sending him a present, since he has so much more wealth than we do; we're just sending him a little toy to amuse his Son who may like to see how our children dress."

We are sending this little costume to Your Reverence. I don't know if it's a good idea to give it to the King, however, because our Indians are currently afflicted with smallpox, and the garment may have been infected. I did have it with me before the disease broke out, but even so, when it's the King who's involved, better safe than sorry.

About the nuns who have recently come to New France, and what they are doing

In 1639, Madame the Duchess of Aiguillon endowed a house for a religious order in the New World; she had ordered it to be built in honor of God. Then the Ursuline order needed someone to lead them here, and an "Amazon," an amazing, heroic woman, miraculously came forward to bring them to this far corner of the world. It is indeed amazing that—at the very moment that God inspired the Duchess with this plan to build a Hospital for Indians who would otherwise die in the woods without medical treatment, and while she was thinking that perhaps the Hospital nuns from Dieppe might come here to staff her new building—God also caused a modest, virtuous noblewoman elsewhere in France to plan a training school (seminary) for the daughters of our Indians, and to staff this school with Ursuline nuns. And God worked things out so that all these projects were realized at the same time, so that the nuns could all cross the ocean together, and so that the Indians would receive the simultaneous double benefit of having both a new Hospital and a new school.

It would be rude of me were I not to say a few words here about the second lady I mentioned. She's from Alençon; her name is Magdelaine de Chauvigny; she is the daughter of Monsieur de Chauvigny, who was, before his death, the Elector of Alençon. She has wanted to be a nun ever since she was a child, but her father married her to a gentleman named Monsieur de Peltrie; this man died five years later, leaving her childless and a widow. She was in the habit of reading the Jesuit reports from French Canada, and, as soon as her husband died, she began to think seriously about how she could help educate the little Indian girls there. She prayed that God would help her accomplish this, and, having decided to give up everything for this goal, she asked God to give her a sign if He approved of this project and her role in it. Soon after, she became deathly ill and doctors felt that she could not recover. She nonetheless made a vow to go to New France. The doctors returned and found her much improved. Without knowing of her vow, he joked, "Madame, your disease has left for Canada." He had no idea how right he was, she laughed!

When she felt better, she thought constantly about how to implement her plan. But her father wanted her to marry again and threatened to disinherit her if she would not. She saw that her father was not going to change his mind and, realizing that she would spoil her plan (since she'd lose all her money) if she did not at least seem cooperative, she pretended that she would consider a remarriage. Her father was soothed, he died soon after, and she kept her inheritance. Then, immediately, she divided the property with her sister and left for Tours. Monseigneur the Archbishop of Tours welcomed her warmly and was pleased to hear of her plans. Admiring her courage and virtue, he decided to help her however he could. The Ursulines at Tours also received her gladly, fulfilled her life-long wish of becoming a nun, and assigned her another brave and virtuous nun to accompany her. Overjoyed, Madame de la Peltrie returned to Paris with two Ursulines. Mother Cecile of the Cross, an Ursuline, was also chosen from the Dieppe Convent to join her.

When we heard that a ship bringing the beginnings of a Jesuit school, a hospital and an Ursuline convent, was about to dock in Quebec, we could hardly believe the good news; as we approached the water's edge, we saw that it was true! As the nuns disembarked, they fell on their knees and kissed the ground of New France, which they already called their "beloved country." The ocean crossing had not damaged the nuns in any way; consecrated to God, they were as fresh and healthy as when they had left their home in France.

The Governor welcomed them with great ceremony; we led them to the chapel where a *Te Deum* was sung; the cannon boomed out. Then we took the nuns to their temporary housing. Over the next several days they were taken to the Jesuit residence at Sillery, where the Indians also live. When they saw these poor people gathered in the chapel, praying and reciting the Creed, the nuns wept. They then visited the families who had settled there in nearby cabins. Madame de la Peltrie, leading the group, hugged every little Indian girl she came across, astonishing all the Indians, as they are much more reserved about these things.

The Jesuits who arrived with them got to work right away baptizing Indians. Madame de la Peltrie is already the godmother of several. She ran here and there, wanting to be involved in everything having to do with the Indians.

As soon as the visit was over, the nuns went into seclusion. The three nuns whom the Archbishop of Rouen had sent went to live and work in the hospital. The three Ursulines went to live in a private house. Soon after, six Indian girls came to be with Madame de la Peltrie and the Ursulines at their school, and they got to work teaching them their lessons. But if ever we can build a larger house for the Ursulines, and get enough supplies, there will be so many Indian girls who come that I don't know how the nuns will manage!

The three nuns in the hospital really didn't have appropriate lodgings, their luggage had not yet arrived, and sick people were already being brought to them for nursing. We lent them our straw beds and mattresses so that they could begin their charitable work. They had sick people but no medicine. Our Governor helped with all that he could give. It wasn't possible to handle all these things at once, and at first it was at times necessary to turn away some of the sick. Even so, since the Indians do nothing at all for one of their own who is ill—considering them as already dead, like someone living already in another world— here the nuns did everything they could, and the Indians were very impressed.

By the way, I must add that we see four great endeavors that are all related: gathering the Indians into settlements, establishing a hospital, founding a school for little Indian boys, and one for Indian girls. The first initiative is crucial to the success of the other three. If the Indians remain nomads, then their sick will always die in the woods and their children will never be educated. But when the tribes stop being nomadic, and learn to farm in settlements, the hospitals and schools will be put to good use.

To persuade the Indians to settle, members of the Company of New France have said that sedentary Indians will be given the same inducements as those granted to French settlers; some cleared land is set aside as a dowry for Indian girls entering into Christian marriages; and supplies and gifts are stockpiled for the Christian Hurons when they come to trade in Quebec. One good and pious person has given a hundred coins to finance the wedding of an Indian girl whom a Frenchman of good character would like to marry.

About the hospital (From the 1646 Report)

The nurse-nuns arrived in Quebec on August 1, 1645. They were overwhelmed with patients as soon as they got here. The reception area of the hospital was too small, so we quickly put up some cabins in the hospital garden. There was not enough furniture for so many people, and they had to cut the blankets and sheets they had brought into two or three pieces. So, instead of resting after their journey, the nuns were so busy and overwhelmed that we thought they might get sick and the hospital would fail. Sick Indians were arriving from all over the place, the smell was hideous, the weather was horribly hot, there was not enough unspoiled and good fresh food, and these poor nuns, having just arrived in a totally strange new land, had little time to sleep and many hardships to endure. From August 1 until the month of May, more than a hundred patients were admitted to the hospital, and over two hundred Indians were treated there, either with first aid treatment or as overnight patients. As many as thirty Indians slept overnight at the hospital on any given evening.

I have taken what I'm about to tell you from the correspondence of the Mother Superior of the order. "The sick people's patience amazes me. I have seen many who are completely covered with smallpox, burning up with fever, who hardly complain at all, who obey the doctor's orders, and who are grateful for the smallest thing we are able to do for them. They are able to take the medicine that we brought from France, and this is helping them; we can also bleed them to help reduce their fever. The Indian mothers love their children so tenderly that they take the medicine given to their children into their own mouths and then pass it into their children's mouths."

Most hospitals observe the custom of washing the feet of the poor on Maundy Thursday. Our Governor wanted to participate in this ceremony, so mass was said in the hospital chambers in the morning, and all the nuns and Indians took communion, then the men lined up on one side and the women on the other. The Governor began to wash the men's feet and the Chevalier de l'Isle and other Frenchmen did so, also. Madame de la Peltrie, Madame de Repentigny, several other Frenchwomen, and the nuns humbly and tenderly washed the Indian women's feet. God knows what the Indians thought of having such respectable people kneeling at their feet. Afterwards, there was a buffet meal for everyone. One Frenchman who was not able to be present gathered his household together in the evening and observed the foot-washing custom with them.

About the Ursuline school (From the 1642–43 Report)

Now that the Ursuline nuns have established themselves here in Quebec, I'll tell their story. This school is one of the most wonderful things about Quebec and a great help in housing and converting the Indians. The nuns left their temporary lodging for their permanent home on November 21, 1642. The building is large and well built. They have found a good, deep well in the foundations of the structure, which is a great help. It's also a very safe place to be in, the safest in French Canada, about a hundred feet away at the most from the fort. Many Indian girls, both day students and boarders, are there, as well as the daughters of the French settlers. Many Indians come often to visit them; they also get help or take some lessons. The nuns' front room doubles as a classroom, and those Indians who come to visit take their lessons in that room with the students. These activities cost money in addition to the expenses for room and board of the regular students, and these people also need to be fed. I haven't said anything about Madame de la Peltrie, because a year ago she left to be in Montreal when the new school was founded there.

This year the nuns added a chapel on to the school and made the structure larger so as to house more nuns and students. They've only just begun work on the addition, and more remains to be done than has yet been accomplished, but we must have patience. Canada teaches us the need for that.

Concerning the residence in Sillery, and about the Indians' life there

About 35 or 40 families of Christian Indians live in the little town of St. Joseph called Sillery, only a few miles outside of Quebec. They live there year-round except for when they go hunting. Many nomadic Indians come to stay with them from time to time; we help them out and take the opportunity to teach them about Christianity. This may not seem like many people if you don't know much about how nomadic Indians live, but actually it's quite a good number and a real improvement on the life the Indians led before they became Christian.

The Christian Indians at Sillery have a good reputation; from Tadoussac and Miskou, even in the Huron country, other Indians admire how they live. The families who live in Sillery are either Montagnais or Algonquian. The Montagnais tribe lives closer to Quebec and the tribe takes its name from the mountains [*montagnes*] where they live. The Algonquians are in the backcountry; some come from the island and others from other areas near Huron country; some are neighbors of the Montagnais and mingle freely with them. Because they are Christian, and due to the influence of the Frenchmen they've met in Quebec, the latter are peace loving while many of the other groups, although impoverished and practically without resources, are still oddly prideful. Because of their attitude, it is harder for us to convert the other Algonquians and Hurons who come through the territories on their way to Quebec.

So far we've only been able to build four little French-style dwellings for all these Indian families. We plan to build two more this fall; we began construction on them last winter and have been given some more money to help us finish the project. The houses are built either facing the Jesuit residence or facing the hospital, separated from the residence by a low hill. The Montagnais have chosen to live near us, while the Algonquians occupy the houses near the hospital; the chiefs live in the French-style houses but the other Indians still live in native wood structures, each tribe staying together, until we can put up some more small buildings for them.

The main advantage of the French-style houses is the little attics in which the Indians like to store their supplies and belongings. Otherwise they lose them, having no place to keep them in. We haven't been able to do much more because for every house we build we must first clear a proportionate amount of land. In the beginning we had eight men working at Sillery but now there are only four, and the money that Monsieur Sillery had set aside to be used for their upkeep after his death is still tied up in the French court system. Also, it is even harder to maintain these dwellings than it was to build them.

Now I'll describe how the Indians spent their time in Sillery. Ships left from Quebec for Europe on October 7 last year, and their departure left us in peace and quiet, so that each man didn't have much to think about except his family's needs. Our Indians here in Sillery, and some others who have joined them, continued to fish for eels; every year from September to the end of October they fish for them in the St. Lawrence River and they catch a lot of eels, saving them to take to the annual trading party in Quebec. When they catch a lot, like this time, the French salt and store them but the Indians smoke them, each setting aside supplies for the winter. The Indians leave their huts and go fishing; they camp just a gun's shot away so that the fishes' entrails, scooped out before the eels are smoked, will not give them diseases. When they have finished fishing, around the beginning of November, they return to their cabins and stock their lofts with smoked fish.

Just when they had finished their chores, thirteen canoes with Indians from the Atikamegues arrived. They had come to spend the winter with our Indians, and also to take lessons from us. Father Buteux, who had come from Trois-Rivières to spend the winter in Sillery, was in charge of giving lessons to both the Montagnais and the Atikamegues.

They lived together and spoke the same language. Father Dequen was assigned to teach the Algonquians.

This is what we did all winter: Father Dequen went to the hospital every day and said mass for the Algonquians to the men, women, and children who came to hear it. The chapel and the sickrooms were often filled. Before mass, Father Dequen would translate the prayers aloud into the Indian language, and they all repeated them. After noon, I taught catechism to the Algonquian children, who gathered in the hospital sickrooms, as eager and ready to learn as any French child. If only they were as disciplined, they'd learn just as well as the French do. When they remembered their responses, I'd reward them with a knife, or a piece of bread, or a rosary; sometimes I'd give the tallest or the smartest a hat or an axe; this is a good way to help out these children who are all so poor. The children would run through the cabins showing off their prizes, and the parents were very pleased with their children's love of learning.

At prayer time or during catechism, the hospital nuns would often sing hymns that had been translated into Algonquian. The Indians love to sing, and they really sing well. When the Indians didn't have much to eat, we'd eat a bit of corn bread (*sagamite*) after catechism. The nuns contributed to the overall expense and usually, in addition to nursing the sick, the nuns also had two or three cabins-full of the poorest Indians to feed. This care can really be expensive, but our conscience will not let us stop providing for their needs. That's what the situation is with the Algonquians.

Father Buteux spent his winter the same way. Since the Montagnais and the Atikamegues had moved a bit back into the woods on a small hill near Sillery, he had to go there every day after mass and in the evening, when he gathered the men and women together. The snow was three or four feet deep. I used to see him every night, when it was already dark, leaving with a lantern in his hand. The wind often blew out the light, and he often fell head-over-heels in the snow. People who knew him in France would be amazed at his courage and perseverance, as he had never been in good health there.

This is how the Indians spent the early winter. Toward the middle of January, the snow lying thick on the ground, they left their cabins at Sillery and went about a quarter of a mile away from Quebec, where they made hunting sleds and got ready to hunt. They stayed there about three weeks. Father Buteux followed them, and stayed with them in their cabins. Although it was very cold and snowy, they traveled about a quarter-mile every day to come to hear mass in Quebec. They usually went to the Ursuline chapel, where Father Buteux gave them lessons. They also frequently visited the nuns, and practiced saying their prayers in the parlor with them. The Ursulines were very kind to them, feeding them and giving the Indians whatever they needed. They do the same for the Montagnais and the Algonquians when they come to Quebec. This sort of expense is to be expected, when ministering to the Indians.

At the beginning of February, the Indians all left their huts to go into the woods to hunt moose. The day after they left, while I was walking from Quebec to Sillery, I found one cabin filled with twelve or thirteen invalids, old men and children. The Indians had told me about them the night before, and had asked that they be taken to the hospital. When I came, they covered themselves with their bark blankets and followed me as best they could, and went to the hospital for the rest of the winter, at first in the sickrooms and then in the cabins nearby.

The Indians hunted for about two months, and several came back for Easter. Each cabin usually has a piece of paper that lists the feast days. Jean Baptiste came back with his group on the Wednesday before Easter, and so they were all present the next day for the foot-washing ceremony at the hospital. Then we had a great feast. Five Hurons who had spent the winter at Sillery and who took lessons there were really impressed by this festival. Father Brébeuf explained it all to them, and they shared this information with their tribe.

Toward the end of April, all the Indians again came together. Each returned to his own hut and got his cabin ready, put away his supplies, prepared his pelts, then came to take lessons. When the snow had finally melted, each one went to his field and got the soil ready for planting. It was wonderful to see how ready they were to work! But this did not last; they had just finished planting corn when we got news that there was an Iroquois war party in the area. Our Indians formed groups of warriors and went to the forts at Richelieu and Three Rivers to fight off the Iroquois. They soon returned, very depressed, to Sillery; they had heard about the King's death and the death of the Cardinal. Also, since no arms or supplies had been shipped to them from France, the Indians split up into small groups and went hunting near Tadoussac, trying to avoid the enemy while waiting for the ships to bring help.

❄ ❄ ❄

About the hospital (relocated from Quebec to Sillery)

Canada burst into tears when we heard of the deaths of the King and the Cardinal, but the hospital especially went into mourning, and for good reason: Madame d'Aiguillon, its founder, has been personally affected by the sad news. She loves the nuns like a mother, and they share her sorrow.

Let me tell you what has happened at the hospital. In addition to being an impressive structure and a place of philanthropy, the hospital also helped to support the Indians and paid many of the expenses for their upkeep. Although the village of Sillery is still small, it certainly would never have gotten as big as it has without the help of the nuns. This was hard work for them; it often took a whole day for them to go to Quebec to find the herbs they needed or to get a few eggs for an invalid's diet. The nuns were so eager to help the Indians and to encourage them to settle here that they actually left the hospital in Quebec and relocated to Sillery, just as they had left the comforts of their home in France to come work in Quebec. They realized that if the French got sick, they were still able to travel to Sillery, but, if the Indians got sick, they had no way to get to the hospital in Quebec. The hospital in Quebec was turning into a hospital for Indians, without any Indians there.

Although everyone was afraid of the Iroquois, that concern did not stop anyone from going to Montreal or to other towns along the river, so the nuns did not think this worry would stop anyone from getting to Sillery. Also, since their building had already been finished in Quebec, the nuns could always go back there if there were any concern over safety in Sillery. If any more Frenchmen came, they could establish their own hospital in Quebec, and that would be good for the colony and help nearby Indians.

The nuns have helped over a hundred Indians in the hospital at Sillery this year; the Indians are from various tribes, such as the Montagnais, Algonquians, Atticamegues, Abnaquiois, and Hurons from the

Tadoussac and the Saguenay areas, as well as some other tribes from father away. As I write, an Indian woman is slowly dying here. Father Buteux brought her here when he returned from Tadoussac. She comes from the Saguenay region, about thirteen days away. Five or six French workers have also been helped at the hospital; they came down with a disease while working at the fort in Richelieu, and would have died had they not been brought to the hospital.

A widow named Louise had a daughter named Ursula who was married to a captain in Tadoussac. Ursula got sick and, after suffering for two or three years, finally came to the hospital in Sillery. She was in the sickroom and then, at times, in a nearby cabin, where, eventually, we had to give her Last Rites. Her mother had decorated the little cabin with bark, like a prayer chapel, and, like Indians do, she hung new, embroidered beaver and moose pelts on the walls. She put the most beautiful one on the sick woman's bed, covered the floor with leaves, and hung more from the rafters. Then she borrowed a crucifix, two candlesticks and candles from the nuns. She put these near her daughter's bed. The whole neighborhood came to hear mass at the dying woman's bedside. Her mother had her buried with great solemnity, and put in her grave many objects of value, such as beaver pelts and porcelain. When the nuns reminded the mother that she was poor, and that buried possessions couldn't be used by a corpse, the woman responded, "But you people buried your sister in her beautiful dress and with great honor" (this was Mother de Sainte Marie, who had died two years ago).

Now I'll write about the Iroquois prisoner whom the Algonquians brought to the Jesuit residence last year. The prisoner and his captors landed across from the hospital, and all of our Indians went to see him. They were kind to him, brought him into all of their dwellings and had him dance for them. He obeyed, although his body was covered with wounds. Afterwards, two of our head Indians took the prisoner to the hospital, where the nuns took him in. They called the doctor in, and the sick ward was filled with Indians curious to see the prisoner and his wounds. I was there, and what I saw horrified me. He was brave and did not cry out while the nuns bandaged him up; he used sign language to tell what had been done to him, but did not show any anger at those who had tormented him. Luckily, there was a sick Abnaquiois, a man named Claude who had been baptized, and this Christian understood the Iroquois language. The prisoner was happy to meet Claude; he was also amazed at how kind the nuns were to him. Claude explained to him that the nuns devoted their lives to caring for others, and that they had vowed never to marry. The Iroquois was very impressed. He recovered fairly quickly and, returned to his own country. There, he told everyone how kind the French and the Christian Indians had been to him. He shared the Good News of the Gospel.

Ves tibus pretiosis exutus, ac pauperi
donatis, sacco ac fune praecinctus
Christi domini paupertatem amplectitur.

10

Plate 1. *"Ves tibus pretiosis exutus, ac pauperis donatis."* Ignatius preached
Christian charity to everyone, recognizing Christ in the other: what would
become the Society of Jesus' dictum of *cura personalis*. Here, on a chilly,
star-studded evening, Ignatius takes off his cloak to offer it to a man
shivering in rags.

Plates 2a and 2b. *"Nautae suis . . ."*
and *"In Hispaniam rediturum a navi . . ."*
Traveling the globe to bring Christ to
those who had not heard of Him, the
Jesuits faced great hardship. They
embarked in small boats, setting off
on their mission with courage and
faith. Sometimes the sea voyages alone
were a terrible trial.

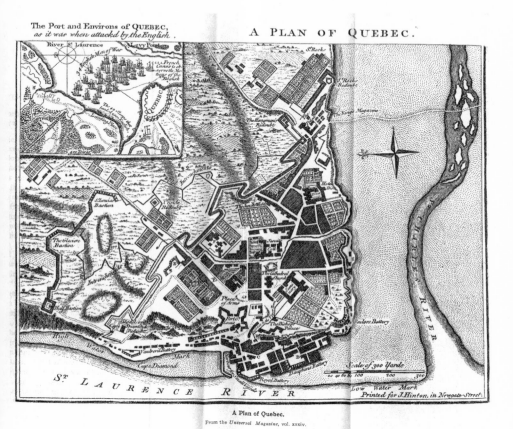

The Port and Environs of QUEBEC,
as it was when attacked by the English.

A PLAN OF QUEBEC.

A Plan of Quebec.
From the *Universal Magazine*, vol. xxxiv.

Plate 3. An early eighteenth-century map of Quebec City.

Ad ædem S. Petri in monte aureo contendens,
rem sacram pro salute Codurij facturus, in medio
Sixti Ponte resistit continuo, coelumq; tantisper
intuitus, ac diuinitus de eius morte admonitus,
Redeamus, inquit, socius mortuus est.

62

Plate 4. *"Ad aedem S. Petri in monte aureo contendens, rem sacram . . ."* Ignatius experienced many visions and special spiritual revelations that strengthened him in his faith and encouraged him to form the Society of Jesus. Jesuits in the New World also chronicled similar confirming paranormal phenomena.

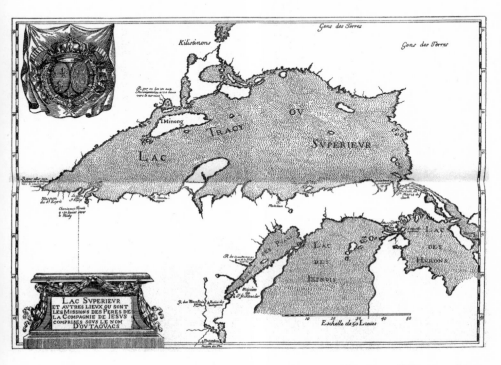

Plate 5. "Jesuit Map of Lake Superior, and Parts of Lakes Huron and Michigan." This map shows the names of various Jesuit missions. Some Indian names for the missions are also included.

PENAUBSKET ALNAMBAY UDENEK, OLD-TOWN INDIAN VILLAGE.

CORPUS CHRISTI'S DAY AT
OLD-TOWN INDIAN VILLAGE,
ON THE PENOBSCOT RIVER.

Plates 6a and 6b. The missions to the Abenaki resulted in well-established towns, where Jesuits lived among the Indians, teaching them the Christian faith and ministering to them. These are two representations of missions to the Abenaki on Penobscot Bay in Maine.

ALNAMBAY ULI AWIKHIGAN,

KISI TUNESSA

Eugin Vetromile, S. J.,

ALNAMBAY PATLIAS,

ULIHALAKONA

PENAUBSKET, SYBAYK, ULASTOOK, MICMAC,

TEBA MINAKTAKIK ETALAUNSISIK

WANBANAKKI ALNAMBAK.

YO PEMIKATOOK NEKUTAM-
QUÀKE NSANSOOK KESSAK-
TEKOY TEBA NONINSKA
TEBA NEKUTANS.
PENAUBSKET ALNAMBAY
UDENEK,

TEBA KANDOSKIK.

NEW YORK:
EDWARD DUNIGAN & BROTHER,
151 FULTON STREET,
1856.

INDIAN GOOD BOOK,

MADE BY

Eugene Vetromile, S. J.,

INDIAN PATRIARCH,

FOR THE

BENEFIT OF THE

PENOBSCOT, PASSAMA-QUODDY, ST. JOHN'S, MICMAC,

AND OTHER TRIBES OF

THE ABNAKI INDIANS.

THIS YEAR ONE THOUSAND EIGHT HUN-
DRED AND FIFTY-SIX.
OLD-TOWN INDIAN VILLAGE,
AND BANGOR.

NEW YORK:
EDWARD DUNIGAN & BROTHER,
151 FULTON STREET.
1856.

Plates 7a, 7b, and 7c. One of the eventual results of the project of inculturation was the production of missals and catechisms and prayer books in the native languages. This was a slow process, as the Jesuits, although gifted linguists, were initially very frustrated in their efforts to learn the Indian tongue. Such abstract theological concepts as *sin* or *redemption* were not easily communicated across cultures. These pages from a later Indian prayer book, called *The Indian Good Book*, represent the Jesuits' endeavor to proselytize in their listeners' idiom.

PRAYERS IN MICMAC LANGUAGE.

Morning Prayers.

The letter *g* before *e, i,* has a soft sound, and it must be pronounced as we do in the Latin words *magi, genus.*

The Micmac Indians pronounce the letter *k* in two man-ners—the one has been explained at the beginning of this book; the other has a peculiar kind of sound, broken as it were in the throat, and of which I cannot give an idea on paper. When the *k* is to be pronounced in this manner, I mark it thus (*k*.) *Ch* pron. as in the French, so *cha, che, chi, cho, chu,* pron. as the French do in the words *chandelle, Michel, chose,* &c. If *ch* is suspended without a vowel, it must be pronounced in the same manner.

Ph has the sound of a *p* bent to an aspiration, making the noise of an *f* and *h* together.

ECHKITPUGOWEY ELAJUDMANK.

M'chet dechi uchkitpagwèl deli mawi elayudmamk.

✠ Tan dèlwigit Wègwigit a*k* Euschit, a*k* Wegi—uli Nixkam. N'delietch.

Egelèg nigmatoot mu negwèch ula k'tedli dèlmanenu K'chi Nixkam kijul-kuchp; mèchtaïl o*k*och a*k* m'chel tàn

19*

Generalis quamquam inuitus, diuq̄ repugnans,
eligitur ; atque in æde, quæ extra vrbem
visitur, Sancti Pauli quarto solemni voto se,
ac societatem suam Romano Pontifici obstringit.

58

Plate 8. The Society of Jesus was not an entity organized to serve parishes. It was intended for missionary work. As such, its focus and energy derived from daily reception of the Eucharist. Here members of the Society of Jesus receive Holy Communion, which strengthened them for service.

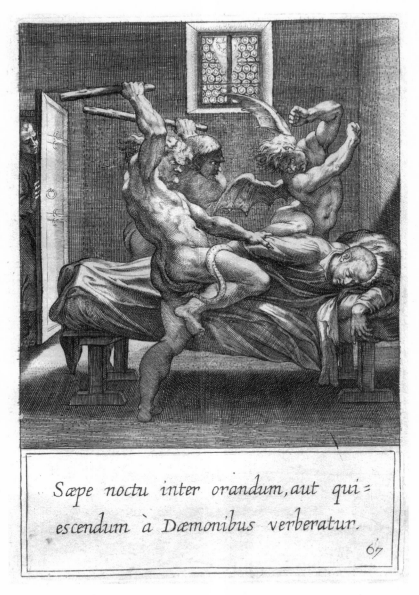

Sæpe noctu inter orandum, aut qui=
escendum à Dæmonibus verberatur.

67

Plate 9. Not only the Indians, but also the Jesuits of the time believed in the existence of evil spirits. At first, the Indians feared that the Jesuits were embodied evil spirits. Here, Ignatius experiences torment at the hands of demons.

Plate 10. The Indians who did respond to the Jesuits' message became very devout in their observance of the Christian faith. Here, a youth in native dress kneels, holding on to the Jesuit priest's chasuble as he celebrates the Eucharist. An image of the crucified Christ can be seen through the window of the church.

Plate 11. La Mère Marie de l'Incarnation—the first Superior of the Ursuline convent in New France (1600–1672).

LA MERE MARIE DE L'INCARNATION.
Premiere Superieure des Ursulines de la nouvelle france decedée a Quebec en odeur de Sainteté le dernier jour d'avril 1672. agée de 72 ans 6 mois 13 j.ᵈ

Plate 12. Madame de la Peltrie (Marie Madeleine de Chauvigny). Inspired by reading the Jesuit *Relations*, she came to the New World and was responsible for the first hospital, l'Hôtel-Dieu, being built at Quebec. The hospital cared for whites and Native Americans alike.

Plate 13. The first Ursuline convent is in the background; in the front is Madame de la Peltrie's dwelling. The convent burned in 1650.

Foeminam phtysi ad interitum pro=
perantem sanitati res tituit.

47

Plate 14. Her desire to participate in the Jesuit mission in French Canada may
have effected the miraculous cure of Madame de la Peltrie. Ignatius ministered to
poor women and street prostitutes, as well as gaining the ear (and access to the
finances) of noblewomen. The Jesuits continued to minister to women, and to
involve both European and native women in their mission in the New World.
Here, Ignatius cures a woman near death.

Multos sæpe Energumenos liberat crucis signo.

46

Plate 15. *"Multos saepe Energumenos liberat crucis signo."* The Jesuits were acknowledged as mighty men and powerful presences, in part because they performed exorcisms of Indians possessed by demons. Here, Ignatius cures a female hysteric.

Plate 16. A young Indian child assists the Jesuit celebrant at mass. The acolyte has brought forward to the altar the elements of water and wine. Part of Jesuit instruction of the natives concerned teaching them about the Eucharist. Father Daniels describes the piety and devoted service of the native Christian boy, Robert Satouta.

Plate 17. The Jesuits instructed native youth in the appropriate Christian ways to woo and to wed. Here, a properly instructed and pious Native American girl kneels to pray her rosary.

Plate 18. *"Vita Beati P. Ignatii Loila. Societatisies Fundatoris."* The frontispiece from the *Life of Saint Ignatius Loyola* shows his portrait in the center medallion, some of the Jesuit martyrs at the bottom, other members of the Society of Jesus around the sides, and two historiated medallions of the missionary activities of the Jesuits in England and in India, Japan, and Florida. Canada was the next missionary endeavor to be undertaken.

AD MAIOREM DEI GLORIAM:
TO THE GREATER GLORY OF GOD

Father Jogues, born in Orleans, France, in 1607, was about thirty-five years old when he came to the New World. He had been well educated in France, and was shy and introverted by nature. He was also very devout. When he heard of the Jesuit mission to Canada, he decided not to pursue the literary career that he had been contemplating, and instead offered himself to do whatever work might need to be done.

Although he was bookish, he was also a great athlete, much admired for his ability to outrun almost anybody. On June 9, 1642, however, he did not even try to run. He and his "people," Huron converts to Catholicism, were heading down the St. Lawrence River in canoes to trade with other Huron villages. About forty other people were in the canoes. Four of them were French and the remainder Huron. Two of the Frenchmen, Rene Goupil and Guillaume Couture, were called *donnés*—men who had not been ordained priests, but who were very religious and offered their services to help the Jesuits without pay and "for the glory of God." Suddenly, an Iroquois war party leaped out from the land near one of the islands that fill the river and the Lake St. Pierre region.

Father Isaac Jogues had with him the yearly report of the Jesuit mission for 1642–1643 which he had been planning to send. This year, the report had concentrated on Jesuit successes in establishing a mission among the Hurons. However, when the Iroquois captured Father Jogues, the report, rather than being sent safely to Europe, was lost. The Jesuit Superior, Father Barthelemy Vimont, reconstructing what he could from other Jesuits, subsequently authored this account so that there would be no gap in the records. The first part of the *Relation* includes a note scrawled by another Jesuit to the Superior, instructing him of Father Jogues's capture and of the report's disappearance. The remainder of the *Relation* is penned by the Superior.

Meanwhile, Father Jogues was still in captivity, threatened daily with torture by the Iroquois, forced to labor as a slave, and given as an "adopted son" to an Iroquois woman whose spouse had been killed in a battle with the Hurons. The practice was meant to compensate the widow, and was certainly more humane than putting a captive to death, but could also prove humiliating, depending on the woman's disposition toward her captive.

Father Jogues was eventually liberated—after witnessing first-hand the death of both *donnés*—by a Dutch trader who purchased his freedom from the Iroquois and arranged for Father Jogues to sail back to France. During his months-long captivity, Jogues had been mutilated by the Iroquois; they had bitten off his little finger and cut off his left thumb. Back in France, Father Jogues posed for a portrait, almost defiantly displaying his missing thumb and finger as he clasped his hands before him in prayer.

Father Jogues stubbornly and bravely went right back to Canada shortly afterwards, where he was again captured by the Iroquois. This time, they put him to death.

Relation of what happened in New France (1642–1643)

by Father Barthelemy Vimont

Your Reverence is not going to be pleased. Unfortunately, I can't send you this year's report. Most of the report, which talks about our activities among the Huron people, is now in the hands of the Iroquois. Last June 9, near Montreal, forty Hurons, Father Jogues (and his correspondence, including the report) were taken captive near Montreal by the Iroquois. Father Jogues has managed to get word to us that those papers have now been returned to him, but he is unable to send the report to Your Reverence, as he is still a captive.

So I am sending Your Reverence the report for this region, minus Father Jogues's part of the report. My report includes stories of great virtue and the increase of new Christian converts. However, my report also, regrettably, will tell you about threats of war and a lack of cooperation from the Iroquois. Luckily we have had reinforcements from France. Otherwise, the Iroquois would have already blocked our missionary activity as well as our trade. Hardly any rivers are safe for us to travel on to the Huron now; all our luggage was stolen from us when we went up river last year, and this year our baggage was again stolen as we were headed back down. As I write this, I've just found out that our baggage has yet again been taken. Our only hope is that Father Le Jeune, well acquainted with the situation as it stands here, may be able to persuade some Europeans to give support to our cause. This is what Governor Montmagny, and the people of Quebec, have begged me to request.

The colony of Quebec is the main way—really, the only way—we have to convert these tribes. There is no better way to help us get more converts than to send material aid to the colony of Quebec. Thank God, bit by bit we are indeed growing, overcoming the hardships of long winters, few workers, sparse trading, and our awareness of how very far away we are from Europe. Nonetheless, almost all of the French families are now able to grow their own subsistence crops of wheat, rye, peas, barley, and other grains. Usually, they are able to set aside a six month's supply. They are beginning to understand the needs of this soil and seasons. Our work is well under way, but we need help and helpers. Our Governor has constantly tried to help us; anyone else would have given up long ago! Father Bressany is in charge of giving religious instruction to the French here in Quebec, and has gotten great results with his preaching. Father Enemond Masse, although very old, has worked hard beside him, and helped to teach the inhabitants. Father de Brébeuf and I have come to Quebec on every holy day and every Sunday to hear confessions, speak words of encouragement, and to minister to the Québecois.

Father Charles Raymbault died this year and went to be with Jesus. Father Raymbault had cared very much that the Québecois get off to a good start and he also worked to convert the Indians. While still in France, for several years he had been in charge of our affairs there, and had done so well that he had asked to be allowed to come to work among us to establish a new church here. So, at the request of the Jesuits already there who knew of his courage, he was sent to live with the Hurons for four years. The Jesuit Fathers hoped eventually to be able to send him out to more remote villages as a missionary. Since he needed to be able to speak Algonquian in order to do this, the Jesuits sent him and Father Charles Pijart to an Algonquian people called the Nipissiriniens. There were great difficulties associated with this mission, and the journey was long and hard. After he had arrived, he became ill and very thin and feeble, eventually the Fathers had to bring him back here so that they could give him food and medicine. But God called him to Heaven, and October 22 of last year he passed away, having been sick for over three months. The Governor, who had admired him, had him buried right next to the tomb of Samuel de Champlain, a monument commemorating Champlain's well-known endeavors on behalf of New France.

Now I'll tell you about Jean Nicolet's life and death. He was an interpreter and also an agent for the members of the Company of New France. After living in this area for twenty-five years, Nicolet died shortly after Father Raymbault. What I can tell you about him will also make our situation in this new land more clear. He came to New France in 1618, and, believed to be well suited by temperament and his excellent memory to learn the Indian language, was sent to spend the winter with the Algonquians. He was the only Frenchman to stay with the natives for over two years, and always went with them on their travels and trading trips. He experienced great hardship, including incredible fatigue and hunger, frequently going without food for eight days and even, one time, surviving for two months by eating nothing but tree bark.

He helped in the peace negotiations when four hundred Algonquians went to make peace with the Iroquois. If only they had kept their promise! There is no peace now, and we are constantly threatened by the Iroquois, which makes it really difficult to continue our work of converting these tribes.

After making the peace treaty, Nicolet lived for eight or nine years with the Algonquian Nipissiriniens, and frequently was mistaken for one of them; he had a separate cabin and fished and traded for his needs. He also regularly took part in their tribal councils.

Eventually, the Company of New France recalled him, appointing him interpreter and agent for the Company. The Company delegated him to travel to the nation known as the People of the Sea, several hundred miles west, in order to make peace between them and the Hurons. He set out from Huron country with seven Indians, and they crossed through the territory of several nations in their travels. When they arrived at the nation of the People of the Sea, they stuck two sticks in the ground and hung presents on them in a display of peaceful intentions; otherwise, the Indians might have taken them for enemies and slaughtered them.

When Nicolet was two days away from the land of the People of the Sea, he had sent one of the Indians accompanying him to bear greetings to the People of the Sea. They were pleased, and when they heard that a European had come to visit with them, they sent several young men to greet him. They called him Manitourinou, the "wonderful man." They met him, carried his baggage, and escorted him into their village. Nicolet had put on a Chinese silk robe embroidered with many flowers and birds. At the sight of the pistols he carried in each hand—which the People of the Sea called "carrying thunder"—the women and children were frightened and ran off.

The news of Nicolet's arrival spread quickly, and several thousand men assembled to speak with him. Each of the chiefs had prepared a feast for him; at one of the meals they served over eighty beaver to eat. They made peace; Nicolet went back to Huron territory, and then later he went to Trois-Rivières where he continued to work as interpreter and agent for the company. He was respected for his work by both French and Indians. When he was able, he helped the Jesuit Fathers in converting the Indians, as he had great influence with them and was skillful in dealing with them.

Mr. Olivier, chief agent for the Company of New France, went back to France last year, and when he left, Nicolet came to Quebec to fill in for him. Nicolet was glad to get back to Quebec, where he was pleased to see so much religious devotion, but his joy was short-lived. A couple of months after he arrived, he traveled to Trois-Rivières to help free a captive Indian there, but he died in a shipwreck en route. Heading for Trois-Rivières, he left Quebec in Mr. de Savigny's boat around seven o'clock at night, but before they got to Sillery, a big wind blew up from the northwest and sank the sloop. The passengers held on to the boat and so did not sink immediately; Nicolet had time to say to Savigny, "Save yourself; you know how to swim, but I don't, so I commend my soul to God. Please take care of my wife and daughter."

The waves ripped the passengers from the side of the ship, which was overturned near a rock. Savigny sank by himself into the water and swam among waves as high as mountains. The boat was not far from shore, but it was pitch-black and so cold that a heavy frost froze the edges of the river. Savigny, exhausted and despairing, began to sink, begging God to save him; shortly afterwards, his feet touched ground. Half dead, he dragged himself out of the water and came to the Jesuit house near Sillery. There he remained without speaking, for quite a while; finally, he told us what had happened: of the loss of Nicolet (whom the whole country would mourn), the deaths of three of his men, and the loss of most of his furniture and supplies. Savigny and his wife showed great patience and courage in the midst of this tragedy. The Indians in Sillery, hearing of the Nicolet's death by drowning, ran to where the shipwreck had taken place, and mourned his passing.

Even more bad news followed: the death of the Cardinal Duke of France who had done so much for Old France and also for New France. We had been hopefully awaiting the results of his endeavors on our behalf, when we learned of his death.

A Miscou Indian boat came to Tadoussac and delivered all this bad news on St. John's Day. The remaining ships in the trading fleet arrived even later than usual this year, causing a lack of supplies for us and for the Indians. Finally, on the day of the Feast of the Assumption, God sent the ships to us. Just as we were beginning mass, two sails showed up on the horizon as they made their way into port; we were all so relieved and excited, and even happier when we found out who was on board: Father Quentin and three Jesuits—hard workers who were also good at languages—Fathers Leonard Garreau, Gabriel Druillet, and Noël Chabanel. Three nuns—braver than most women—were also on board: two hospital nuns from Dieppe, Normandy, named Mother

Marie de Ste. Genevieve and Mother Anne de St. Joachim, and Mother Anne des Seraphins, a Breton Ursuline nun from the Convent of Plermel. These women had courageously endured the dangers of the sea crossing, their fears of savages, and the unhelpful attempts of other Europeans to persuade them to remain in France where they were safe rather than embark on this mission.

Iroquois raids and the capture of Father Jogues

There are two groups of Iroquois: the neighbors of the Huron and the Santweronons, who are as many or more in number than the Huron tribe. The Hurons used to dominate the area, but now the Iroquois are far more powerful. Other Iroquois called the Agneronons live in the Trois-Rivières area. There is a Dutch settlement nearby and the Iroquois trade for guns there. At present, they have over three hundred muskets, and are very expert at using them. These are the Iroquois who attack our Algonquian and Montagnais converts and are always spying on the Hurons along the River. They slaughter them, burn them, and steal their furs; they then trade these pelts with the Dutch for powder and more muskets, and then they are able to dominate and wreak havoc on the whole region. This is what is starting to happen now, and unless France sends us some help, that is how it will soon be everywhere. Since the Montagnais and the Algonquian people, our neighbors, have had their numbers so reduced by disease, the Iroquois don't worry about any opposition from them; when peaceful Hurons come down to trade, carrying no weapons, if they run into any Iroquois they just flee and, if captured, do not struggle and are tied up and slaughtered like sheep.

Formerly, the Iroquois came in big groups at times during the summer, but after they left the River was safe for navigation; this year, however, they've changed their ways and have divided into smaller groups of twenty, thirty, fifty or a hundred, stationing themselves along all the tributaries of the river; if one group leaves, another comes to take its place. These are small groups of armed warriors which set out continually from Iroquois territory for ours, intending to occupy the entire River and outlying area, and to ambush anyone who travels along it; from these outposts they make surprise attacks on whoever comes along—Montagnais, Algonquians, Hurons, and French.

We've learned from letters sent from France that the Dutch are encouraging the Iroquois to harass the French to make them give up and leave. It's hard to believe that the Dutch, being allies of the French, are doing this; however, the way the Iroquois are behaving is consistent with such a plan. The Dutch should put a stop to this behavior, (as our Governor has done here by preventing our Hurons from attacking the Dutch).

The Iroquois movements into our area this year have had a terrible effect. On May 9 of last year, as soon as the ice had broken up on the river, eight Algonquians came down the river to trade pelts with the Hurons. They had paddled their canoes all night through a hard frost, and they stopped just a bit away from Trois-Rivières to make a fire to warm themselves. After only about a half an hour, eighteen Iroquois attacked them from the woods, killing two, imprisoning the others, and stealing all the furs. Father Buteux had been through that very area, accompanied by three Hurons, only two days previous. It is a miracle that the Iroquois did not take him and his companions captive.

A month later, on June 9, another group of forty Iroquois attacked Montreal. They saw sixty unarmed Hurons coming down the river in thirteen canoes. The Hurons were headed to Trois-Rivières to trade their furs. They were carrying correspondence for us as well as the most recent report to the Jesuit Superior. The Iroquois attacked them, took twenty-three Hurons captive, beat to death three Frenchmen who were doing some carpentry work only a few steps outside the settlement, and took two others captive. The Iroquois spent the night celebrating their victory, and, when morning came, they beat thirteen of the Huron prisoners to death. The ten who were still alive, and the two Frenchmen, along with all the pelts and plunder from the captured canoes, were taken away across the river in triumph . . . and those of us who watched them go were helpless to do a thing about it.

Eight or ten days later, one of the French prisoners managed to escape. He told us that the Iroquois had kept them tied up for two days, but had not otherwise injured them.

There's no way that fighting back will work against the enemy: we don't know where they are or how many they are, and they are trained to run and hide in the woods, which we French are not. Attacks against them would just risk more loss of French lives, since usually only a small party of Iroquois strikes while a much larger number waits in hiding to reinforce them.

While this group of forty Iroquois was in Montreal, another similar group was on Lake St. Pierre near Fort Richelieu. They had three or four Hurons with them—two of whom were brothers of the famous Huron convert Joseph, of whom the authors of other *Relations* have written. The Iroquois had taken these men prisoner, along with Father Jogues, the year before. Both brothers managed to escape to Trois-Rivières around nightfall, where they told Father Brébeuf all that they knew: that Father Jogues was alive; that he had had the chance to escape last year, but wouldn't take it because he did not want to abandon the Huron captives. The Iroquois assaulted him, beating him and the two Frenchmen, Cousture and Goupil, with their fists and with big clubs. Two hundred Iroquois from another war party, returning from their attack on Richelieu, were angry because they had lost five of their group and had several others wounded. They also roughed up Father Jogues. While traveling, they did not tie up Father Jogues, but when they arrived in the Iroquois village, they bound him, stripped him of most of his clothes, attacked him, cut his left thumb off, and crushed his right index finger with their teeth (although he is still able to use it a little).

The Hurons who escaped also told Father Brébeuf that two Dutchmen, one on horseback, had come to the Iroquois village to ransom Father Jogues, but that the Iroquois refused to release him; that Father Jogues had given one of the Iroquois a long letter to bring to the Jesuits; and that some of the Iroquois were talking about returning Father Jogues to us, but the Hurons didn't believe a word of it.

Other Hurons, having been taken captive earlier and in other attacks, escaped, came to Trois-Rivières, and confirmed this information. The Governor, hoping for Father Jogues's release—and for peace if at all possible—put together a group of four sloops and went, ready for war or for peace, to Fort Richelieu to see if the Iroquois would negotiate. But they would not show themselves and just went deeper into the woods as soon as they saw the boats, only returning to keep watch at the river's edge for Algonquians and Hurons when the boats had left.

On August 15, twenty Algonquians left Trois-Rivières, planning to look for the Iroquois near Richelieu. Near Lake St. Pierre, just a few miles away from the settlement, they broke into two groups, one of which ran into Iroquois almost immediately. Some Iroquois as well as some Algonquians were killed, but more Algonquians were lost than Iroquois. The Algonquians ran away, but some were taken prisoner.

While all this was taking place near Lake St. Pierre, two other groups of Iroquois were scouting near Fort Richelieu; with them was a captive but treacherous Huron who had agreed to help the Iroquois. They put him in a canoe alone and he went up to the fort, requested admission, and, once inside, lied and said he wanted to talk about making peace between the Iroquois and the French. He gave them some beaver pelts as token of good faith. They asked him if there was any news of Father Jogues; he pulled out a letter and gave it to them, then got ready to go. They told him that the letter was addressed to the Governor, who was either in Quebec or in Trois-Rivières, and that he had to wait for an answer. He asked them to shoot off the cannon, and they did; shortly after, three or four canoes full of Iroquois showed up, paddling steadily toward the fort. Those in the fort ordered them several times to stop, and, when the Iroquois kept on coming, shot at the canoes. The Iroquois ran into the woods, abandoning their canoes and baggage. It was not clear if any were wounded or dead.

I've enclosed a copy of the letter from Father Jogues that the Huron traitor brought from the Iroquois to give to the Governor. Unfortunately, we have lost the three other letters that Father Jogues wrote to us.

From the Iroquois village, June 30, 1643

Sir, This is the fourth letter I've written to you from my captivity among the Iroquois, and I no longer have time, or enough paper, to repeat what I've already written to you. Cousture and I are still alive. Henry, who was captured in Montreal, is also with us; he was brought here on the night of St. John's Day, was not beaten at the entrance of the village and neither were his fingers cut off, as the Iroquois did to us. All the other Hurons captured are also still alive.

Watch out for yourselves: new Iroquois war parties leave daily and, until autumn, the river will not be safe. They have at least three hundred guns and there are seven hundred Iroquois braves who know how to use them. They can reach the river by any of three tributaries; it's a bit harder for them to get to the fort near Fort Richelieu, but they will still try.

The Iroquois say that if those who killed the French in Montreal had known of what you've done—freeing some of their number, the Sokoiois, from the Algonquians—they would not have attacked Montreal; they had begun their attack in winter, and news of your actions had not reached them in time. Just the same, a war party headed by Mathurin's man (Father Brébeuf knows who I mean) left recently, the same kind of party that captured us last year. They plan to capture and kill more Frenchmen and Algonquians.

Do not let your worry about us stop you from fulfilling your mission to God's greater glory.

As far as I can tell, the Iroquois plan to capture and kill all the Hurons, to absorb this nation into theirs and, thereby, control the entire territory. I pity these poor people, many of whom have become Christians, others of whom want to be and are preparing for baptism. When will we find a way to ease their burdens? When they are all captured?

I have received several letters from the Hurons, along with the *relation* seized in Montreal. The Dutch have tried, and continue to try, to ransom us, but the Iroquois refuse, and I think they always will.

I am aware that I may be here a very long time, and I accept whatever is God's will. I have decided not to escape, even if I have the chance, because my presence here comforts the other Frenchmen, the Hurons, the Algonquians, and I've also been able to baptize more than sixty people, some of whom have since died and gone to be with God. I take hope and comfort from this, and from God's will, which is my will, too.

Please have prayers and masses said on our behalf, and especially pray for me, who desires to be

Your humble servant, Sir,

Isaac Jogues, S. J.

The letter speaks volumes in a very few words; it is well-drafted even though Father Jogues had to write it with a maimed hand; it is written in a more elegant and thoughtful way than any piece of literature could ever be.

"Do not let your worry about us stop you from fulfilling your mission to God's greater glory," he writes. He might as well say, "Forget about me. I am as good as dead. If you attack the Iroquois, they'll kill me, so I no longer consider myself to be among the living. My life belongs to God; do whatever you need to do for Him, and forget about me." How strong is a heart whose hope is set on Jesus! His goodness cannot be overcome, but triumphs gloriously even in the hardest time of trial.

"I have decided not to escape, even if I have the chance, because my presence here comforts [others]." God loves the noble and generous spirit of Father Jogues! This man, who is in constant pain, says that he would not escape from this torture even if he could.

"My presence here comforts the French, Hurons, and Algonquians." There are two Frenchmen held captive along with Father Jogues, many Hurons, many Algonquians, some of whom are Christian and others who want to be converted. So how could Father Jogues, a good shepherd, his heart on fire for God, abandon his sheep? He is no thief, no hired hand who would abandon the sheep to the wolves. We weep when we read these words, but we are also strengthened by them and by his example. Some of us are almost jealous of his conviction. To give up one's life for God is no bad deal.

"I have baptized more than sixty people." These must be his fellow captives, Hurons and Algonquians, and maybe even a few Iroquois children who, dying, pray to God for the souls of their parents. "I take hope and comfort from this, and from God's will, which is my will too." What wonderful words! And who better to comfort poor Father Jogues than his Father above, Whom no one and nothing can ever take away from him. The two Frenchmen who are with Father Jogues amaze us, too, with their courage, especially Guillaume Couture. He had the opportunity to escape, but could not abandon Father Jogues: "No," he says, "I'd rather die with him; I can't leave him; for the love of him and for the love of Christ, I'd rather die in the flames these tigers ignite to burn me." Spoken like a faithful friend. He certainly had nothing to gain by saying this—except his soul.

The letter says that an Iroquois war party had set out, headed by "Mathurin's man" (a Huron who'd been captured by the Iroquois and who'd turned traitor to his people, on whom he now wages war). Since he knew the paths on which the Huron travel, he went to ambush them there; he did the same thing that time that Father Jogues was captured. The Hurons call him "Mathurin's man" because, before he joined the Iroquois, he had brought to the Jesuits another young Huron man by that name; the Jesuit Fathers were impressed with Mathurin and eventually encouraged him to go to France and devote his life to God; he became a Capuchin monk.

In addition, this letter was written partly in French, partly in Latin, and partly in Indian idiom, so that, were it to fall into the wrong hands, no one would be able to understand everything that Father Jogues meant for our ears alone.

The Governor, who was in Trois-Rivières, wrote back to Father Jogues. I wrote him a long letter, too, and sent Father Brébeuf to Richelieu to talk with the Huron who had brought the letter. But the poor man wasn't much help because he was afraid that when he went back, if he let on that he'd been having discussions with us the Iroquois would think he was a spy. So he declared that he would not go back to the Iroquois, but would remain with the Hurons instead, and we couldn't change his mind. So we got no help from him, and Father Jogues got even less help, since we were unable to have our letters taken to him. With no news from us, he was also at risk daily of being put to death, because the Iroquois suspected that we had harmed the captive Huron messenger whom they had sent.

FAMILIARITER: THE THEOLOGICAL
SENSE OF DAILY LIFE

In late sixteenth- and early seventeenth-century Europe, the devil was a well-known presence, and witches were feared and discerned everywhere. When the Jesuits came to the New World, they found this cosmogony replicated. Not only did the Native Americans whom they met believe in Manitou (the Great Spirit), they also believed in witches and demons. They also accused the Jesuits of being witches and sorcerers (in this way acknowledging their power at various times.)

Indeed, supernatural power or spiritual insight was regarded by Native Americans as neither positive nor negative, but rather as a gift or tool that could be used for good or for bad effect, along a continuum. This view, of course, was very different from the Christian dichotomy between Heaven and Hell or God and Satan, causing much incomprehension at first between the Jesuits and their potential converts.

Father Le Jeune first encountered native beliefs about death, ancestors, and the spirit world when he (together with Father Brébeuf and some other Jesuits) was lodged in Indian cabins prior to a great procession and feast. In the hut were over a hundred bundles stuck up in the rafters of the structure. These turned out to be the decaying skeletons and bones of the Indian dead, which were carefully set aside for periodic veneration by family members at the "Feast of the Dead." Although the

Jesuits had a Catholic reverence for sacred relics, they had never seen an instance of ancestor worship before. The veneration of non-sacred, indeed secular, bones shocked and disturbed them.

The Jesuits sought to reorient native thinking so that witches and demons pointed to their opposite: the Christian God. In order to make this shift happen, the Jesuits had to become conversant with the native description of the metaphysical realm. They could then refute some of it, while also making comparisons and analogies between other aspects and the Christian understanding and depiction of the spirit world. By familiarizing themselves with native lifeways, the Jesuits were able to speak a language that made sense to the natives and ultimately converted many of them. This strategy was one Ignatius of Loyola had termed *familiariter*—familiarity, he averred, does not breed contempt; rather, it fosters understanding, communication, and conversion.

In this cluster of several related letters written by Father LeJeune in 1637—entitled "Concerning sorcerers, and whether or not they are in league with the Devil," "Concerning their customs and beliefs," "Concerning their customs and their beliefs," and "Concerning discipline at the Huron school, and some characteristics of the students"—the reader can trace the stages of this strategy of *familiariter* or what we today call inculturation. The process passes from observation to conversancy, to metaphor and simile-making, to reeducation, to institutionalized education for the young (the Jesuits founded a training school or seminary for native youth), to conversion.

The Jesuits interpret the everyday beliefs and habits of the natives, using phenomena from the natural world (such as what appears to be a native grasp of the properties of lightening long before Benjamin Franklin) and religious customs such as the "shaking tent" in which a prophet divines the future, reading them into a sense that will lead the native in the direction of a Christian understanding of the world.

❊ ❊ ❊

Concerning sorcerers, and whether they are in league with the Devil

The Montagnais Indians call "Manitou" anything in nature that is beyond human control, whether it be a good or a bad force. That's why, when we talk about God, they call Him "good Manitou," and when we talk about the devil, they call him "bad Manitou." Now, there are certain people in the tribe who have a familiarity with the good or the bad Manitou. We call those people who claim to be conversant with the bad Manitou "sorcerers." That's not to say that the devil makes himself evident to them in a physical or obvious way as he does to sorcerers and magicians in Europe; it's simply that we don't know what else to call this presence or force. Sometimes, these people act like real witches do. For example, they cause the death of others by casting spells, or by cursing someone, by Manitou's evil workings, or by poisons that they brew up. This happens so often among the Indians, at least they *think* that it happens, that practically everyone I've seen die thought his death was due to witchcraft. That's why they don't have any doctors, just these sorcerers, and they go to them to get the spells removed that they think have been cast on them. Indeed, they nearly all die in an anorectic state, languishing away and drying up so that they are nothing but skin and bones when they are buried. This is why they are all very afraid of sorcerers, and never dare to anger them, because the sorcerers can, they believe, kill people with their black arts. The sorcerers are also in great demand, because they are able (or so they claim) to take sickness away. It's really pathetic to see how the devil plays with this people's minds, and they are amazed that we so readily mock and resist their "sorcerers." They figure we're able to do this because we have a greater knowledge of Manitou than they do.

They also think that there are some men among them who have nothing to do with the devil; these are tricksters who do the same sort of things as do the sorcerers, in order to have the people give them gifts. One day, as we were criticizing sorcerers, one of the Indians who was there and who was thought to be a sorcerer, said loudly: "As for me, I don't do anything wrong; my father used to beat his drum to make sickness go away; I saw him do that; I'm just doing what he did; that's all there is to what I do."

Now, as the Indians are dying daily, they say that there is no longer a Manitou or sorcerer among them [who can cure them].

The sorcerer's job is also to interpret dreams, to explain the words of a song, and to talk about the omens of birds. The ancient Romans had oracles, who did the same. The [sorcerers] say that when you had a vision of a lot of moose flesh, it was a sign of life; but if you dream about bears, it's a sign of impending death. I've already said several times that these sorcerers sing and beat their drums to cure illness, to kill enemies during wars, and to help hunt animals. Pigarouich, the sorcerer I mentioned above, once sang to us the song that he said helped hunters. He just said the words "Iagoua mou itoutaouj ne e-é," which he repeated several times with different low and heavy tones, although they were fairly sweet to the ear. We asked him why he sang in this way to hunt animals. "I heard this song in a dream," he said, "that's why I remembered it and have used it ever since." He asked us to teach him what we sang to cure illness and to have good hunting, promising us that he would sing the songs word for word.

Now I'll describe one of the ways that these evil men use to kill their fellow man. Someone told me that they tried to use these devilish tricks against the French, but that they were unable to make them sick. If the Christians were to know what he could do, they'd have great respect for this ability. A sorcerer wanted to kill someone in his worship place, and caused "spirits of the day" to come, or those "spirits who make the day" that is how they name them, but we call them demons. After summoning the demons, the sorcerer sent the demons to find the soul of the person or persons they wished to have die. If these people belonged to another tribe, the sorcerer changed their name so that, if the person's relatives got wind of what had happened, they could not take revenge on the sorcerer. These demons brought the poor souls to the sorcerer in the form of stones, or in some other shape. Then the sorcerer would beat them with swords or axes, so that the blood ran out of them and the sword or axe was totally covered with blood. Once he had done that, the person of whom the soul had been struck fell sick and eventually died. That is how these poor people are tormented by demons.

When an Indian hates someone, he consults a sorcerer to have that person killed, but they say that if the sick person dreams of the person who has bewitched him, he will get better and the sorcerer will die. These demons make them believe that they love the people of the tribe, but that the evil Manitou has forbidden the people to give good things to the demons, even though they'd like to.

They imagine that he who desires the death of someone, especially if he is a sorcerer, is usually able to make his wish come true, but that the sorcerer himself will also die after he has caused the death of another. It's a strange thing to see how these people seem to get along so well yet hate each other so intensely in their hearts. They never seem to get angry at each other and rarely come to blows, but deep in their hearts they wish each other ill. I don't know how to reconcile this with the good deeds they do and with the help they routinely give to each other.

One of the sorcerers or tricksters told me that sometimes the devil talks to a certain Indian, but you can't see anything, you just hear the demon's voice. The demon will say to him, for example: "you will find a stone lying on the snow, or in such and such a place, or in the heart or shoulder of an elk or of another animal that you slay; take this stone and you will have good luck hunting." This particular Indian swore to me that he had found such a stone in the heart of an elk, and that he gave it to a Frenchman. "That's why," he claimed, "I am no longer a successful hunter."

He also said that the devil communicates with him through dreams. A moose came to someone in a dream and said to him, "come to me." Upon awaking, the Indian went to find the moose that he had seen; when he had found it, he threw his spear at it and the beast fell down dead; when he had slit it open, he found some hair and a stone inside the body; he took this stone and kept it in a safe place; and he always had good luck and was a good hunter.

In addition, he said that the demons teach them to make ointments out of toads and snakes to kill those whom they hate. If he's telling the truth, there can be no doubt that they are in league with the devil. I believe that this superstition comes from a custom that the Indians have: each has his own special little bag, and no one is allowed to look inside it; they would get so angry if someone did that, they'd practically kill him. They don't want anyone to see their magic stones or whatever they're hiding, and one Indian once said to me that you can tell if an Indian has begun to believe in God if he'll give you such a stone or prized object.

Makheabichtichiou told me that, while he was still a boy and was hunting alone in the forest, a demon came to him. The demon was dressed and decorated like an Iroquois, and was flying through the air. "I stopped short," he said, filled with fear. "The demon stopped, too, right near me, and all the earth around him began to shake. He told me not to be afraid, that I wouldn't die right away, but that he couldn't guarantee the same where some of my people were concerned. Finally, I saw him rise up in the air and disappear before my very eyes. Stunned, I went back to my cabin. I told my countrymen what I had seen, and they took this to be an evil omen, and said that some of them would be killed by their enemies. Soon after, a man came to tell them that one of their fasting hunters had been separated from the others and set on and massacred by Iroquois braves." If fear, which makes the imagination see things that do not exist, wasn't what totally confused this man, it was probably the devil himself who had appeared to him, even though the man was not himself a sorcerer.

One Indian told me that they believed that these demons are cross-eyed, one eye looking up and the other staring down. Since I've already talked about these beliefs in other *relations*, I won't say anything more about them here. Let's instead try to answer the question that I asked at the beginning of this letter: namely, do these sorcerers truly communicate with the devil? If what I have just said is true, there can be no doubt that the demons do at times show themselves to these men; but up until now, I had believed that the devil himself was deceiving them, filling their brains with mistaken thoughts and filling their will with evil urges. But now I am persuaded that there is no real appearance taking place, and that everything their sorcerers do is no more than trickery that they've invented in order to profit from it in some way. I've begun to doubt everything they say and do, and even to lean in the opposite direction, for the following several reasons.

I said before that, when they want to consult these spirits of the day, they erect dwellings by sticking posts in the ground, tying them together and stabilizing them in a circle, then covering them with robes and coverings. Then, when the sorcerer has gone into this tent, and when he has sung and invoked these demons, the "tabernacle" begins to shake and to move about. Now, I always thought that the sorcerer himself was making it move, but Makheabichtichiou spoke to me with complete honesty, and the sorcerer Pigarouich explained all these tricks to me with great sincerity, and they claim that it was not the sorcerer who was making the tent move, but rather a wind that came up strongly and blew the tent. As proof of this, they told me that the structure is sometimes so strong that a man by himself would not be capable of moving it; nonetheless, you can see these buildings shake, bend here and there, and you'll have to admit that there is no way that one man could cause all that agitation. When I was spending the winter with the Indians one year, I saw one of these occasions when they consulted a sorcerer in such a structure; I saw some tall young men erecting it; I saw it shake, not with violence such as had been described to me, but still with a fair amount of force, and for such a long time, that I found it hard to believe that a man would have enough strength to keep up such a deception. Even so, since I didn't have the chance to verify whether the structure was firmly established, I still believed that it was the trickster himself who was moving it about.

Further, those whom I've just mentioned, as well as others, have strongly assured me that the height of this structure, as high as seven feet or thereabouts, sometimes sways all the way down to the ground, so violently is it shaken. In addition, sometimes they could see the sorcerer's arms and legs lying on the ground or even sticking out of the back end of the "tabernacle," while the upper part was moving very strongly. Whether it's the devil, or the wind coming into this little building and blowing into it so ferociously, something blows the sorcerer every which way and makes him feel like he's falling into a pit; the earth seems to open beneath his very feet; and he runs, terrified, out of the tent—and it continues to shake and move about for some time after he has left it.

Anifkaouaskoufit, a young Indian, told us that Etouet (the chief of Tadoussac), upon entering into his "tabernacle" (which he calls his "Apitouagan"), had his loincloth thrown clear out of the tent and his body was raised up so that those who were looking in could no longer see him; finally, they heard him fall back down, letting out a plaintive cry like a man who had fallen from a great height. Once out of this devilry, he said that he did not know where he had been, nor could he remember what had happened.

The same Indian told me in all confidence, because he was our house servant and we were giving him instruction in the faith, that he and another companion were once on an iced-over lake during winter, and they saw a sorcerer fall into a trance, during which he was raised into the air by no apparent mechanism, then he disappeared immediately right before their eyes. That evening, they found his garment, but without his body, and several days later he returned all confused, unable to say where he had been or what he had been doing. I've said above that sometimes, during periods of famine, someone will disappear and will never be found; they claim that this happens and, when it does, it's a very bad omen for them and means that the bad Manitou will eat them all up.

Even more, this young Indian said he had seen with his own eyes the sorcerer named Karigouan (with whom I've spent the winter) pull a stone out of his bag, put it on a leather shield, and burn it up, without the stone having been heated.

Finally, Makheabichtichiou told me that the Algonquians, who live farther up the St. Lawrence River, predict the future by interpreting the flames of a fire—but because this is not that different from what the Iroquois do (and Father Brébeuf has already talked about this in his letters), I won't explain that further.

All this evidence just goes to show that the devil does indeed communicate at times with the poor Indians, and so they are greatly in need of earthly and spiritual assistance to pull them out of this sad state of servitude that oppresses them.

Just as I was finishing this letter, Father Pijart came in, just back from Huron territory, and he brought me a stone, sent to me from Father Brébeuf. This stone was used by a sorcerer in this way: trying to dress the wounds of a sick man, the sorcerer placed this stone into the fire, left it there so long that it got all red and covered with flames. Then the sorcerer went into a trance, pulled the burning stone out of the fire, took it in his teeth, ran like a madman around the cabin of the sick man, threw the stone—still throwing off sparks—and was not at all injured by doing all this. Father Pijart was an eyewitness to this event and, since the stone was fairly large, he wanted to see if it had burned the sorcerer's lips or tongue. He found that, in fact, they were unharmed, which made him believe that this event could have only transpired through the agency of a demon. I am sending that very stone to your Reverence. It still bears the marks of the sorcerer's teeth: since it was on fire, it became like bone, softer than stone, and that's how, gripping it in his teeth, the sorcerer made the two marks that you can still see on it.

Concerning their customs and their beliefs

I won't repeat what I've already said on this subject, but I do want to add the new information that I've learned. If I repeat myself, it's because I've forgotten what I already wrote, or because I want to explain something in more detail. Among the superstitious acts that sick people rely on to try to get cured, they often have some man, woman, or child stay near them, imagining that this will help them regain their health. They are so insistent on this point that a sick person will often ask for a person to be sent to stay with him, and his request is nearly always granted. A person who refuses such a request would be judged discourteous, even though the task can really be unpleasant, because it's necessary for that person to stay right by the sick person, doing nothing other than sitting near him.

They give potions to their sick people to make them vomit; they boil leaves and cedar branches, and then they drink the broth to prevent getting dysentery. Father Buteux claims to have seen a child cured in a very short time in this way, after having been given such medicine.

They throw bear fat into the fire, to cause it to sizzle, believing that this noise will help them catch more bears.

Father Buteux asked an Indian why they stuck their spears into the ground with the sharpened end up, and he answered that, since thunder has a soul, if it sees these naked blades, it will turn away, and will stay far from their huts. Father Buteux asked another Indian where the noise of thunder comes from. He said, "it is Manitou, who is vomiting up a large serpent that he swallowed; every time his stomach heaves, he makes this great noise that we hear." Actually, the Indians have often told me that lightening is nothing more than these serpents falling to earth, and they see this in trees that have been struck by lightening, for they claim to see the shape of the snakes imprinted in twists and serpentine shapes around such trees. They even say that they've found large snakes underneath trees struck by lightening. Here's a new way of looking at things, indeed!

The Indians having come out badly in a recent war, they sent one of their people ahead like a herald, and he cried out the names of those killed or captured as they approached their village; the daughters and wives, hearing their relatives named, covered their faces with their hair, burst into tears, and clothed themselves in black. When they return from battle, and are about to set their faces toward the journey home, they hang on a tree as many small wands as there are of braves, perhaps to let their enemy know, should they pass by that place, how numerous they were, and just how far they had ventured into enemy territory, to intimidate them. I can't think of any other reason for this.

In the sparring of their war parties, they shout out each time that they take down one of the enemy (if they are able to see this), and I think they do this to encourage themselves and to express their satisfaction.

They believe that the earth is flat; that its ends are cut off perpendicularly; and that souls go to the farthest end, that of the setting sun. These souls then erect huts at the edge of precipices, beneath which there is nothing but water. The souls spend their time dancing, but sometimes as they frolic near the edge of the precipice, one of them may fall into the abyss, and right away is transformed into a fish. There are trees at the edges of the precipices, but their trunks are so smooth that the souls are not able to hold onto them to stop their fall. I've already said that Indians imagine that these souls can eat and drink. Let me also add that they believe that souls can marry, and that children who die on earth remain children [in the afterlife] at the far end of this earth, and there they grow up, just like they would have done had they remained in the land of their birth. This mischievous belief is one of the hardest for us to disabuse them of. First, we tell them that, if the earth is entirely flat, the ocean would quickly submerge it. Then, we explain to them that it would be daylight at the same time everywhere on the globe. However, it's noon here, while it's night in France during the winter. We assure them that our ships sail from rising sun to setting sun, and that we've never found such a "country of the souls." They are astonished when we tell them about the lands below the Equator, and they laugh as if we were telling them a great joke (just as many people with more intelligence than they have also scoffed at this in the past).

We often tell them that, if souls could eat, they would get old and die—yet they believe these souls to be immortal. Besides, if they can marry and have children, but they never die, the whole earth would be filled up with souls and you'd run into them everywhere, forever since

going to this land of the setting sun, they would not have stopped prolif-
erating. They muse over these explanations and other arguments that
we present to them.

Here's an amazing explanation for a solar eclipse: they say that there
is a person—be it a man or some other sort of creature—who really
loves humanity; he got angry with a very bad woman, and sometimes he
wants to kill her, but he refrains from doing so because that would kill
daylight and then the earth would be covered with eternal night; this
bad woman is the wife of Manitou, and she is responsible for the death
of any Indian who dies. The sun is her heart; therefore, anyone who
kills her, kills the sun forever. Sometimes, when this man gets mad at
her and threatens her with death, her heart trembles and gets pale; that
is what happens, they say, at an eclipse of the sun. When the sun of
justice does not shine in a soul, that soul is not even able to see the sun
shining before her very eyes. The Indians differ greatly as to this belief,
so it's difficult to know for certain what they actually do believe. Alas!
How hard it is to find any certainty in the midst of such confusion!

They believe, or at least this is what Makheabichtichiou has told me,
that everyone will die, except for two people, a man and a woman; that
all the animals will also die, except for two of each species; and that the
world will in this way repopulate itself, out of that remnant.

I've heard them tell a lot of fables—or at least I think that the most
intelligent among them consider such tales to be fables. I'll just mention
one, which seems really ridiculous to me: they tell how once a man and
a woman were out in the woods and a bear threw itself on the man,
strangled him and ate him, then an enormous hare jumped on the
woman and devoured her, but did not eat her child (which was still in
her belly, since she was about to give birth). A woman passing by that
spot shortly after the attack was astonished to find the child alive; she
took it, raised him as her own son (nonetheless calling him her "little
brother"), and gave him the name Tchakabech. This child never grew,
but remained as small as an infant in diapers, yet he had extraordinary
strength such that he used the tall trees of the forest as arrows for his
bow. It would take too long to tell all the adventures that this man-child
had: he killed the bear that had eaten his father, and found in the bear's
stomach his father's mustache, untouched; he also killed the great hare

who had eaten his mother, and found her ponytail still in the hare's stomach.

To make a long story short, this Tchakabech, wanting to go to Heaven, climbed up a tree, and when he had almost reached the top he blew hard against the tree, which grew and grew as the little dwarf breathed on it, so that it reached all the way up to the sky; there, he found the most beautiful country he had ever seen; everything was incredibly beautiful, the earth was fertile; the trees were tall and straight; having looked around thoroughly, he came back to tell the news of this special place to his sister, to try to convince her to go with him to Heaven and to live with him there forever. He came down out of the tree, building cabins in some of its branches to lodge his sister on her way up. At first, his sister didn't want to come, but he described the beauty of that land to her so persuasively that she decided to brave the difficulty of the journey. She brought with her one of her young nephews, and climbed up the tree, Tchakabech following behind so he could catch them if they fell, and at each rest-stop they found a cabin waiting for them, which helped ease their fatigue.

Finally, they got to Heaven and, so that no one could pursue them there, the man-child broke off the end of the tree, so that it no longer reached up to the sky. After having admired the landscape, Tchakabech went to set out his traps (or, as others call them, snares), hoping perhaps to catch an animal. When night came, he went to check on his traps and he found them all ablaze, and could not go near them. He went back to his sister and said to her, "Sister, I don't know what is in my traps, all I can see is a big fire, and I did not dare go near it." His sister, suspecting what it was, said to him, "Oh, my brother, this is a real problem! I believe that you have caught the sun in your traps. Quick, run back and release the sun. Perhaps as the sun was going by during the night, it fell into the trap unawares."

Tchakabech, astounded, went back and, having looked carefully, realized that indeed he had trapped the sun in his snares. He tried to set the sun loose, but he couldn't get close enough. By luck, along came a little mouse. He grabbed it, blew on it, made it get big enough so that he could order it to untie the snare and release the sun. The sun, finding itself again free, continued on his daily route. While the sun was caught in the trap, there was no daylight on the earth below, but no one can say how long this lasted; nor can they say what happened to the man-child. I've heard that Muslims believe that the moon has fallen out of the sky and broken into pieces. Mohammed, wanting to put the moon back together, picked it up, rubbed it with his sleeve, and in this way glued the pieces back together and put the moon back in the sky. This tale about the moon is about as believable as the one I've just told about the sun.

To conclude, *beati oculi qui vident quae nos videmus*. Blessed are those to whom God's goodness teaches truth. What will they give in return to Our Lord for this great gift? A firm faith, and a solid resolve to live according to the precepts that this faith teaches us, because those who do not follow the paths lit by the light of faith, deserve to stumble in darkness.

Concerning the Huron school

Our glorious Father and Founder Saint Ignatius having been informed by several sources that his children were running into serious problems in pursuing their holy endeavors, responded nonetheless with great joy; he said that God's business begins in difficulty and pettiness, but ends in glory: up until now, he had a poor opinion of the establishment of our Company in any province, because he always heard how well received we were and how everyone was so pleased with our efforts. There was no resistance up until now. If crosses and suffering are the most solid bases for a building that is destined to raise its height up to the Heavens, the Huron school [that we Jesuits have founded] is well-established: its birth was full of difficulty, its first progress was filled with sadness, so I beg God that it may end up being established with joy and peace.

Your Reverence having told us that we should try to start such a school, God seems to have inclined several good souls to start one. I already wrote about this to Father Brébeuf, so that he would send us a few Huron youth: immediately, the Jesuit Fathers in the area made it their job to find some; they choose, from quite a few, about twelve very nice young people, and they designated Father Antoine Daniel as the caretaker of these young shoots. These determinations having been made, Father Daniel sailed down to the area, hoping that his students would soon get ready to travel in their relatives' or in their friends' canoes. For all of them to come together in one big boat would be impossible, since they did not have any boats or sloops, but only very small birchbark canoes. But when it was time to separate the children from their mothers, the extraordinary tenderness that an Indian woman has for her children stopped everything in its tracks and almost ruined our great plan for these youth. But one brave young man named Satouta, went up to stand by the Father, and spoke of staying with him and even of going to France, should he want that. He was very happy, and continued, even in the midst of great difficulties, never changing his mind about staying with us to be taught.

When Father Daniel arrived in Trois-Rivières, where we—along with the twelve young Hurons who had been sent to us—had been long awaiting his arrival, we were astonished to see with him only this one young man (and he was already nearly an adult). We didn't let ourselves get discouraged, though, just because of this one problem; instead, we trusted in God and in the help of men. All the signs are that soon several young people, accompanied by their parents, will come to stay with the French. Monsieur the General is doing his best to make this happen, as I wrote in my last letter. Lord Nicolet and other interpreters are doing what they can to help; sometimes they talk to one Indian, then to another. They give them gifts, Father Daniel prays and begs the children to remain with him, and he begs their parents to allow them to do so; these efforts have had some effect, but usually, if they stay with us for the night, they leave in the morning. Finally, since it's this people's custom to assemble to discuss matters with us French before they go back to their land, Monsieur the General had the young brave named Satouta sit next to him. He was the only one who persisted in his plans, so the General honored him before everyone else, prepared a feast in his honor, and sent presents to his friends. All this made the Hurons think that we loved their tribe, but still did not convince them to leave their children with us. When the assembly broke up, we lost nearly all hope of being able to start the Huron School that year, but suddenly Our Lord, implored by the prayers of both New and Old France, touched the hearts of one of the Indians. This Indian got a large group of Huron together and strongly exhorted them to consider the good points of such a school, and of the good things that would come to them as a result of such an alliance with the French. The Chiefs then ordered two young men to keep Satouta company and to remain with us. I'll leave it to your imagination whether this news raised our spirits, and whether it helped us to feel hopeful again about our project, which had really begun to flounder!

We can truly say that *Deus deducit ad inferos & reduci[t], attollit & deprimit, exaltat & humiliat.* Now here we were with three young men instead of the twelve young students we had been expecting. Since we were running short on time, Monsieur the General put us on board a ship with these three young men and sent us to Quebec. We had only just arrived when another group of Hurons, arriving in Trois-Rivières and hearing what had happened, gave us three more young pupils, who Lord Nicolet also brought to Quebec. Some time later, other Hurons, who arrived in Trois-Rivières, offered some more of their children to us, saying that no one was talking about anything up and down the St. Lawrence River except for about the decision that some Hurons had made to remain with the French, and that they'd talk even more about it when they got home, and very enthusiastically. Now, since there was no one who could have an official meeting with them about this, some interpreters came down to Quebec to explain it all to them. It was actually Divine Providence that they didn't send us any more pupils, because we would not have had enough food and supplies to provide for them.

So this is the way that the Huron School started in great difficulty. We took great care of our young pupils, we dressed them like Frenchmen, we gave them underclothing and other necessary items of apparel. We housed them in a hut set apart for this purpose, along with the Father who was to care for them. Everything seemed peaceful. Our Frenchmen really enjoyed seeing the young Indians who were so eager to live in the French way, and each of the Indian youths seemed very content. Yet he who bases his contentment for any length on time on anything other than the Cross will soon regret it; one of these young men was of a rather depressive temperament, and asked, soon after arriving, to be allowed to return to his home, since he did not feel able, as he put it, to get along with the others.

As this was going on, a Huron chief, having heard in Trois-Rivières of the new school, came down to Quebec to see the young men and to encourage them to do well, especially one of his nephews who was part of the group. This good old man (for he was at least sixty years old), having seen the discipline that was observed in the school and the good treatment that was given to all those of his tribe, exclaimed, "Oh! We will have a lot to talk about when I get back to our tribe! My children, you are indeed lucky to be so well cared for; you know that at home we don't have good food like this; take heart, be well behaved and obedient; observe everything that you can about the French so that you can teach us about it when you come back home; you'll be fit for high office when you return, and people will really admire what you've learned here."

The poor young man who had wanted to leave, seeing that those who were staying received such praise, changed his mind; but, since we could see that he was more unstable and less mature than the others, we expected him soon to change it back again. Father Daniel asked him, in front of his schoolmates, if he had anything to complain about as far as the Jesuit treatment of him was concerned. "Not at all," he said, "you have been very kind to me, but I have trouble getting along with my schoolmates." He had arrived without clothing or blanket, and we sent him back to his people well dressed. We don't spare any money when it comes to winning the hearts of the tribes.

When the Indians give you their children, they give them to you naked as the day they were born; that is to say, as soon as you have them, you must dress them and then return the blanket they'd been delivered in to their relatives. You must house them and feed them well, and even so, some of the Indians still think that we should be grateful to them! I could say more: usually you have to give presents to the parents, and when they live nearby, you must assist them for some time with their living expenses. That's their custom: if someone, seeing his friend childless, gives him one of his own to console him, the one who has received the child must give presents to the parents and friends of the child. This custom requires that we spend considerable sums of money, but God will help us meet those needs, if it is His will.

Now I'll get back to my story. This young man having left, the others who remained did so well and lived so peacefully together that we were very relieved. They were happy, even joyful, and obedient; in short, it seemed to us that we had weathered every storm, and that, after the rain, good weather was on the horizon. But suddenly one of the leaders of the group came down with a very high fever. We had him bled, we cared for him night and day, and gave him medicine, and we ardently prayed to God for him to recover his health, but after all this, the young man, having suffered for a long time, was at death's door. Father L'Allemant baptized him, and soon after he gave his spirit up to God. Alas! That death was a great and painful loss to us, especially to Father Daniel who cared for the boys: he had spent night and day by the bedside of the dying boy, doing everything he could to keep him as comfortable as possible, and, even so, Father Daniel had been compelled to see the boy die before his very eyes.

This boy had just been buried when Satouta became ill with the same sickness: the poor young man was a model of humility and of patience in his distress, his serious and kind nature showing itself. We gave him purges, had him bled as we had done with his deceased friend. We did everything we could to save his life, but Our Lord willed that things should be otherwise. We baptized him, and soon afterwards his soul gained entry into Heaven. In this way, what we might call the "two eyes" of our school were shut in very little time, its two "pillars" toppled. For, there is no denying it, those two boys had exceptional qualities for Indians. Loving God's ways, even though we could not understand them at all, Father Daniel (and other Jesuits), having worked so hard nursing the boys, became sick himself, and we thought he, too, would die as his students before him. Our Lord gave us back his life, however, so that he could continue to care for the other students who suffered from lesser ailments: and, thank God, they are better now.

It is true that the deaths of these two young men laid us low, especially since their presence had given us great hope of eventually converting their entire tribe, but something that happened just shortly before their death really worried us: Tsiko (that is the name of the first dead young man), was joking around with one of the more stupid Frenchmen. He got angry and challenged the Huron to fight, and they actually threw a couple of punches, although without doing each other any harm. But the Huron fell sick just a few days later, and accused the Frenchman, blaming his illness on the blows to the head that he had taken. We inspected him and found no bruises or contusions and, indeed, the cause of his death was not this light cuffing, but of excessive eating, as I will explain. However, since he had told his friends what had happened with the Frenchman, we were quite worried as to what turn events would take; if the Huron were to decide that one of their children had died by violent cause, they would kill as many French as remain in the area. The same thing happened when Satouta died. This poor young man, embracing a Frenchman and running his hand over the Frenchman's face, offended the latter (who thought he meant to pull his nose); he pushed the Indian away roughly; some bystanders even claimed that he struck him; that's why the Huron picked up stones to protect himself, and the Frenchmen put his hand to his sword, or so I am told. I am sure that he did not hit him hard enough to really hurt him. Nevertheless, since this poor Huron fell sick and died soon after, we were again afraid— especially because an Algonquian, who knew Satouta's parents, was present at this poorly played tragedy. These two events could have ruined everything for us. Our Lord, by His great goodness, reestablished order. May He be blessed forever by angels, and by men, and by every living creature!

I was in Trois-Rivières with the Governor when I received the bad news, and it came to us watered-down, too, for fear that the Indians might get angry. The true cause of their death was actually a result of the change in climate, exercise and diet: the boiled corn or buckwheat broth that the Indians usually eat is neither firm nor solid like French bread and meat. These young people, greatly enjoying whatever we served them to eat, ate constantly, in such a way that they killed themselves with gluttony. To keep this from recurring, we gave the rest of them food that was mixed: half Huron-style, and half French-style, and they were healthier that way. Add to this the fact that the Indians, when they get sick, have no idea how to protect their health; if they are hot, they go somewhere cool, throw cold water on their body, without bothering to think that a dose of medicine or a good sweat would do them more good.

Let me say a few more words about these two young men. Satouta, who was named Robert when he was baptized, was the grandson of Tsondechaoüanouan, who is like the leader of the country. Everything concerning trading, sailing, and all the news of the nations where the

Huron travel over the St. Lawrence River, comes to him: he is so well-known that if you want to talk about the Huron to tribes farther away, you just say what you have to say in his name. He keeps up with everything going on in the Iroquois nation as well as in the neutral [Tobacco] nation, not to mention the disputes that he daily settles between his own tribesmen.

This chief had promised his grandson, our student, to give him his name and to let him take over his leadership role for the whole country, but Our Lord settled things otherwise. This poor boy, realizing that he was sick and about to die, very courteously thanked all those who were watching over him and all those who cared for him. Father de Nouë told me that this boy was so gracious in receiving others' care that the Father often came away from the bedside deeply touched and amazed. Father Daniel, who has given me his memoirs of what happened at the school, notes that this sick boy often turned toward the crucifix and said: "My God, You have made me Your son and I have taken You to be my Father; save me therefore if it please You; have pity on me; wipe away my sins, which I hate and which I promise never again to commit." At other times he would say, "Jesus, my Chief, since you have suffered so much so that Heaven might be opened to me, make sure that I do not fall into the fires of Hell: may I instead see you in Heaven."

He was greatly troubled by some dream or evil premonition. "What do I see?" he would ask, "What are those people doing? What are they telling me to do?" "Do you not know those people?" the Father asked him. "No," the boy answered, "and I don't know what they are doing." Then the Father encouraged him, making him understand that the devil, furious that the boy had been baptized, was trying to make him relinquish the faith he had embraced, but that, if he would only hold firm, God would not abandon him. So then, speaking to the demons, the boy said, "Go away, evil ones, stay away from me, I abhor you! I recognize no Master other than He who made the heavens and the earth, and He who has chosen me to be His child. Oh! My God, do not abandon me; I will never abandon You. My Chief, You have paid my way, I belong to You; You have bought my way into Heaven; give Heaven to me!" The pains of his sickness increasing, he often sighed sweetly and said, his voice interrupted by weeping, "My Chief, take pleasure in seeing how I endure this; take this in payment for my sins;

what I suffer is indeed very little compared to Your suffering; but please let Your suffering and mine be joined so that there will be sufficient to buy off my sins and to buy my way, pardoned, into Heaven."

He took great delight when I said to him, the Father reports, that God looked down from Heaven on his suffering, and that the more patiently he endured it the more he was becoming like Our Lord, the more God loved him, and the greater, as a result, his reward would be in Heaven. Finally, having endured another two days and one night after his baptism, showing great faith and hope, he gave his soul up to the Creator, all ruddy and bathed in the blood of His beloved Son Jesus Christ our Savior.

His classmate, named Tsiko, who died before him and who was called Paul, was the son of Ouanda Koca, a Chief who always spoke well of his tribe and who, as a result, was much loved; his son was even better than he, because he had a natural gift of eloquent speech. In the evening, when I occasionally would ask him to make some small speech, Father Daniel relates, he would adorn his speech with metaphors, with dramatic renderings; without ever having studied the art of rhetoric and without being of noble birth, he would nonetheless compose elegant dialogues. He would warm himself up as he spoke, polishing his speech with graceful and innocent figures of speech, and both his schoolmates and I would be lost in admiration. He was not as well educated as Robert Satouta, who was on familiar terms with the Jesuits, and Paul Tsiko had never heard of the Christian faith before coming to our school. But he had a wonderful disposition, and all who knew him loved him. The passion that he showed for the Faith as he was receiving instruction in Christianity is the reason why we baptized him as he lay dying, even though he had already become deaf as a result of the illness.

Concerning discipline at the Huron school, and some characteristics of the students

No group of people is as difficult to discipline as the tribes of America. All these Indians are like wild donkeys: they are born, they live and die in totally unconstrained freedom; they have no idea what a bridle or a fishhook are; they think it's a joke when we talk of overcoming our passions; and their highest philosophy is to slake their thirsty sense with whatever they crave. Our Lord's Way is very different from such degenerate behavior: His Way gives us guidelines and prescribes healthy limits beyond which we cannot step without offending both God and reason. Now, it is really hard to put a yoke—however sweet and light that yoke might be—on the neck of people unaccustomed to disciplining themselves or to bending their will to anything, be it earthly or heavenly. I say it's difficult, but not impossible; in fact, I am coming to think that it is beyond the power or the work of men, but that it is an easy thing for God to do. We are all amazed how young free spirits, used to following their whims, can be caught in Christ's net so easily, such that there is no being more docile than a Huron schoolboy! That's not to say that great dexterity is needed to bring them along; kindness and infinite patience are also necessary, because any asperity or sharpness makes Indians rebel. I truly believe that these young people, finding themselves three hundred miles away from their home, become more obedient as a result, but I have to say that their sweet nature and obedience is also a great gift from God. Since they were very proud to live a French lifestyle when they first came here, the Fathers have let them know that we all regulate our conduct; we don't just do whatever we feel like doing, but rather we are rational beings, and we do things after having planned them. We advised them that they'd do well to imitate us in this and, seeing that they were willing to do so, we drew up a little "rule" (or order of daily discipline) that they stick to every day with great obedience and humility.

In the morning, after they get up, they pray to God, they thank Him for having created them and for preserving their lives. They ask Him for His help and His grace so that they will do nothing to offend Him during the day, and then they offer everything they do to Him, dedicating themselves to the Holy Trinity, in whose honor they recite the Lord's Prayer three times as well as saying the Hail Mary three times to show honor to the Blessed Virgin. They also recite the Apostles' Creed and some other prayers. After having prayed they go to chapel, where they attend mass up until the offertory. They are always on time for mass; in fact, as soon as the bells for mass have rung, you can already find them in the chapel, and we've many times offered their example to several of the French who are not nearly so devout in this respect as are the Huron students.

After mass they have lunch, and then we help them learn to read and to write, and then they have a brief recess. Then Father catechizes them, explains to them the mysteries of our faith, and they are always very attentive to this.

When it's time for dinner, they set the table themselves with the help of a couple Frenchmen who live with them, and after dinner they go worship and adore Our Lord in the chapel. They say this little prayer: "My God, I thank You for having kept me in safety from morning until now; keep me safe for the rest of the day, forgive my sins, and help me to sin no more. Everything I do, I offer to You. Give me Your grace so that I may live in the right way."

After this, we have them read a bit more, then we let them amuse themselves, take a walk or get some exercise; they often go hunting or fishing or use their bows and arrows, or clear some ground for a garden, or find something else to do.

In the evening, after supper, they examine their conscience and also kneel to say their prayers, then they go to bed. To have been born a savage, yet to live with such daily discipline, is an amazing thing; to be a Huron and not be a thief (which, in fact, they are not) is another miracle; to live at liberty (so that they aren't even expected to obey their parents), yet now be willing to do nothing without first getting permission, that's a third miracle.

Let me tell you about some things that their teacher has observed about these students.

One of them having offended one of the French, and having acknowledged this in his examination of conscience at bedtime, he first went to ask the pardon of the man he had offended; he did not want to fall asleep without having asked pardon for his sin. Another student, who did not get up early enough to go to mass, was so distressed by this that he was in tears. The Father told him that he was not required to go to mass, but this didn't make the student feel any better. Finally we just sent him off to the chapel to say his prayers there, which consoled him.

It's wonderful to see, also, how these students get along so well together, the youngest deferring to the oldest, yet the older boys never ordering the younger ones about in a highhanded or prideful way, but always in a loving, respectful way, in testimony of their love for them. They are all so united that if anyone offends even the least of them, they all feel offended.

It does my heart good to hear them recite the Apostle's Creed in the presence of everyone gathered in the chapel. To encourage them to do their best, the Fathers chant a stanza in French, then the Huron students chant the next stanza in their language, then they chant all together the third stanza, each in his own tongue, and somehow it's harmonious. This pleases them so much that they sing the Creed everywhere and all the time. We also have them recite their catechism in public, so that their faith will be better established. I've heard the French, the Montagnais, and the Hurons all sing together the articles of faith, and even though they were speaking in three different languages they harmonized so beautifully that it was a pleasure to hear them!

"They've begged me," the Father said, "to baptize them, and to try to get me to say yes; they've given me every reason they could think of to persuade me to baptize them, assuring me that their good will was beyond question, and that they had vowed never to leave us Jesuits." One of them said that he would gladly do everything that Christians do: "I will fast," he said, "I will resist evil thoughts that the devil puts into my head; I no longer have impure dreams, so I don't even have to ask God to keep such dreams away, but now I pray to Him to keep any and all evil thoughts from me." Another Indian said that if we baptized him, he would be better and wiser, and would learn more quickly what we are trying to teach him.

One day, the Father explained the Ten Commandments to them, showing them the difference there was between these wise and reasonable commands and the things that their sorcerers tell them to do. "They order you," so he said, "to throw parties; they get people from different tribes together and perform all sorts of ridiculous and disgusting rituals; and they say all this will help sick people get better; but these poor folk get no relief from their suffering. Rather, they are bedeviled by shouts and noise, and whittled to the bone by the greediness of the medicine men, to whom they must give many presents. When we hope to get something, we do not ask for the aid of demons, stones, rocks, or waterfalls; we don't have silly ceremonies like you Indians do; our only hope is in God, who can do all things, who knows all things, and who is goodness himself."

Then one of the natives began to speak and said, "There's another thing we do that is even more upsetting than you know. When we want to have a successful hunt, we fast—sometimes for up to a week, we do not eat or drink anything, and we also cut ourselves so that blood covers our body. Now we can see that this is not a good thing to do."

These good students, on their way to do something, or coming back from an errand, go to the chapel to ask for God's help, or to praise and thank Him for his aid. Our Lord has enabled them to see that He expects such thanksgiving from them, because, if they forget this duty, an accident or something unfortunate happens to them. One day, they went hunting without permission, and without first having prayed to God for help. They got lost in the woods, and they were not able to find their way back to the residence until after having been out a very long time in the snow and cold; they acknowledged that this misfortunate had happened to them because they had acted in the Indian [and not the Christian] way. Another time, having left without having attended chapel, and planning to cut down a tree, one of them almost killed his companion when his swing of the axe went wild. They came back ashamed and confused. The Father asked them if they had said their prayers in church before leaving. Without answering, they went immediately to ask God's pardon for the sin that they had committed. One of them who had not gone to pray, coming into our residence too quickly and slamming the door, caused a large beam of wood to fall on his head and was injured. The first thing that another of his companions said to him was, "Did you go to chapel when you came back to the residence?" The wounded young man admitted that he had not, and they said, "Well, look, that's the problem." He showed them some of his cuts and bruises and as they were bandaging him up, one whispered to another, "everything bad that happens to us is a result of forgetting to honor God."

The Father explained to them about the Passion of Our Lord; then, talking to them about the eclipse of the sun, and about the earthquake that had happened recently, they answered that they had heard about such happenings in the past, but that no one had been able to explain (until now) how they happened. "People still talk," they said, "about a great darkening of the sun. They thought that the big turtle, whom they believe holds up the earth, changed position so that his shell blocked out the sun." Those who do not know God have even more shadows in their souls than the earth has when the sun is hidden. They respect the truths that we teach them much more than the fables that they tell.

When Father de Noüe set out for the native cabins, which were about seven or eight miles away from Quebec, two Huron students wanted to go with him. When the Montagnais saw them, they offered them elk meat to eat, but, since it was Saturday, the students refused this meat. The Father told them that, since they had not yet been baptized, the students did not have to observe this commandment of the Church. "That doesn't matter," they said. "We do not want to eat it, because you are not eating any of it." The same Father told me that these good boys prayed on their knees so fervently, and made their examination of conscience so thoroughly, that he was deeply touched.

It is true that God saddened us with the death of some of their schoolmates, but He also has consoled us by the docility and deference that those still alive show to us. They are proud to live a French lifestyle, and if anyone is rude, they call that person a "Huron" and demand to know how long it's been since he came from Huron country. They humbly bow to the French, putting their hand to their hat to greet people politely. All our Jesuits and the lay brothers have commented to me on how willing the Indian boys are to do things our way. This is not to say that the pupils can't be spiteful or grumpy at times, but that sort of emotion doesn't last, and usually they are very sweet-tempered.

The oldest of them became willful and did something he should not have done, and for some time he was quite obstinate. When he came to Quebec, Father Daniel told me what had happened. I called the young man to me and asked him if, having done so well for so long, he really wanted to sacrifice everything just for a fit of anger. I told him that I had seen promising signs of how he walked in Christ's way, so that it would be a grave spiritual fault were his behavior not to continue along this road, and God would be very upset were he to stray; as for us, we had nothing to lose, but he'd pay the price himself, especially if it was true (as I'd been told) that he'd stopped praying regularly. He answered that, indeed, he had been very angry, believing that we had tried to force him to believe in God, and, to show that he could not be intimidated he had been unruly; he said that he had stopped praying to God in public, but that he still prayed to him in private. "Don't worry when we get upset with each other," he told us, "this sort of thing happens a lot in our tribe, even among our closest relations, but we don't hate them or stop seeing them. Here, Father Daniel is like our father, so when we get a little upset, that doesn't mean we're going to leave him." His answer relieved me, and reinforced my thought that it's important to discipline these people with great care, because the threat of eternal fire really turns them off. Once we've been able to convince them and train them, then we need to teach them about hell; it's that awareness that will keep them from straying in the long run.

Here's something that happened that really reassured us: on the eve of the Feast of the Assumption, they decided to get together to clear some ground and plant some seed and then to build a little house in the Indian style. When we first heard their plan, we took it with a grain of salt, thinking that they are young and easily change their minds, but their accomplishments far surpassed our expectations. Little by little, they began to prune trees, and when spring came, they prepared a large stretch of ground; the amount of work they put in astounded us. An unfortunate thing happened to them around this time: the Indian corn they had planted was either too old or too dry; at any rate, it didn't come up. They were more successful in building their house, even though they didn't really use it; they had constructed it to hold their wheat and corn, which never came up. Now, even if their work didn't have any great worldly result, I think it's likely that it had a significant spiritual effect; seeing that they were well supplied with food and with tools, and that the French thought highly of them, they decided to do everything they could to convince their parents to let them stay with us, and not just for the next year, but for the rest of their lives. They hoped in this way to convince some of their countrymen to join us, and to encourage some young women from their tribe to come here to be taught Christianity and then become their spouses.

If this plan works, it will be a great accomplishment to God's glory, and will greatly please the directors and the associates who govern these lands. First of all, in just a few years there could be a small town of Huron Christians right here. Such a group would be very useful in evangelizing others through the contact they would have when trading; the

Montagnais Indians, who are nomads, would learn from the Huron example and would begin to settle down. Secondly, the directors and associates of the Company of New France would effectively have hostages already in place to ensure the safety of the French in Huron territory; this would also protect trade with the Hurons and with other Indian tribes farther away. Indeed, if the wandering tribes saw the Hurons living as settlers and as our neighbors, they'd stop making war whenever they feel like it, because they would know that the Huron, being under our protection and living among us, would not abandon us and, besides, knowing the woods as they do, and running as fast as any other Indian, the Montagnais would fear the Huron more than he would any Frenchman; thus, we could use our weapons to protect the Huron settlement, while they could hunt for themselves and for us and also repulse any enemies. Anyone who thinks long and hard about what I've just said will conclude that we should spare no expense to have a Huron settlement be established near us. The Huron who already live with us certainly are willing to have this happen.

Here's another proof of their regard for us: As the ships from France were slow in arriving, the crossing having been long and difficult this year, we were short on food and we wondered how we would feed these poor children. I asked the Governor for advice. He's a brave man. He told me that he'd gone to a great deal of trouble to get these young men here and that he could not bear to send them back, because they were so willing and so well behaved. "We must deprive ourselves," he said, "and give them some of our own rations." The Governor is well aware of the significance of this school for God's glory and for the trade of the Company of New France. When we quoted his reply to the students, the eldest said, "That's a good thing; it would have been a bad idea to send us back, because we've already decided to stay with Echon (that's their name for Father Brébeuf) and Antoine (Father Daniel); we'd rather suffer a little here than go back to where we were and where it is so dangerous."

SPIRITU, CORDE: PRACTICE, HEART, SOUL, AND WORSHIP

By 1642, the Jesuits had four residences (at Quebec, Notre-Dame des Anges, St. Joseph, and Trois-Rivières) and were administering the sacraments on a regular, daily basis to the natives in the area. However, despite this success, the Jesuit impulse was always to harvest more souls and, in some frustration, Father Vimont wrote to the Superior that "the door to Christ will remain forever closed" to nations above Quebec, if more creative and fruitful ways were not found of evangelizing the nomadic, often hostile tribes. As one historian put it, "two forces were battling for the mastery of Canada: on the one side, Christ, the Virgin, and the Angels, with their agents, the priests; on the other, the Devil, and his tools, the Iroquois" (Parkman 568). Father Vimont, the author of this letter, himself called the Iroquois "the scourge of the infant church." Frequently, Algonquian and Huron converts to Christianity were taken captive by warring Iroquois bands, tortured and killed. Those who managed to escape recounted horrific stories to Father Vimont, who shared many of them with the readers of the *Relations*. A strong spirit, a stout heart for Christ ("*Spiritu, corde pro Christi* . . ."), and the daily practice of devotions were Ignatius's prescription for such a troubled situation, and Vimont set about to apply it. His aim and hope was to protect the fledgling congregations, nurture new converts and claim—and keep—

souls for Christ. This *relation* clearly attests to Jesuit successes but also to the ongoing nature of their struggle to save souls. The unrelenting opposition they faced was a characteristic of the Jesuit mission in French Canada (whereas it was not always the case elsewhere; witness Matteo Ricci's great success with the mandarins in China).

❧ ❧ ❧

Relation of what took place in New France in 1642

My Reverend Father,
Peace of Christ.

Events in this country have forced me to send one of our Fathers to France so that he can describe the state to which Iroquois hunting parties have reduced the newborn Church. I believe that he who worked the hardest to establish this Church would be the most likely to be able to communicate how urgent it is that help be sent to us so that we can resist these barbaric depredations. And, in fact, I was right, because, although he's only been in France a short time, he has met with several well-placed people, with whom he has shared the great spiritual riches that, it is to be hoped, will come from these vast lands where there is practically a numberless quantity of tribes who only need to hear the Gospel in order to become Christian and know their Creator. This would have already happened, at least in part, had demons not placed great obstacles in our way. They saw that all the French living in these far-flung outposts of the world lived in a much more holy way than they did in France, and that the Indians, formerly subjected to these demons, were daily being freed from their bondage. So the demons decided to do battle to defend their stronghold from [us Jesuits].

Now, since it was going to take a good show of strength to put these demons down, our emissary back to France had to seek out powerful people who had both the desire and the ability to help out in the New World. So he went first to talk to Madame the Duchess of Esguillon, who was most interested in the conversion of the Indians; in fact, because of her strong devotion to the blood that Jesus shed for us, she founded a charitable organization for sick Indians, and there she helped them to see the wonderful healing power in the blood of Christ. As a result, she took it upon herself to talk about the mission to Cardinal Richelieu, explaining to him the dangers facing Christian faith and the French colony if help was not sent to reinforce them against the Iroquois. Her conversation was so fruitful that he promised her that he would send substantial aid to arm us against our enemies.

With this assurance, the Father set sail for New France, much relieved to have seen in France such eagerness for the salvation of native souls. He witnessed this zeal not only in religious orders and people who devoted their lives to God, but also in many high-born men and women who, not satisfied with simply telling him of their support for the conversion of the natives, actually wanted to contribute financially to our mission and supply what was needed to settle these wandering tribes; God, who looks with favor on such charitable giving, will remember their good deeds and reward them a hundred times over. The joy that the French and the natives felt at receiving this assistance is beyond belief; their fear of the Iroquois had so discouraged them that they were constantly in fear for their lives, but as soon as the good news came that reinforcements were on their way and fortifications were to be built to defend against Iroquois raids, they lost this fear, took heart, and lifted their heads with as much assurance as if the fort had already been built.

It is true that such fortifications will be very welcome, but, as they do not get to the root of the problem, since these barbaric tribes go to war like ancient primitive warriors, the door will not be completely open to Christ and danger will not have entirely left our colony, until the Iroquois have either been won over or wiped out.

Further, I hope that Your Reverence will take great joy in, and be consoled by, the beginning of what you have ordered us to do. If you have the time to read the letter I've attached, you'll see in it that your wishes (expressed in your earlier letter of consolation and encouragement to us) have been carried out.

It is true that this joy will be somewhat diminished when you see how the Iroquois are a true plague of the new-born Church; they kill and confound new converts by weapons and by fire, and they have sworn eternal war on us French: they block all the mouths of the St. Lawrence River, hampering trade and threatening to ruin the whole country. Father Jogues, if he wasn't killed immediately when the Hurons were defeated by the Iroquois, is still held captive by them along with two of our servants and twenty-three Christian Hurons (those studying to be baptized). However, this fact, thanks be to God, does not discourage us, nor do we lose hope that this tribe will be converted, it just compels us to beg for your prayers and holy sacrifices on our behalf. I therefore ask your special prayers and I remain your humble and obedient servant,

Barthelemy Vimont.

Quebec, October 4, 1642.

Concerning the general state of the country

The first ship that arrived at Quebec this year set off a false alarm, dampening the joy that the arrival of a ship from France usually evokes in the hearts of both French and Indians. One fleet, we were told, had been defeated by a ship from Dunquerk, and Lord Courpont, crossing the English Channel at the same time, was either taken prisoner or thrown overboard and all the crew either killed or imprisoned. This news upset everyone, but then, when we learned that all the ships had reached port safely, our joy was even greater because our sadness had been so intense. The whole colony made it through the winter in good health, Lord Montmagny, our Governor, was both good to us and much loved by all, keeping the peace and good order of the colony; everyone honors and respects him, and if there is any unrest it's due to the self-interest of a disturbed individual, not the colony as a whole. We have, indeed, no enemies here but our own selves; there are very few other problems. Lawsuits, ambition, greed, dirty living, the desire for revenge—the demons you find in Europe—are barely present here, our woods not offering occasion for such sins.

Our wheat crop came up very well, and some who live here harvested more than they need to feed their family and animals (which thrive in this country). The day will come when everyone who lives here will have livestock. *Labor improbus omnia vincit.* Hard work conquers everything. There is much work; it's hard work to create a new country. The growing season is much shorter here than in France, even though we're at the same longitude and latitude as La Rochelle.

Virtue, courage and joy have made their dwelling in houses dedicated to God; sweet and gentle girls who would be afraid of a snowflake in France are not daunted by mountains of snow here. Hoarfrost can lock them in their houses, and a big, long winter filled with snow and ice can cover them from head to toe but will cause them no harm; it will simply give them a big appetite. The European humid cold would bother them, but Canadian cold is a stinging cold; in my opinion, it is more pleasant, even if more severe.

We have four dwellings or residences here. Our Father Superior, and Father Jacques de la Place usually stay in Quebec, Father Enmond Masse and Father Anne Denoue stay in Notre-Dames des Anges, Father Jean de Brébeuf, Father De Quen, and Father Joseph du Peron stay in St. Joseph. Father Jacques Buteux and Father Joseph Poncet stay in Trois-Rivières. All the Fathers and brothers are in good health, each works according to his vocation, and God will reward them at the end of the day according to the price and worth of their endeavors.

To imagine the state—good or bad—of the country, you should not only take a look at the French who are the healthiest ones there, but also look at both our Indian friends and our Indian enemies. Those who we call the Iroquois are real devils; they go to war winter, spring, and summer; they have massacred several Hurons and many Algonquians; they have captured Frenchmen and killed some of them, they still have one of our Jesuits, and they have killed numbers of our people. I'll sum up what I think of all this later; let me just say here that, if we don't soon have peace with these barbarians, or if we don't wipe them out, the country will remain in very bad shape, the door will remain forever closed to the Gospel in the nations above Quebec, and travel routes will stay infested with brigands.

But let's look on the positive side; let's see how these new Christians are behaving, especially those who live in St. Joseph (known around here as Sillery). There are a good many signs that faith in Christ is taking deep root in their souls, among them their constant attendance at mass, their thirst to hear God's Word, their diligence in following His Commandments, the punishments that they themselves are beginning to mete out to offenders, and their zeal to defend and increase the faith. Morning and night you'll hear the bells ringing for public prayer led by a Jesuit in the chapel. Those who have gone hunting all pray to God together in their cabins before leaving, one of them saying the words aloud and the others repeating word for word. They don't go on any trip before being sure that they are right with God, and the first thing they do when they get back is to go to chapel and thank God for having kept them safe; if they go for a month without confessing their sins or taking communion, they complain about this sin to a Jesuit who tries to remind them that moderation in all things is desirable: the respect that they owe to these great mysteries means they should not use them lightly. They are so happy when we tell them a feast day is coming up, they try to remember them season by season; they ask for a little calendar or a list of saints' days to take with them when they go hunting or trading for an extended period of time; they cross off each day as it goes by, noting those on which they cannot work, those on which they are to fast or not eat meat, so that they can strictly observe them if at all possible.

They are revolted by the superstitions they used to believe in, and if anyone invites them to a ritual dance or a feast which is not suitable for a Christian, they answer, "we love prayer; we have ceased from such foolishness and don't ever want to go back to it."

That's enough for you to be able to tell what these new converts are like in general, now let's talk about some specific details.

❊ ❊ ❊

Concerning the converts' good deeds and good will

Non omnis qui dicit mihi Domine, Domine, intrabit in regnum coelrum: Not all those who call on God's holy name will enter into the Kingdom of Heaven; it's not enough to lift your hands in the air, they must also be filled with hyacinths as an acceptable sacrifice to the Lord.

In short, good deeds must accompany protestations of faith; then you will be welcome in Paradise; we shall recognize who is a Christian by his actions.

Easter Day usually falls at a time when the natives go elk hunting. Some of them really wanted to take communion on Easter Day, so they left their hunting camp and drying racks and headed straight for Quebec, where they meant to arrive by Good Friday, but the bad weather slowed them down. The next day, we saw them on the river, which was iced over, and they came shouting: "Christ the Lord is risen today; that's what it said on the calendar we have; we came to confess our sins and to take communion." They crowded into the Ursuline chapel and asked if mass had already been said; some of them had enough time to make their confession, and we heard the others' confessions the next morning.

It's a pleasure to see how these good people arrive in Quebec or at St. Joseph in their little birchbark canoes which they carry on their shoulders or on their heads to keep them out of the water; then they go to church and hear mass. Having done that, they go back quietly to their hunting or fishing, happy to have done their duty as good and faithful Christians to God and His church. I've heard that our Frenchmen have been most edified this winter, seeing these new plants bearing fruit, these converts dropping everything to attend church when the bell calls them. I've hardly ever seen (says Father De Quen, who wrote the memoirs I'm sharing with you here) since I've been in New France, worse weather than on the Feast of St. Andrew last year. It was snowing heavily and the wind was blowing the snow about like tornadoes or very heavy rain; it was so thick that you could hardly see heaven or earth. I thought that our new Christians, having gone into the woods to seek shelter from the cold and to continue their hunting, would not come for mass that day; the weather would have been excuse enough, and the roads were not clear. But I was astonished to see the entire chapel filled up. I praised their courage, and let them know that such good behavior was very pleasing to God.

"I think," Father De Quen goes on, "that these good souls are enlightened by the beauty of the Eucharist and enabled to recognize the truth of our faith; they gain strength to stand against their countrymen's jibes; they are charitable so as to be compassionate to unbelievers and encourage them to share in the happiness that the converts experience." "It really makes us sad," they tell us, "to see our relatives and friends remain under Satan's power. They make fun of us; but we still love them. We hate the things they do, we detest their superstitions, but we do not wish them ill. They are angry that we believe in God, but, no matter what they do, prayer is dearer to us than our lives; we would die rather than stop coming to mass."

Having heard of the Algonquians' death at the hand of the Iroquois, the converts who were at St. Joseph wanted to console those who had survived the massacre. They followed their own traditions but sanctified them with true Christian fervor. They held a big feast, invited all the leaders of the Algonquian tribe who had come to visit them, and had three things to say to them. That is, they gave them three presents: the first was given to dry the tears they had shed over the death of their people; the second, to bring back to life the nephew of one of the Algonquian chiefs; the third and most beautiful was given to encourage those who showed a disposition to pray: they invited them all to become Christians. These Algonquian notables, whom God does not stop trying to bring to His mercy by means of all these plagues, accepted the first two things and held the third in abeyance so they could discuss whether to accept it or not: for whoever takes hold of a present given by an Indian pledges to do what that present says. One member of the tribe, seeing that the present mentioned God and invited whoever received it to pray aloud to Him, said loudly, "I can't think straight any more, I wouldn't know how to pray; the Iroquois have taken my head and my spirit away. I can't see anymore; my tribesmen are dead. When I see great boiling cauldrons filled with the flesh of my dead enemies, when my stomach and my guts are stuffed with them, then my spirit will return to me." Rage and vengeance, characteristics of demons, reign in these barbarians' hearts. But these wolves become lambs when Holy Baptism clothes them in the grace of Jesus Christ.

A small group of converts, wanting to show that faith does not take courage away from he who converts, decided to go into battle at the side of those who were not converted. The Christians prayed to God, while the non-Christian Indians feasted and did superstitious dances: they yelled, they sang, they screamed, they mimed hideous poses in which they would murder their enemies. Then they all set out together, but they had only gone part way when the non-Christians split off from the Christian Indians. Whether because the former scorned the latter or because they were afraid to enter enemy territory, they decided to go hunting animals instead of hunting down men. Our good converts, however, continuing their route, came stealthily upon a small group of Iroquois. They pulled up short, talked among themselves about whether they should kill the Iroquois or bring them back alive, should God give them the victory. On the one hand, the glory of bringing back prisoners seemed good: that's the sweetest pleasure an Indian knows, to drag after him his enemy tied and gagged so as to make a spectacle of him before the tribe. On the other hand, the converts, realizing that they probably wouldn't be able to stop their tribesmen from throwing themselves on the captives and killing them, figured it would be better to kill the Iroquois right away, instead of looking like heroes but causing their victims greater suffering. They rushed at the Iroquois, killed every one of them and, now in possession of the dead bodies as well as the goods the Iroquois had been carrying, they knelt to pray, thanking God for the victory. Then they picked up the scalps and dead bodies of their fallen enemies and returned triumphantly home to St. Joseph. Before even going to their homes, they went to church. This really made the other Indians look bad: they had mocked the converts for their piety, saying that they were cowards because they did not take part in the traditional dances.

Another Christian convert always fasted on holy days; if he ate fish on Friday, he salted it and saved it for that day, and if he didn't have much luck catching fish, he bought bread from the French, and that—plus a little water—is all he would eat; when he was out hunting in the woods and had only meat at hand, he went without eating as long as he could, then, realizing that he had to eat to live, he knelt and prayed to God: "You who created me, forgive me if I offend You; I do not want to offend You and you know that it is against my will and only because I am starving that I eat this meat; You would not want me to die, and so I am now going to eat, in the name of the Father, Son, and Holy Spirit."

This same convert, having met a sick Christian woman far from the Jesuit residence, did everything he could for her; she was about to die so he gave her the good counsel that God inspired him with, and while the other women wrapped her in a shroud he dug her grave, and then he made a wooden cross, stuck it at one end of the grave and, speaking aloud, he prayed this prayer: "You who created us all, have pity on this woman who has just died; she believed in You, be merciful to her, forgive her sins and carry her soul up to Heaven; and you, good woman who has just died, pray for us when you are in Heaven. Pray for those who are baptized, that they may keep the faith; pray for all others, that they may believe in Him who made all things." When he had finished praying, all the Christians present said their rosary for the poor woman's soul. When they had finished, this good convert covered the grave over, said his rosary twice more before leaving, then went into the dead woman's cabin where he spoke so eloquently of eternal life and of the happiness of this woman in Heaven because she had died a Christian, that everyone who heard him was comforted.

When he left the cabin to go hunting, he hung a small crucifix that someone had given to him to a piece of wood covering a lean-to, and he talked to God, kneeling on the ground and joining his hands in prayer: "You can do all things, give me something to eat, I beg you; feed my people, they belong to You, you made them: nothing is impossible for You, give them something to eat, they beg You as I do; feed us, You are Our Father, they speak truthfully: You are Our Father and if You feed us we will always believe in You; if You have no food for us, we accept that, too: You are our Lord and we will never stop believing in You, obeying You, and loving You."

A good old woman said to one of her daughters who was near death: "My child, believe with all your might in Him who made all things, *SunKa SunKa* (strongly, strongly), and you will go to Heaven where you will live forever, you will see Our Father, and He will give you a new life that will be without end. Take heart, my daughter, your suffering will end soon; in a little while you will feel no more pain. When you come into the Lord's House, tell him: 'Have pity on my mother, take pity on my brothers and my sisters, let them come be here with me'; tell Him to think kindly about us." After the death of this child, this good old lady met the Jesuit who had baptized her daughter, and she said to him: "My poor daughter whom you baptized is now in Heaven; she obeyed God, she never gossiped and she never slept around, she never got angry but was always peaceful, and she never upset anyone. Ever since she became a Christian, she carried her rosary around with her all the time, that's why I hung hers around her neck and buried it with her in the grave; I am sad that she is gone; but I'm even sadder that one of my children died without being baptized." Then she stopped and asked, "Where is that poor child now?"

A new Christian having done something wrong, he approached one of the Jesuits with these words: "I am sad that I have angered God; if I had known what I should have done, I would have done it. Tell me, Father, because I am sad," and, indeed, his depression showed on his face. "You should have gotten on your knees and begged God to forgive you for the love of His Son who gave His life for you." "I did that," the new Christian answered, "but unfortunately that doesn't seem enough to me to appease the Great Chief whom I offended." As he said this, the tears ran down his face, and he began to sob so much that he couldn't talk and he had to put off finishing his confession the next morning. All he could say was, "I have offended God."

Another new convert went even farther. This is what Father Buteux, who wrote this account, said about him: "This good man waited for me on his knees for a full half-hour after mass; seeing me about to leave, he stopped me: 'I offended God, I want to make my confession.' He was beside himself with grief. 'I woke up in the night and I couldn't get what I'd done wrong out of my mind,' he said, 'I got up, I went into the woods and I cut switches off the trees and whipped myself until I couldn't stand any more. Once I've confessed my sin, I'll need to do it again. Tell me what I need to do to placate God.'" "I will hear your confession," the Jesuit said; he was moved to tears. "I will give him a penance three times harder than I would ever give a Frenchman for the same offense." "Is that all you're going to tell me for such a big sin; make me carry something that will tear my muscles; order me to fast; do not be afraid, I have angered God, I want to make it up to Him." The Jesuit Father answered, "I do not want you to fast today or even tomorrow. Right now it's a festival day; there will be feasting in all the cabins to celebrate the Jesuit whom God has called to us, Father Le Jeune's, arrival here." "But that's why," the young man said, "I have to fast. I need to be punished; I have offended God; I should not be allowed to rejoice with the others; I will stay away from the feasting, and, if I am forced to go, I will pretend to eat and no one will notice that I am fasting." This good repentant man could indeed say: *Dolor meus in conspectu meo semper* ("my eyes, beholding my sin, can only see objects of sorrow").

"That's not all. He came to find me in my room, as soon as I had arrived, to tell me his regret—at least, I think it was the same young man, the one about whom the Jesuit just told the story; he showed me his bloody hands, he had made deep cuts in his fingers, and I asked him why he had done this! 'Oh, Father, I am so sorry that I have angered God, and I also was the reason why others offended Him, so I have cut my fingers to show them that they should not do as I did, and to teach them that those who are baptized should never again do any evil thing.'"

Someone else gave me this account: one of the two chiefs of the St. Joseph tribe was so touched by God and so zealous for the faith that he felt responsible for the smallest misdeed of any of his people; he could not sleep until he had rectified things. Not long ago, coming to make his confession to one of the Jesuits in the residence, he said to him, "My soul is peaceful and glad when I see that my people pray; it feels like my heart is at a feast; but when I see one of them detour from the right road I am so sad, my heart is uneasy like an unstable man, I can't get any sleep, and all I can do is think of how to fix the problem." His wife, whom he had converted to Christianity, is his equal in piety; some time ago, when she was sick, a Jesuit went to visit her accompanied by Lord Giffart, the doctor in Quebec. After he took her pulse and thought about her malady, he told her to take heart, she should not be too depressed because she wasn't going to die of what she had. This good woman looked at him as though he were crazy and said, "Does the doctor know that I've been baptized?" "Yes, he knows," the Jesuit answered. "Why then," she asked, "does he tell me not to be upset and not to worry, because I'm not going to die? Is God not my Father? Does He not set the course of my life? Why would I be sad about anything that my Father might plan for me? Let God do as He will, He is my Master; I am a Christian and nothing here on earth will make me sad." The doctor was not expecting such an answer from a woman who had been raised a pagan; there are certainly many learned men and civilized women in France who would not be capable of making such a statement.

A newly baptized Indian, greatly upset by a difference of opinion between him and one of his tribesmen, kept silent, but felt like his heart was going to jump out of his chest. "Very well," he said to himself, "It's better to lose this argument and my reputation for being brave, than to do something unworthy of my baptismal vows." Then he went right away to find the priest who had baptized him, so that he could ask him how to discipline his heart and its evil desires. The Jesuit was very impressed with this man's goodness. May God bless all those who, by their prayers or their actions cause heavenly dew to fall on this vine newly planted in Christ; truly, it shall bear good fruit.

A young Indian who had been married for a short time took it into his head that he didn't want to live with his wife anymore, and this thought made him very depressed. The devil described to him the many pleasures of the flesh that he could experience were he to leave the wife he despised and find another more pleasing to him. But his guardian angel reminded him that we will be rewarded in heaven for any evil desires we control or repress here on earth. Then he remembered the vows he had made before God and to his spouse; he wanted to remain faithful to her but he was tempted to be unfaithful; he went back to his spiritual director, begged him to give him some solution to his problem, which he believed to be a great sin. The Father led him to the Reserved Sacrament, had him pray to God there, and then he asked that his confession be heard. He wept copiously. Just the thought of switching wives seemed such a grave crime to him that he begged to be sent to prison, or that he be put in a deep grave, or that he be publicly whipped. Seeing that his requests were denied, he went into a small room off of the chapel and, finding a rope, beat himself so brutally all over his body that the Jesuit heard him: he ran to him and ordered him not to brutalize his body as a penance. The devil, who does not love a spirit of mortification, left him immediately, and his temptation evaporated.

We had always thought that Indian marriages would cause us problems; the freedom to have several wives and to get rid of them at a whim, is a great obstacle to Christian faith, but it is not insurmountable: grace is more powerful than human nature. The Chevalier de Montmagny, wanting to explain the sacred sacrament of marriage to his converts, made a big deal out of their weddings, holding a big feast on the day of the nuptials, inviting several French dignitaries, and having a Eucharist celebrated in church. There, the priest was sure to talk about the stability of marriage and of the importance of obeying God by being faithful. The Indian chiefs are the first to enjoin newlyweds to stay together; these good people demonstrate a naïveté and simplicity that is unknown in France. The priest who performs the weddings, when he is just about to conclude them, makes sure to let one of the chiefs present speak; the chief calls out, "Wait, Father, I want to be heard!" Then, speaking to the husband and wife in front of the altar, he says, "Be warned, you're one step away from being married; if you go any farther, you cannot go back. Your word is a bond that will bind you so closely that you may never cut it. Shut your mouth if you do not want to be so united if you speak, may your words be like iron and never break; now you are still free, no one is forcing you to get married; but if you take these vows, we will compel you to keep them: Now, speak or remain silent." Then, turning to the priest, he says, "Go on, Father, continue, I have said what I had to say." This straightforwardness reminds me of the good old days, when nature walked garbed in simplicity more beautiful than any dress-up costume that a more civilized nation could produce.

While I'm on the subject, I'll make it the conclusion to my letter. Here is a new way to take each other in marriage. I've heard that, formerly, when a pagan Indian loved a girl, he would go see her at night and ask her in secret if she liked him. If she said that she didn't want to wed, the young man would drop the matter; even if she answered that he should not come to her to pursue his suit, he'd continue to court her. We disapproved of this way of acting, so the Christian converts fixed the problem: now, they ask us for permission to court a girl. Look how some of them behave at present: they paint the picture on a piece of bark of a young man and a young woman holding hands, as they would be when they got married in church, then the suitor asks one of his friends to deliver the picture to his beloved.

Now, even though the artwork might not be professional quality, the girl knows what it signifies. If she likes the young man, she accepts the painting; if she says that she can't understand what the picture is showing, it's as if she were saying that the young man doesn't have a chance. Then he'll go away, and you don't have to worry that he'll beat up a successful suitor: he has too much pride to let himself be upset because of his feelings for a girl; it's weakness to let oneself be overcome by love's tyranny or by the demon of hatred. The unsuccessful suitor will instead congratulate the successful suitor whom the young woman loves.

Concerning the belief and good deeds of the Christian converts

One of the Jesuits who teaches the Indians in the Residence at St. Joseph, while reading one day a list of sins that afflict people before baptism, began to talk to the Indians about some native superstitions such as the spells they try to get demons to cast, or the spirits of the day, or pacts with the devil whom they worship through the medium of a certain mysterious stone (which I've mentioned elsewhere). One good Christian spoke up saying, "Look, Father, there are many among us who still believe in this sort of thing. Let's go into the cabins and search everywhere; we will find small idols hidden away. No one brings them out when you're around, but those who have idols carry them with them into the woods; the devil tempts them and makes them believe that they'll have bad luck if they get rid of the idols, they will have no success at hunting. In this way, they stay locked up in their old habits. I don't wish them any ill, but I want them to leave off worshiping demons and stick to the narrow way to Heaven, and that's why I'm telling you all this."

This zealous man hoped so fervently that the natives would be converted, that one spring he left and went to other nations far from French habitation, offering them gifts and inviting them to believe in Jesus Christ. The year before, he had also gone there and had some success, as Father Ragueneau wrote to me this past year: our Hurons who, last summer, went to trade at Ondstasaka (I believe that this is the land of the Saguenay people, the place where our zealous convert went) reported to us that both day and night they held public prayer services, and they were taught to sing the same songs as Charles Tsondatsataa had heard sung by the Christians at St. Joseph. As a result, the Hurons concluded that these tribes had come to believe in Christ, and that all the western tribes are converted and under God's blessing; the conversion of other tribes continues, and even those whom we've not yet evangelized are beginning to convert by the others' example. I am as persuaded as Your Reverence is that these words of the Father are true words.

This same convert was especially devoted to images of the saints, and he had several that he always kept with him and carefully protected. Unfolding one of these images to show to one of our Frenchmen the other day, he kissed it with great humility. When he came to the crucifix, he kissed that three times. "Here you see," he said, "the portrait of Him whom I love above all things." He gave such reverence to the crucifix that you could see that he truly loved Him who had so much loved the whole world.

This poor man, finding that he had married an unbelieving woman, left her one morning, as Saint Paul had advised. ("Be ye therefore not unequally yoked . . .") Some Christians rebuked him for leaving her; they reproached him, saying that he was just giving lip-service to his faith; and that a true Christian would never leave his wife. He was really upset by this, because he could not imagine loving a woman who did not love God; and, besides, she was of a very haughty temperament. He was depressed all day, and he slept very poorly that night; each time that he woke up, he prayed to God to let him know His will for him, whether he should take back his wife or divorce her; then he was able to fall asleep, comforted to know that all was in God's hands. He dreamed he saw a group of Frenchmen, and several of our Jesuits, who were saying to him, "Divorce this woman; she has no spiritual understanding." When he awoke, he decided to have nothing more to do with her, and he really disliked her from that day on. But, as he could see that there were some who still criticized him for this, he said to the Jesuit who was his spiritual director, "Father, if you order me to stay with this woman who has so often laughed at God and who treats me like her slave, I will do what you tell me; I will ignore my emotions and my dreams; I could go astray if I just kept my own counsel without listening to you; I will know I'm doing the right thing if I allow myself to be guided by you, whom God has given me for a guide." The Father, astonished by this courage and strength in the soul of a man whose sweetness was utterly in contrast with the nastiness of his mocking and disdainful wife, ex-pressed the hope that God would touch her heart and change her mind, and, at present, she is in fact taking religious instruction, claiming that, while she once mocked at religion and laughed at prayers, her soul has been changed and she feels differently. The good Christian convert went back to her, on the condition that he will leave her once and for all if she does not remain firm in the Faith.

When a young girl answered the catechism questions with great suc-cess, the Jesuit who was questioning her wanted to give her a gift, and he said aloud, to encourage her to do well again, that he regretted having nothing in his possession that was worthy of commemorating such an admirable effort on her behalf. An Indian woman, overhearing him say this, answered, "Alas, Father! Learning is itself a great treasure. You shower this child with riches when you teach her the path of salvation;

it's worth more to know that than to have all the gold in this earth." I think that this woman was a relative of the one who had said aloud to Our Lord, "Beatus venter qui te portavit, ubera quoe suxisti:" she understood the truth of Scripture, "omnia aurum, in comparatione illius, arena est exigua" ("gold, in comparison to this, is worthless").

Another woman who was blind gave a hard time to an Indian who was laughing at Christians. This unbeliever, seeing that the Christian converts were getting into boats one Sunday morning to go hear mass at Quebec, also got into the boat, and as they were leaving, he cried out, "I love you all more than I love my own family," and pointing toward where the sun sets, he said, "That's where my ancestors have gone; that's where I want to go; that's where my brothers will surely go; and not into your churches." This good blind woman, hearing what he said, retorted, "If you love your countrymen so much, why did you abandon them to the Iroquois last winter? You were afraid of being burned at the stake, but, if you were truly a spiritual person, you would be even more afraid of the fires of hell where you will surely go when you die. You are good for nothing! He who created you will either burn you in hellfire or grant you glory when you die." This good woman, although blind, saw clearly when it came to matters of faith; she led an innocent and blameless life.

Victor Sechkine, getting ready to go trade furs, came to confession. After having made his confession, he said to his confessor, "Father, pray to God for me and for my wife, as well as for my child. I know what holy prayer is able to accomplish. You see my little daughter? God gave her to me twice: while we were in the woods on our big hunting excursion this winter, she became ill, and I expected her to die. My wife could do nothing but cry. 'Tears,' I told her, 'will not revive your child: let us cast ourselves on the mercy of Him who gave her to us, and beg Him to give her back to us.' They got on their knees and prayed this little prayer, more filled with emotion than with words: 'You who made all things and who preserve all life, you made this child and gave her to us; she is sick, You can cure her, so please do cure her, if You so will; if she lives, she will believe in You, she will obey You when she is grown; if You do not cure her, I will still believe in You and I will not complain, because you are Lord of my life. Do as You will.'" "The next morning," the convert said, "my daughter was in as good health as you see her in now."

The Indians having returned from hunting, one of our Jesuits gathered the leaders together and said to them, that he would be very pleased if they would settle some of the disagreements that arise among them from time to time; but that he was amazed that they had allowed a young woman who had been baptized to leave her husband. The chief who had jurisdiction over this woman answered that he had tried everything to get her to do her duty, but that nothing had worked; he agreed to try one more time, however. When you leave this gathering, he said, ask among your people in private and see what should be done about this woman's disobedience. They all decided on a severe course of action: good advice didn't set her straight, some said, perhaps prison will! Two chiefs decided to take her to Quebec and to ask the Governor to put her in a prison cell. They set about doing this, but, having seen them coming for her, she ran away; she fled into the woods with them chasing her. Having caught her, they declared her condemned to prison until she came to her senses. Since she was trying to get away, they tied her up and put her in a canoe going to Quebec. Several young non-Christian natives, seeing the violence with which they were handling her (because Indians really do hate violence, and usually do not use it; it is far from their custom as heaven is from earth), threatened them, saying that they would kill anyone who put a hand on that woman. But the chief and his Christian people answered bravely that there was nothing that they would not do, or that they would not endure, to show their obedience to God. Their resolve silenced the pagans and the woman was taken to Quebec, but when she saw that she had the choice between being put in a tiny cell below ground or returning to her husband's house, she humbly begged them to take her back to St. Joseph, promising to be more obedient in the future. Such legal proceedings would raise no eyebrows in France, because it is customary to act this way, but they do among this people, where everyone believes himself to be free as a birthright, as free as the wild beasts in the forest. Here, it's almost a miracle when some act of justice is accomplished. Some Indians, having heard that in France those who do not behave are put to death, reproached us frequently with being bad people, with causing our fellow men to die, with lacking a spiritual nature. They asked whether the relatives of those whom we condemned to death sought vengeance. The unbelievers felt this way, but the Christian converts came to acknowledge the importance of carrying out justice.

When a certain convert, on fire for the Faith, urged that pious acts be performed, another said to him, "Stop, people will get angry with you! Those who haven't been baptized will hate you." "That doesn't matter to me," he answered, "I'm not afraid to die. Let them kill me, let them tear me to pieces. I will not stop doing what God asks of me just to satisfy their lack of belief. My life is not more important to me than my Faith."

I mentioned in the preceding *relation* a particular Huron named Charles Tsondatsaa, who was baptized last year in the little church of St. Joseph. This good convert came this year, with several of his tribesmen, to visit the Christians at that church. These good people welcomed them warmly, invited them to feast with them, after having demonstrated their goodwill and exchanged presents all around. A chief from St. Joseph stopped them in the chapel of St. Joseph after daily public prayers. Hurons and Algonquians were worshiping there. Speaking to Charles Tsondatsaa, this chief said, "Brother, you know very well that you were baptized last year in this church. You became our brother in Christ in this very place. Let me tell you what is on my heart, now that I see you about to return to your country. 'This man is baptized,' I say to myself, 'he has become a child of God; that is all very well and good, but what will happen to him when he rejoins his tribe, which does not believe in God? How will he resist the attacks that will be leveled at him on all sides?' I had these thoughts when I was not in your presence. My soul felt weightless, with no ballast, since I did not know what you would become. I worried about you all winter long. I eagerly waited for spring, when I could hear news of you. Then someone told me that you were on your way down river, and that you were still living a good Christian life. My fears evaporated, my soul grew strong, my heart rejoiced. 'What a good man,' I thought to myself. 'But it is God who gave him this strength,' my heart said to me, 'It's God who gave him strength and courage; we should thank God.' And that, my brother, is what we did, out of love for you."

After this little speech, Charles answered as follows: "My brother, ever since my baptism I have held firm in the Faith; my feet have stood on level ground; my body has not shifted; I have never been tempted to stop praying, and I never will stop praying; He who carries the earth in His hands, as you say, it is He who has helped me, and He will continue to help me, for He is good. I wish that all people in my tribe would believe as I do: they will come to believe, little by little, and I know some who already pray, but so far there are only about thirty of us who are firm in the Faith. We do not stumble, just like you all; we held firm all winter against the criticisms of unbelievers; they have assaulted us on every side, but our souls were not overcome. So, take heart, my brother, be brave and may the rest of your good people be equally courageous; do not be afraid; half of us do not believe at all, but *we* believe entirely. Pray God for our safety during our return trip." After this exchange, they said goodbye to each other.

The Christians from St. Joseph learned that Father Vimont was going up river to Trois-Rivières and that he was going to meet with some of the Huron Christians. They asked him to take with him some bundles of smoked venison so that the new converts could feast on them. They were sending them in token of their love and affection. This took place in our residence, with great joy among all the converts; they were so uplifted by this charitable act, something not customary among Indians (who only love good things for themselves).

I'll conclude this chapter by describing an act of gratitude that we witnessed. The Governor went up river to the Iroquois, to get them going on building the fortifications of which we've already spoken. A Christian chief went to meet him and talked to him about it in this way: "We Indians, since we were not raised in your country, don't know how great chiefs who work to defend the country should be honored. I don't know what I should do or what I should say. I've looked, and I can't find anything to say except for these two words: 'Good for you, great chief! Leave now to become the master of the earth and the savior of your country. May God, who can do all things and who is all goodness, be always with you!' That's what my tongue has to say, but this is what I'm thinking: 'May it please God to make us a great nation here, and that, with all our voices joined, we may speak strongly and mightily, so that the whole universe will hear what we say. Farewell, savior of our country, thank you for defending us; go with peace, and come back again to see us so that we may again cry out: our chief has come back; the savior of our country has returned; it is because of him that our women and children and all of us are still alive! Without his protection the enemy would have kept us from being able to plant, farm, and harvest our wheat.' This is what I wish every man around here would say, but we cannot speak: illness, and our enemies, have torn out our tongues. Let us, nonetheless, try to talk to you one last time. Farewell, savior of the country. May He who made the world be your guide and protector as you sail." This eloquence did not come from classical rhetoric, neither Aristotle nor Cicero taught the chief to speak like this; but a more loving, innocent school—the school of the heart—taught him.

Having communicated to them his joy at their good wishes, the Governor asked them what they planned to do during the summer. "There's no need to ask us this," they said, "You are our leader: command us, and we will do it; we've made up our minds a long time ago to obey your wishes." That's the answer they gave him, and that's the end of this letter.

CONCLUSION:

INCULTURATION ASSESSED

In conclusion, the historian Francis Parkman's assessment of the grand project of the Jesuit Fathers in French Canada may yet be—some decades after Parkman's monumental study, *France and England in North America*—the most fitting summary: he deems the Jesuit order "a vast mechanism for guiding and governing the minds of men, this mighty enginery [sic] for subduing the earth to the dominion of an idea." It is possible that he overstated his case; the syncretism we have observed suggests that "a mighty enginery" might be more aptly stated as "a well-disciplined mission directed toward saving souls" with those souls being acknowledged to have individual worth and cultural distinctives to which the Jesuits sought to appeal rather than to coerce. The aboriginal response to this ideology of conversions was mixed—receptive on the part of Algonquian, especially Huron, but those gains were ultimately undone by Iroquois militarism. The period of struggle for mission and conversion, however, left a lasting legacy of great value, not only theologically and ethnographically but also in terms of literary influence. The *Relations* remain a formative text for much of North American literature and history, and left their mark on European audiences as well.

The experience of Jesuit inculturation was an in-spirited encounter. Through the Holy Spirit—often called the "Umpire" in sixteenth-century theological parlance, the negotiator, intermediary or even the "translator"—the Jesuits were enabled to discern the inherent goodness of their potential converts, or to determine appropriate avenues of receptivity for such conversions. When they offered them Christianity, they appealed to that "best self," which they visualized through Ignatian practices and verbalized in the *Relations*.

What you have just read is a narrative woven of excerpted voices, a constructed dialog that sounds again the words and hearts of both Jesuits and Native Americans. In reading these paraphrases from the original French, you heard the concerns preoccupying the Jesuits—the fears, pride, and hopes of their native interlocutors—and saw the ways in which each began truly to listen and be fully present to the other. The thematic clusters of the letters were ordered chronologically. The themes highlighted Ignatian spirituality as well as attested to the Native American appropriation, and reinterpretation, of Jesuit teachings for their own purposes. That the Christian message remains the same, yet in some mystical way becomes *other*, is undeniable. This is the strength and the beauty of inculturation: what is best from both cultures comes to the fore, and the work of proselytizing does not efface or distort the native culture, but rather enhances what is best within it.

When the cultures clashed, as is inevitable, and when value judgments arose, the Jesuits were quick to call themselves to an even stricter accounting than that to which they subjected the native lifeways. And if at times the Jesuit project seems strange or excessive to our postmodern ears, we should remember and acknowledge the gracious self-sacrifice with which they gave themselves to this mission; if they were not always right, if they did not—to our minds—always respect the native culture as they should have, it was not because they were callous or unsympathetic, but rather because, for them, the stakes were death or life. They did what they did out of love for Christ and the "other."

Thus, this text teaches us the integrity of a different time, place, and people, and coaches us in how to listen deeply for the past as it whispers the truth of its aims and achievements, failures and heartaches, trials and triumphs—and it does so from two very different standpoints, languages, and lifeways that converge, as is fitting, in the Cross. They do not lose their former identity, but they do take on a new one.

Whether clothed in a loincloth, wrapped in a blanket, or wearing breeches, clad in buckskin or in black robes, the figures of this narrative ultimately are all clothed in Christ. The Jesuits did, indeed, "enter in through the [other's] door" of cabins, huts, tents, and long-houses; yet many were the Indians who willingly walked through Jesuit residences, chapels, schools, and Ursuline hospitals.

"We go in by their door, in order to come out by ours," said Ignatius—and Jesuit and native, Frenchman and "other" were all changed by this entrance, this encounter with the cross of Christ.

APPENDIX: CATHEDRALS OF ICE
Translating the Jesuit Vocabulary of Conversion

The Jesuit *Relations* is an important document not only for historical reasons, but also because of the complex vocabulary, both theological and literary (to date unexamined in an interdisciplinary way) through which the work of evangelization is carried out between the Jesuit Fathers during the foundational moment of French Canada and the Native Americans—Algonquian, Huron, and Iroquois—with whom they interacted. In a tripartite typology of space, story and spirituality, this essay finds that *relation* fully lives up to its seventeenth-century meaning of *relayeur*, acting as an interpreter or translator between two cultures, two world-views and a European and Native faith system. Both Jesuit and Native interlocutor change and evolve because of the process of translation, necessary to convey theological concepts, that transpires between them.

"In some places," wrote a Jesuit Father from his hut in the Canadian woods, "there appeared prodigiously high bodies of ice swimming and floating, elevated by at least 40 arm-lengths, swollen and large as if you'd put several castles together, and as if the cathedral of Notre-Dame in Paris, with a considerable portion of the Ile-de-France, its houses and palaces, were floating down the river toward you."[1] The juxtaposition in

This essay first appeared in the *International Journal of Canadian Studies* 23 (2001): 17–34.

1. *Relations*, I, xiii ("Le voyage et arrivée à Port-Royal"), 29. "En aucuns endroits apparoissoyent hauts et prodigieux glaçons nageants et flottants, eslevez de 30 et 40 bras sees, gros et larges comme si vous ioigniez plusieurs chasteaux

this epistolary evocation of the wildly divergent images of artificial palaces, castles and cathedrals, the constructions of human hands, with towering icebergs, the products of a powerful and capricious nature, points to cultural difference yet also conjoins the two in a coherent impression: a translation between two cultural modes of understanding and experiencing the world. In the Jesuit *Relations*, a collection of first-hand accounts of proselytizing and missionary activity in French Canada, written from 1611 to 1672, an Old World mentality struggles to make sense of an alien New World through a process of textual and theological translation. The image of the floating cathedral sets the tone, for to describe an iceberg as that pinnacle of European cultural production and manifestation of faith, a cathedral, requires a process of translation in and of itself. The cathedral becomes the metaphor for rendering the new, North American experience into terms comprehensible to Europeans, just as, vice versa, European theology needs to be shaped into forms and figures that will evoke Native American assent. The notion that the cathedral is floating, moving despite its massive bulk and, presumably, firm foundation, symbolizes the willing transference of the fundamentals of Catholic theology to a new place and a new auditor: the bringing of the message of salvation to those who have not yet received it. In return, another process of translation occurs, this time reversing the focus, so that the Jesuit Fathers, rather than reading nature in terms of European constructions, scrutinize the sky and natural phenomena—for instance, the glamorous pyrotechnics of the Northern Lights—for divine insignia. In short, they learn to become more like the Natives, even as they proffer their message of salvation: as for the former, nature looms large as producer of signs and wonders, proof of God's dominion. As opposed to "castles" and "cathedrals," which still give preferential status to the Europe they have left behind, the terms of the terrain to which the Jesuits are relocated now become the primary signifiers.[2] And the

---

ensemble, et comme vous diriés, si l'Eglise nostre Dame de Paris avec une partie de son Isle, maisons et palais, alloit flottant dessus l'eau." When French original is provided, translations are mine. When only English is provided, translation is Thwaite's or, alternatively, is cited in English by another author.

2. See, in this respect, the entire chapter of the *Relations* entitled, "A quelle occasion nous nous arrestasmes a Saint Sauveur" (Chapter xxiv).

architectural referents—castles, cathedrals—become oriented toward a construction appropriate to this North American context: the base to be laid is the message of faith, and that must precede any sort of restructuring of the Natives' heart: one of the Fathers refers to God as the architect who has a blueprint for restructuring the human spirit (*"l'architecte qui fait et deffaict ses plans et modeles"*), and advises that "you've got to lay this foundation (*"base"*) before raising the capitols (*"chapiteaux"*) topping the columns of an edifice [of faith]."[3]

This important document has received little attention *as text*, and although it has been examined theologically (Berthiaume compares it to the Golden Legend, a medieval collection of saints' lives[4]), employed historically (by Francis Parkman, for instance) and utilized comparatively (as a precursor text for other European works concerning cultural relativism, among them Voltaire, Diderot, Montesquieu and Rousseau), it has not been put into an ethnographic framework,[5] which would necessitate a concomitant attention to its literary value, for the interplay of voices that animate it.[6] The document is also distinctive as a collaborative effort, so the voices that interweave throughout the text are not

3. "Quant à moy j'estime un tres grand profit en ce que nous avons tousiours mieux et mieux descouvert le naturel de ces terres et pays, la disposition des habitans, le moyen de les pouvoir ayder, les contrarietés qui peuvent survenir au progrès de l'œuvre, et les secours qu'il faut opposer a l'ennemy. L'architecte qui fait et deffaict ses plans et modeles . . . ne se pense pas pour cela avoir rien faict en son premier et second essay." *Relations*, Chapter xxxiv, 62.

4. Pierre Berthiaume, "Les Relations des jésuites : nouvel avatar de la *Legende dorée*" in *Figures de l'indien*, ed. G. Therien (Montreal, 1988).

5. There is the study of Delon, which uses an anthropological lens to view the text in "Corps sauvages, corps etranges." But this perspective nonetheless does not scrutinize the text literarily. Neither does Duchet, in *Anthropologie et histoire au siècle des "Lumières."* I owe some of this bibliography, and numerous other helpful and encouraging suggestions on the penultimate draft of this essay, to an anonymous outside reader for the *International Journal of Canadian Studies*, and I would like to express my gratitude to this (French) academic for his or her invaluable assistance.

6. I also note that this compendious and important text has never received, in its entirety, a treatment that would amount to a scholarly synthesis, or overall interpretive perspective. Such an endeavor would necessitate the work of a team of academics. This would provide an enormous contribution both to scholarship and pedagogy.

always the two poles of European and Native, but also the individual and stylistic "distinctives" (to the extent that those persist after the editing process, which I shall discuss shortly) of various Jesuit Fathers. I list here the early writers (I treat only the first three volumes of the seventy-three volume project—those explicitly dealing with the foundation of French Canada), those of immediate significance to the scope of the present essay, and also those whose voices can be heard most clearly, in a more individual idiom, since the editing process that the Order quickly established did not much affect the earliest texts of the *Relations*: "During the first few years, each missionary wrote to his Superior simply as a matter of confiding in him [the progress of the work of evangelizing] . . . "[7] These earliest writers, then, include Father Biard, who in 1611 went to Acadia with Father Masse, then was later sent back to France by the English; Charles Lalemant, from Brittany, who arrived in Quebec in 1625 where he started the first schools for French children in Quebec; Paul le Jeune, called "The Father of Jesuit missions in Canada," who, encouraged to evangelize by Father Masse, arrived in 1632, was called back to France in 1649, and who penned a *"catéchisme en Sauvage"*; Father Vimont, who came to Quebec in 1629, returned to France, then came back to Quebec from 1639–1659, and who wrote six volumes of the Jesuit *Relations* himself while serving as Superior of the Order; Father Jérome Lalemant, brother of Charles, who arrived in 1638, was working among the Hurons by 1645, was named Superior of the Missions in Canada in 1659, and died in Canada in 1673; Father Raguenau, who came to Quebec in 1636, and was successful in converting many Huron and Iroquois; Jean de Brébeuf, called by the Natives "Black Robe," who came with Champlain and the other first five Jesuit missionaries to Quebec from Normandy in 1625; was the first Jesuit missionary to the Huron, and was martyred by the Iroquois with Gabriel Lalemant at St. Louis in 1649; Father Le Mercier, who arrived in 1635, and served as a missionary for three years at Trois-Rivières; Father Dequen, who also came to Quebec in 1635, and who discovered Lac St. Jean in 1652; and Claude Dablon, who arrived in Canada in 1655, and established a mission at Sault Ste-Marie.

7. "Dans les premières années, chaque missionnaire écrit spontanément à son supérieur sans autre dessein que la confidence." Maurice Lemire, *La vie littéraire au Quebec*, vol. I. Quebec: Les presses de I 'Université Laval, 1997, 41.

Most North American scholarship in the fields of both history and religion focuses on an American religious history that neglects the larger part of North America: the rich, complex story of Christianizing the Canadian natives. In addition, the *Relations* needs—yet has not yet received—a literary interpretation, one coupled with a theological sensitivity: Native destinatees often do not receive language signifiers, as manipulated by the Jesuit fathers, in the way intended. The whole Saussurian dialectic (and problematic) of slippage between signifier and signified yawns widely here, emphasizing the cultural gap, and the shock of two vastly divergent cultural identities. This bridgeable difference is encapsulated in the drama of attempted translation of theological issues, as the Natives are encouraged to adopt a christological understanding that is utterly alien to their mentality. It seems that the Native tongue is well suited to practical issues, to concrete, even artisanal engagement with the world at hand.[8] Yet the French language is inclined toward abstractions, speculations and refinement: in short, a well-tempered tool for theological discussion, but one that often appears useless or extraneous to the Native interlocutor:

> But concerning interior or spiritual actions, which cannot be demonstrated by the senses, and concerning words which we might call abstract or which we believe to be universal—such as "belief," "doubt," "hope" . . . "virtue," "vice," "sin," "reason"—that's where we really had to sweat and strain; that was the limit of giving birth to [a mutual] language.[9]

How can these two come to speak a common tongue? It is a learning process for both sides of the discussion, and this process is, precisely, what has not yet been explored. The muscularity of the translator's task

8. We should recall that the Native language itself, as the Jesuits found it, was not monolithic, for they encountered Algonquian speakers (Micmacs in the east, Abenaki in the area south of the St. Lawrence River, and Algonquians and Montagnais in the north) and Iroquois in the Finger Lakes, Hurons, Petuns and others above Lake Erie and Lake Huron.

9. "Mais aux actions intérieures et spirituelles, qui ne peuvent se demonstrer aux sens, et aux mots qu'on appelle abstraits et universels, comme croire, douter, esperer, discourir . . . vertu, vice, péché, raison . . . en cela it fallait ahanner et suer, là estoyent les tranches de leur enfantement" (Chapter XV).

is highlighted, as the Jesuit Fathers must struggle to craft metaphors and symbols into their verbal representations that will "speak to" this other mind-set. We need to recognize this poeticized universe, in which nature and language somehow conjoin to acknowledge a common metaphysical referent.

For this reason, and others, the *Relations* deserves recognition as one of the *textes fondateurs*,[10] or foundational texts, of North American religion, history and literature. The Jesuit mission to French Canada developed trans-continental initiatives that reached into the forests and bayous, hills and back-country of all of North America, an initiative that can still be glimpsed—and even heard—in the Canadian patronyms and Catholic affiliation of folk in Louisiana and State of Mainers, as well as in the French names of Midwestern and Western towns like Des Moines, Boise and Butte. As the Jesuit Fathers transplanted their theology, through a painstaking process of translation, onto a new soil, they traced the space of an entire continent, and set the template for its history of religious depth and complexity.

The Relational Text: Topography, Translation, Theology

All theology turns on the issues of topography and, eventually, of translation. While religions begin as chthonic, or aboriginal, productions, some religions—preeminently Christianity—survive primarily through a process of exportation, the geographical equivalent of proselytizing. Pentecost serves as the first occasion in Christianity in which the question of translation arises, and it is linked to the evangelizing movement toward the Gentiles: in short, a topographic swerve. When the apostles are visited with tongues of fire, they do not babble or speak in arcane, indecipherable jargon; rather, their experience fulfils the Gospel mandate that, when tongues are spoken, an interpreter must translate. The apostles, through spiritual gifts, suddenly speak all the languages of the world, of which representatives present there hear and understand what

10. The acclaimed scholar of Québécois literature, Aurélien Boivin (Université Laval) asserts that the *Relations* constitutes a *"texte fondateur"* of French Canada and French Canadian literature. This important recognition calls for further work of substantiation, which the present essay in part hopes to supply.

is spoken. In the Gospel, the Holy Spirit provides the words needed to profess one's faith. Significantly, the calendar entry of the feast of Pentecost heralds many conversion accounts in the *Relations*. Spiritual matters construct a new topography into which one cannot effectively venture without the mediation of language provided by the Holy Spirit.

The Jesuit fathers, newly arrived in the New World from the Old, also face the issues of topography and translation. They express concern and consternation, confronted not only with Native American languages they do not speak, but also with the need to convert doctrinal and theological abstractions into concrete concepts that can be understood and acceded to by an alien culture. The earliest letters of the *Relations*, therefore, are the focus of this essay, for they bear the weight of the "shock of the new" and the Jesuits' struggle to translate across Old World/New World boundaries.

> The Fathers, realizing that a full knowledge of the native tongue was essential in the conversion of the Natives, resolved to begin immediately to learn the language. But they ran into an incredible number of obstacles, primarily because they were trying to learn the language without the help of any translator or interpreter. . . . A few other men knew enough of the language to be able to conduct trade or to deal with daily matters, but when it came to talking about God or things having to do with religion, there was the rub: no words existed! What would you have done, if you were in [their] shoes? It's probably true that no one can really understand how hard their task was, unless he were to experience it for himself. It's complicated because, the Natives having no established religion, government, towns, or art, the words and terms appropriate to such things also do not exist: holy, blessed, angel, grace, mystery, sacrament, temptation, faith, law, prudence, humility, government, and so on, are unknown to them. Where would you begin to find all the things that they lack?[11]

11. Chapter XV: "The Return of Potrincourt to France, and the Difficulty of Learning the Native Tongues," *Relations*, vol. 1, 31. (Montreal: Editions du Jour, 1972; a reprint of the Côté edition published in Quebec in 1858). "Les deux Jésuites . . . voyants que pour la conversion des Payens la langue du pays leur estoit totalement necessaire, s'y resolurent d'y vaquer en toute diligence . . . [ils]

The Jesuits' translating enterprise takes a triune turn. First, they must turn inward, exploring the depths and resonances of their own theological vocabulary in order better to understand it, the prerequisite of any competent translator. *Trans-latio*, after all, means at root a *literal* carrying across of a product from one place or recipient to another. Interestingly, when they confront obstacles in understanding, they often express these in terms of real, physical obstacles: obstructions in topography: "when it came to discussing matters of religion, there was the cape [point of land] beyond which we could not explore."[12]

The second turn of the translation is toward Europe. Situated now in the New World, the Jesuit Fathers depend heavily on their Old World patrons and sponsors. To cultivate their continued interest in the enterprise of conversion, the Jesuit Fathers pen weekly or monthly epistles, which they call *relations*.[13] The Superior of the Order then culls the best of the letters, which are disseminated as information and propaganda to appropriate patrons and prospective sponsors throughout Europe.[14] The

---

sçavoyent bien quelque peu, et assez pour la tracque et affaires communes; mais quand il estoit question de parler de Dieu . . . les mots aussi et les paroles propres à tout leur manquent: sainct, Bien-heureux, Ange, Grace, Mysterie, Sacrement . . . Comme[nt] vous en passerez-vous? O Dieu que nous devisions à nostre aise en France!"

12. " . . . et des affaires de religion, là estoit le saut, là le cap-non." (Chapter XV).

13. "L'objet apparent des *Relations* est de raconter ce qui s'est passé au cours de l'année, mais leur objet réel est d'illustrer l'action de grâce sur les ames . . . Quand la publication devient officielle, il acquiert le statut de correspondant: ses textes sont destinés aux bienfaiteurs de la Compagnie. Il glane les faits en conséquence. Ce n'est là qu'un premier seuil de sélection. Le supérieur de Québec rédige le texte définitif." Maurice Lemire, *La vie littéraire au Québec*, vol. I. Quebec: Les presses de l'Université Laval, 1997, 41.

14. The *Relations* were translated into English by Thwaite in 1898; this translation possesses typographical errors and errors in sense, but is also unworkable because it is unwieldy and because its English is stilted, tending to produce a confessional, rather than a scholarly, tone. The letters composing the *Relations* were penned during the years 1611–1672; there are several more modern and complete French translations but all are out of print; the English translation was done in 1898. There is currently considerable interest in narratives pertaining to Native Americans and colonization, as well as in para-literary texts or documents with interdisciplinary character. There is a core of contemporary scholars

Relations is thus explicitly *relational*: in and of itself, it creates a textual link between Old and New Worlds; *relatio* is not merely a letter, story or narration, but a bond that relates one thing to another: the embodiment of *translatio*. Randle Cotgrave's *A Dictionarie of the French and English Tongues* gives "relation" as "a relation, report, recitall; also, the Returne of a writ; the report made, or account given, by an officer of the serving or a execution therefore."[15] Such language describes a charge, a responsibility, a commission, a kind of contract to be executed. Such terminology constantly addresses an audience: "what would *you* do? . . . " The authors of these epistles inscribe a sympathetic reader, as well as a hostile critic ("We came across the polemic written and published against [us]"[16]), in their pages, hoping for what they call an "honorable reader,"[17] such that their rhetoric generally displays a self-protective tone. In this light, the authors spell out their rhetorical plan, which can be summarized under the rubrics of Space, Story and Spirit (these rubrics will be discussed further later in the essay):

1. Space: "the first benefit that the wise reader will gain from the *Relations* is that through the actions, voyages, and events that we shall describe to him, he will become better acquainted with this [new] land . . . "[18]
2. Story: "the second [benefit] is that he will here encounter so many diverse incidents and reversals of fortune that he'll be able to develop great prudence."[19] Thus, the *Relations* will have a shaping, or formative role, in producing a new kind of reader. This is

currently working on the issue of the semiotics of spiritual speech; much influenced by the late philosopher Michel de Certeau and his last book, *Mystic Speech*, their work and that of scholars with similar interests could appropriately and fruitfully be brought to bear on the *Relations*.

15. (London: Dent, 1611): "relation."
16. "Nous sommes tombez sur le Facteur escrit et publié contre les Jesuites," *Relations*, "A quelle occasion les Jesuites allerent en Nouvelle France," xi, 1, 24.
17. "Lecteur honorable" *Relations*, I, xi, 24.
18. *Relations*, I, xi, 25. "Le premier emolument que le sage lecteur en tirera, est que par la praticque, actions, voyages, et accidents que nous luy specifierons l'un après l'autre, il recognoistra mieux ce qui est de ces terres . . . "
19. *Relations*, I, xi, 25. "Le second, qu'il rencontrera tant d'evenements, et si divers, tant de fortunes et incidents avec leurs moments et articles, que sa prudence pourra beaucoup s'y former."

a form of textual proselytizing that parallels the explicit face-to-face evangelism to the Native Americans, and that is striking in that it is directed toward the (at least supposedly) already Christianized European audience.[20]

3. Spirit: "the third fruit will be to recognize God's truly paternal, sweet and admirable Providence for all those who turn to Him."[21] Here, the European and Native American audiences are joined together, in the Jesuit anticipation that *all* will be converted. Such an expectation eliminates the frontier dividing Old from New World, and testifies to the effectiveness of the new brand of rhetoric developed in the *Relations*.

The Jesuits' third translation turn is toward the Native Americans. Armed with a new appreciation for their own theological vocabulary, and aware of the complexities of communicating across cultures and languages, the Jesuit Fathers construct a glossary of working words, one especially reliant on simile and metaphor to make the requisite connections. One of the more striking of these composes the title of this essay: "Cathedrals of ice" is the phrase that an awed Jesuit coins to describe the

---

20. It is interesting that, to some extent, the textual and theological flavor of the *Relations* is oriented to evangelizing a *dual* topography. One of the Fathers notes that the *European* audience is, in some respects, more difficult to convince than the Natives (even though it already possesses the same vocabulary as that of the Jesuits). We hear frustration with the Europeans: "maintenant quelqu'un ayant ouy tout nostre récit . . . nous dira: Or sus, voilà beaucoup de travaux que vous nous avez contés . . . mais quoy? Est-ce là tout le profit quant à l'avancement du culte de Dieu?" ("now someone [European] having heard our story will say to us: Well, that's a lot of endeavors you've described, but to what avail? Is that [small amount] the only profit that you've gotten from this work of saving souls?"—*Relations*, xxxiv, 61.) To which the Father responds: "que partout, et aussi bien en France qu 'en Canada, il faut semer avant que moysonner . . . " ("that everywhere, in France just as in Canada, you have to sow before you can reap"). The text is very fair, and certainly does not have a prejudicial or imperialistic attitude toward the Native interlocutors, on the other hand. We witness respect for the Natives' appropriation of theological concepts once these have been explained in a convincing and compelling way.

21. *Relations*, I, xi, 25. "Le tiers fruict sera de recognoistre une vrayement paternelle, douce et admirable Providence de Dieu sur ceux qui l'invoquent."

magnificent, towering icebergs majestically making their slow passage through the icy Canadian waterways.[22] The word-picture also represents that crystalline moment of translation epiphany when one comprehends, and can express, what has been "other." The image of Notre Dame progressing slowly down the St. Lawrence is a compelling juxtaposition of old and new calculated to elicit a response among the Fathers' European audience. It begins to tell an evocative tale to translate an alien topography.

These image-driven narratives are anecdotes encapsulated by their own dominant images, in a dramatic form of storytelling that we might well term *proprioceptive*: as the Jesuit fathers strive to know this new place, and to position themselves and their theology within it, space and sense find shape in story.[23] Marie de L'Incarnation uses a similar image as she attempts to settle into French Canada, referring to the massive shapes of ice that move slowly and majestically down ice-clogged waterways. This may be a direct borrowing, as Marie's mission endeavor seems to have grown, at least in part, out of her reading of portions of the Jesuit *Relations*: "Four years passed between Marie's first reading of the Jesuit *Relations* and her boarding the boat for Canada . . . She was inflamed at reading Father Le Jeune's *Relations*."[24] At the urging of Fathers Vimont, Lalemant, and others, she herself actually composed letters that were included in later *Relations*.[25] Her *Sacred History*, which she began around 1661, appears to be the first publication by a European in the Algonquin tongue (even though some Jesuit Fathers were working at the same time on preparing catechisms, prayer books and dictionaries in the Native language).[26] Story-telling thus provides a key tool in the Jesuits' structuring of narrative as they adjust to the circumstances generating it, as they configure it for their Old World audience, and as a strategy in facilitating the conversion of the Native Americans.

A *relateur*, according to Cotgrave, is also a rehearser, one who repeats, in a dramatic way, a significant event so as to share it with others.

22. *Relations*, I, xiii. All translations mine.
23. See Natalie Zemon Davis, *Women on the Margins*. Cambridge: Harvard University Press, 1998.
24. Ibid., 80–81.
25. Ibid., 87.
26. Ibid., 86.

The *relation*, therefore, must be interpreted as a kind of intermediary, a document that reports, links and acts as agent. It mediates, as does a priest between God and believer. The *relation* does not exist solely to document an occurrence but, as with a story, requires a scene of reception, an appropriate audience and a change of heart: the very definition of conversion (*conversio*: a turning toward, which recalls both translation and the topographic turn). The story exists in community, a milieu and an audition that it creates textually.

The *Relations* is an epistolary endeavor in which stories shape souls: those of the Native Americans, those of the Europeans, and the souls of the writers themselves, touched and changed by their new experiences and encounters. These stories are textual topographies. They both describe the geography in which the Jesuits have arrived, and with which they struggle to find similarities, knowable qualities, with their prior experience, as well as seek to surpass terrestrial bounds to point beyond themselves to another land, the "far country" of the Gospel. Space, in and of itself, is not sufficient; it must be invested with story to have meaning. The significance with which story imbues space is, here, ultimately, always spiritual. Christian Jacob cites a scene from Père Dainville's relation of 1634, in which a Jesuit father draws, with a charcoal-tipped stick pulled from the fire, a map of North America. His Indian interlocutors are astonished at the map's accuracy, an abstract rendering of a space that they, physically, have experienced. Image, space and story conjoin. Jacob observes that

> this geography lesson in which the drawing accompanies the speech turns the map into a sequential process and a finished object . . . Following the cosmographical overview of the old world is the chorographic description of the new, in which attention is drawn to the specificity of landscapes. Space is dilated at that same time as the descriptive discourse, and is reorganized as a function of a new symbolic center: the spot where the two interlocutors are located. The Father thus narrates his map as he draws it. The map organizes the dialogic space, it disengages a mode of social communication. It has a rhetorical effectiveness.[27]

27. Christian Jacob, *L'empire des cartes*, trans. Tom Conley, unpublished manuscript, 1.2, p. 9.

Translation in at least one form was already a prominent, sacred practice among the Iroquois. Their own religious figures, shamans, excelled in interpretation of dreams, or oneiric translation.

The Jesuits were astonished by the importance the Woodland Indians assigned to dreams. "The divining of dreams," Father Carheil complained, was "the soul of their religion . . ." When Father Lejeune wintered among the Montagnais Indians in 1634, one of them asked, "What dost thou believe then, if thou dost not believe in thy dream?" Writing from Seneca country five years later, Father Frémin observed that "the Iroquois have, properly speaking, only a single Divinity—the dream. To it they render their submission, and follow all its orders with exactness . . . In the case of the Iroquoians, the community as a whole accepted responsibility for helping the dreamer to unravel—or amplify—the meaning of a 'big' dream, and to fulfill its message . . ."[28] For this reason, the Iroquois were already accustomed to multi-level thinking, and adept at juxtaposing dreamed experience with waking experience, finding connections, picking out common threads, crafting interpretive stories and using symbolic language. Once the Jesuit Fathers began to resort to a literary-cultural symbolic system in order to express Christian theology, they found an adept audience. In addition, as is the case with the interpretive charge involving the entire Native American society, translation creates community, one now weaving together both Jesuits and Native Americans: "Nonetheless, the Fathers had no choice; they had to learn the language on their own, asking some of the Natives the names for certain things, which was really not all that difficult—as long as the things were tangible or visible: a stone, a river, a house; to strike, to jump, to run, to be seated."[29] This community is not without strain, however. The translation process mimes the passage from jabbering infancy through adolescence to a linguistic maturity, a transition in which the Jesuits, cultivated exponents of the New World, find themselves surprisingly in the inferior position, the learners' role:

28. Robert Moss, "Missionaries and Magicians: The Jesuit Encounter with Native American Shamans on New England's Colonial Frontier," *Wonders of the Invisible World: 1600–1900*, The Dublin Seminar for New England Folk-life, Annual proceedings, ed. Peter Benes (Boston: Boston University, 1992): 17–34. Quotation is from page 19.
29. *Relations*, I, viii.

But when it came to interior or spiritual actions . . . absolutely no gesture existed that could convey their meaning, although they tried out more than a hundred thousand. While this was going on, some of the Natives, to amuse themselves, mocked the Jesuits' awkward mimes, finding something amusing in their every attempt to communicate . . . It happened more than once that the Natives duped us rather than correctly inform us, even persuading us to use obscenities when we were innocently trying to preach the Gospel. God only knows who came up with such a sacrilegious scam![30]

The muscularity of the Jesuits' struggle to understand the physical push-and-shove of their prose when they speak of translation issues, demonstrates the very real significance of linguistic interpretation in the conversion process:

The worst of it was, after you wracked your brains, asking and searching—as though you'd finally discovered the key to all existence—you found out, even so, that you'd mistaken the shadow for the real thing, and that your precious find had just evaporated in smoke.[31]

The Jesuits need to find a new stock of images that will be effective not only for their European audience, but also for the Native American hearers. Some of the persistence of the Old World cultural stock of imagery can be seen in the following references to detailed architectural components, something unknown to the Native Americans, and not effective in translating to them, although certainly convincing to a European reader: "These are truly great fruits, the confidence and friendship that the Savages have granted to [us] French . . . For it is always true that it is necessary to establish the foundation and base before erecting a column."[32] Prior to such "simultaneous translation" being possible, the Jesuits themselves have to learn to preach in translation, by marrying the Gospel message to the Indian tongue: "We had begun to compose our

30. Ibid.
31. Ibid.
32. *Relations*, I, xxxiv, 62. " . . . c'est un grand fruict que la confiance et l'amitié que les Sauvages ont prinse avecques les François . . . Car touiours faut-il mettre ceste base avant que d'eslever le chapiteau . . . "

catechism 'in Savage' [in the Savage's language], and really began to have success at jabbering in the tongue of our catechumens."[33] The real point at which the Old World and New World conjoin comes in the text when the images are accessible to the experiences of both sets of interlocutors: a "simultaneous translation."

One of the more effective metaphors selected, one that bridges the translation gap, is the multilayered imagery of fire used by the Jesuits. Fire, a folksy necessity in the lives of the Native Americans, also recalls the Pentecost motif of the tongues of fire that conferred the gift of speaking in tongues on the Apostles, as well as significantly reworking the Petrarchan literary conceit of love represented by alternating states of fire and ice.

> The Christian religion will flourish by God's grace in this region, just as it does in Huron territory . . . grace abounds nonetheless, where sin has prevailed for a long time; cruelty has changed into kindness, and wolves into lambs . . . We can see small sparks, they have not surrendered quickly . . . our impatience would have hoped that ice would catch fire, like gunpowder.[34]

Such metaphors not only rework European expectations; they also metamorphose the unknown into the known: "He who can change wolves into lambs has changed a barbarian into a child of God."[35] The literary and linguistic translation expresses the theological transformation, as well.

One reason for the success of the image and metaphor strategy on the Jesuits' part was the faith that Native Americans placed in concrete

---

33. *Relations*, I, xxxiv, 63. "Nous avions composé nostre catechisme en Sauvage et commencions aucunement à pouvoir jargonner avec nos catechumens."

34. *Relations*, I, xxxiv, 93. "La Religion Chrestienne, moyennant la grace de Dieu, florira en ce pais cy, comme elle fait en celuy-là, notamment aux Hurons . . . la grace abonde neantmoins, ou le péché a regné fort longtemps; la cruauté s'est changée en douceur, et les loups en des agneaux . . . On voit de petites estincelles, on voudroit desia se chauffer à un grand brasier . . . Ils ne se sont pas rendus si tost; et nostre promptitude voudroit que la glace prist feu, comme la poudre à canon."

35. *Relations*, I, xxxiv, 93. "Celuy qui peut changer les loups en agneaux, a changé un barbare en enfant de Dieu."

images, and the credence they granted to image-studded stories. In 1637, Père Paul Le Jeune, in the last letter he ever wrote, recorded the extraordinary solicitude and veneration accorded to an image of Jesus by a recent Native American convert. The transformation from a former cannibal to one who gently envelops a sacred image in a soft cloth so that it shall not be scratched is striking.

> At that point, I pull out a beautiful painting of Our Lord Jesus Christ, I uncover it and display it to their eyes, then I begin to speak and tell them that we were not the masters of life and death, but He whose image they see here was . . . I give this beautiful painting to . . . our newest convert . . . our new Christian immediately took the portrait, and began to preach. It's been a long time since I've been so moved by such preaching . . . Finally, our good Christian displayed the little picture and counselled his fellows to no longer eat human flesh, and to now sing praises of our great God. Having said this, he gives me the painting, begging me to wrap it carefully so that it will not be damaged.[36]

An unexpected outcome of the Native American's already highly developed interpretive skills was a form of boomerang effect, wherein the Jesuits' preaching rebounded back on them, compelling them to "walk their own talk," to take responsibility for their teachings. Here, their rhetoric works in reverse, on the Jesuits, rather than on its intended, Native American, audience. One of the Fathers, Père Biard, expresses a certain reluctance to undertake a lengthy and dangerous trek through the snows to a distant Indian village where some of his converts reside. He is persuaded, however—or, rather, shamed into it:

36. *Relations*, I, xxxv, 99–100. "Là dessus, ie tire un beau tableau de nostre Seigneur Jesus Christ, ie le descouvre et Ie place devant leurs yeux, puis prenant la parole, ie leur dis que nous n'estions point les maistres de la vie et de la mort, que celuy dont ils voient l'image estoit . . . ie donnerois ce beau portrait à nostre Neophyte . . . là dessus nostre nouveau Chrestien prit le Tableau et se mit a prescher. Il y a long temps qu'aucune predication ne m'a tant touché . . . En fin nostre bon Chrestien desploiant le petit Tableau . . . [leur dit de ne plus] manger de la chair humaine, et maintenant, [de] presche[r] les louanges du grand Dieu. Cela dit, il me presente Ie Tableau, me priant de le bien enveloppez afin qu'il ne se gastast point."

For, said the [Natives], you have to come back, because Asticou our Chief is sick unto death, and if you do not come, he will die without having been baptized, and will not go to Heaven; you will be to blame, because, as for him, he earnestly desires to be baptized.

This reasoning expressed so simply astounded the Father, and utterly persuaded him to go there.[37]

Finally, the Jesuits' rhetoric is transformed and enriched by the semiotics of Native American speech and their persistent search for signs in the natural world. The Jesuits, too, begin to divine God's will in a way very similar to that of their proposed converts, finding a new book to read in the heavens, the arrangement of the stars, and the fortuitous arrangement of events.[38] Thus, as they translate, they are also translated to a new, non-European mode of being and perceiving, perhaps a demonstration of cultural relativism.[39] Tolerance for other cultures—what happens when real translation takes place—is actually something that the Native Americans must teach to the Jesuits who, in this, are their pupils:

Those who were from Ihonatima said: At any rate, we have our ways of doing things, just as other nations have theirs; when you tell us to obey as master he who you claim made the heavens and earth, it seems to us that you are speaking about toppling the normal order of things here . . . Your ancestors got together and decided who to

37. *Relations*, I, xvi, 45. "Car, dirent-ils, il faut que tu viennes, d'autant qu'Asticou nostre Sagamo est malade a la mort; et si tu ne viens, il mourra sans Baptesme, et n'ira pas au Ciel: tu en seras la cause, car pour luy il voudroit estre baptise. Ceste raison ainsi naifvement deduite, fit estonner le Père Biard, et luy persuada totalement de s'y en aller."

38. *Relations*, I, xxiv ("A quelle occasion nous nous arrestamses à S. Sauveur"), 45. " . . . tous unanimement consentirent qu'il falloit rester là, et ne pas chercher mieux, veu meme que Dieu sembloit le dire par les heureux rencontres qui nous estoient arrivez."

39. Their endeavor does, however, show a similarity with Montaigne's earlier "*Des Cannibales*" in the *Essais*. His concluding comment—"Mais quoy! ils ne portent poinct de hauts-de-chausses!"—is designed to show that value does not reside in externals, yet the condescending European mind continues to try to assign merit in such a superficial way.

worship; we learned differently from our fathers . . . The Jesuits, hearing this, rebuked them that they erred utterly in their beliefs, and that there was no choice . . . all nations must believe in the same way.[40]

The *Relations* frequently take up the question of the urge to penetrate into how an alien culture thinks. In the following anecdote, two vocabularies spar. Finally, the Jesuit use of language prevails, and the Indian woman converts. But she makes the Jesuit fathers really sweat over how to communicate with her. Translation has high stakes in these letters: the loss or gain of a soul. While the tendentious theological system of the Jesuits makes it impossible for them to allow cultural relativism, to some extent some appreciation of the other's mentality is absolutely essential to establishing the grounds of communication.

> On the 21st, we baptized a woman who caught us up on two points . . . she pulled me up short while I was exhorting her to confess her sins . . . answering that she could not do so, since she did not know what "sin" meant . . . [and] that she equally could not define "lasciviousness" . . . I told her that, if such was the case, then I could not baptize her, and that even if I were to do so, baptism would be of no help to her . . . as long as she continued to speak in such a language to me finally, God's mercy moved her; she confessed her sins to us and said she would sin no more; we baptized her.[41]

40. *Relations*, I, xxxvi, 137. "Ceux d'Ihonatina disoient: . . . Au reste nous avons nos façons de faire et vous les vostres, aussi bien que les autres nations, quand vous nous parlez d'obeir et de recognoistre pour maistre celuy que vous dites avoir fait le Ciel et la terre, ie m'imagine que vous parlez de renverser le pays. Vos ancestres . . . ont resolu de prendre pour leur Dieu celuy que vous honorez, et ont ordonné toutes les cérémonies que vous gardez; pour nous, nous en avons appris d'autres de nos Pères . . . Le Père luy respondit qu'il se trompoit tout a fait en son opinion; que ce n'estoit par election que nous avons pris Dieu pour nostre Dieu . . . que toutes les nations devoient avoir les mesmes sentimens . . ."
41. *Relations*, I, xxxvii, 143. "Le 21 nous baptisames une femme, qui nous arresta sur 2 poincts . . . elle m'arresta encore et comme ie l'exhortois à estre marrie d'avoir offense Dieu et luy disois que sans cela ses pechez ne luy seroient point pardonnez, elle me respondit qu'elle ne pouvoit, qu'elle n'avoit point offense Dieu, et qu'elle ne sçavoit ce que c'estoit que du libertinage . . . ie luy representai que cela estant, ie ne pouvois pas la baptiser, et quand mesme le baptesme luy serviroit de rien . . . tandis qu'elle me tiendroit ce langage . . . en fin il pleust à

Perhaps the most moving aspect of the letters, already highly readable, is the way in which the budding relationship between the Jesuits and their Native American converts is described. The Jesuits struggle to forge a language adequate to communicating spiritual concepts:

> He went among the Natives asking questions about the meanings of some of their words that might correspond to those both of our language and of our religion. So that this task could more effectively be accomplished, he left with [one of the Frenchmen] a lengthy and detailed explanation of the principal credos of our holy faith.[42]

They attempt to understand and value an alien culture while nonetheless insistently preaching the Christian salvation message. Sometimes the Jesuits even view the Native Americans more favourably than they do their European counterparts: "They never hurry, which is really unlike us, who never know how to do anything without making haste and sighing a good deal about it, for our desires tyrannize us, and banish peace from our actions."[43] These are vital and dynamic texts, narratives studded with personal witness, anecdotes, descriptions of—and attempts to make sense of—alternate lifestyles and belief-systems.

Story-telling functions in the *Relations* not just as a rhetoric of persuasion, but also in a deeply *ritualistic* sense: to speak is to know, to *in-corpor-ate*, to take on the body and life of another, to hear another's soul speaking. A phenomenon occurs in which understanding, or the ability to enter into relationship with another, transfers from Jesuit to Jesuit or from Jesuit to European reader, to a new configuration, that of Jesuit empathizing with Native American, or of Native American expressing acceptance of European otherness. "The nature of our Natives is flexible, free, not at all malicious . . . They have a very good memory for physical things, such as having seen you . . . [but] there is no way to get them to retain a speech or a lot of words . . . They've

---

la misericorde de Dieu luy toucher le coeur; elle nous advoua qu' elle avoit peché . . . et ne pescheroit plus; nous la baptisames."

42. *Relations*, I, xviii.

43. Ibid., iv. "Ils n'ont jamais haste, bien divers de nous, qui ne suaurions iamais rien faire sans presse et oppresse dis-ie, parce que nostre desir nous tyrannize, et bannit la paix de nos actions."

often told us that we really seemed ugly to them at the beginning but little by little they got used to us, and we began no longer to seem quite so misshapen to them."[44]

Thus, in the *Relations*, storytelling gradually shapes a *spiritual topography*. A textual typology forms a spiritual structuring conceit for the collection. This typology has three components: space, story and spirit or, read theologically, God the creator, Jesus—the incarnation or the insertion of the Godhead into history; and the Holy Spirit—the indwelling force that provides the language for spiritual speech. This is a *Trinitarian* textual typology.

God comes first, as the Jesuits describe the new place they have come to, and try to extend logically, through comparison, metaphor, analogy and simile, France's topography onto and into that new, as yet unknown, space: ". . . these lands being, as we've said, parallel to our France . . . we should be able to expect them to have the same influences, variations in weather and temperatures . . . as in France."[45]

Christ comes next. As stories are told, relationships are constructed. Christ's appearance in human form mandates consideration of the incarnational aspect of all humanity as sons of God. An example is the Jesuits' account of the exemplary death of the powerful sachem Membertou, who had converted to Christianity. Not only do they praise and glorify him for his Christian witness, they also go so far as to cite his own words within the body of their own narrative—a linguistic incorporation that feasts, verbally, on a sort of textual eucharist of the believing convert's body: "He died a very strong Christian . . . Often he would say to them [before his death]: Learn quick our language, because when you learned it, you will teach me [your things] and taught I will become

---

44. *Relations*, I, iv. "Le naturel de nos Sauvages est de soy liberal et point malicieux . . . Ils ont fort bonne memoire de choses corpore lies, comme de vous avoir veu . . . il n'y a pas moyen de mettre dans leur tête une tirade de paroles . . . Souvent ils m'ont dit que nous leur semblions du commencement fort laids . . . mais peu à peu ils s'accoustument, et nous commençons à ne leur paroistre si difforme."

45. Ibid., ii. "Ces terres estant, comme nous avons diet, paralleles à nostre France . . . elles doivent avoir mesmes influences, inclinations et températures . . . "

preacher like you, we'll convert all the country."[46] The verbatim quote of Membertou's English dignifies his last words, and demonstrates the Jesuits' acceptance of him. His body and speech are written into their story about him, as the living bodies of other converts will be gathered into the harvest by his example.

The christological aspect of the relations finds expression in the Jesuits' reliance on the parables as the primary textual prototype for the narratives that they recount to the Natives. They frequently have recourse to Scripture in order to justify their endeavors, and the dense, multilayered parabolic narrative seems to them to work well for Native Americans accustomed to the interpretation of dreams. Their parabolic narratives almost always begin with a general "*on*" or "*quelqu'un*"; this address then develops into a dialogue between "*vous*" and the Jesuits' perspective, "*je*." The "*je*" marks the conversion moment, the point at which translation works: the Jesuits' "I" has the last word in the story. In addition, this narrative itself effects the geographical translation discussed elsewhere in this essay by speaking of Canada and France.

> Now, someone having heard all of our preaching will justifiably say: Look here! You've told us about a lot of undertakings and incentives . . . but is this all that you have to show for your labors? Have you succeeded so minimally in advancing God's kingdom on earth? . . . Hear the words of the Apostle: Whoever labors, it is in hope of bearing fruit. What fruit therefore do you now bring? To this I answer that everywhere, in France as in Canada, you have to sow before you can reap, and plant before the harvest, and neither be greedy nor impatient like the usurers, who expect interest at the same time as profit.[47]

46. *Relations*, I, xvi ("Un voyage faict à la rivière de S. Croix"), 33. "Souvent il leur disoit: Apprenés tost nostre langage: car quand vous l'aurés apprins, vous m'enseignerez, et moi enseigné deviendray prescheur comme vous autres, nous convertirons tout le pays."

47. *Relations*, I, xxxiv ("Quel profit a esté faict"), 61. "Maintenant quelqu'un ayant ouy tout nostre recit à bon droict nous dira: Or sus, voilà beaucoup de travaux que vous nous avez contés, plusieurs entreprinses . . . mais quoy? Est-ce là tout le profit quant à l'avancement du culte de Dieu? . . . Ainsi, a tres bien dit le S. Apostre: Que qui laboure, c'est en esperance de recueillir du fruict. Quel fruict donques apportez-vous de vos travaux? . . . A cela ie responds que partout, et aussi bien en France qu'en Canada, il faut semer avant que moysonner, et

In effect, this narrative is a *mise en abyme* of the process and achievements of cultural and theological translation.

Finally, the Holy Spirit resumes all those concerns of the text that are directed to fashioning a new sort of speech capable of touching the hearts of listeners, but able also to bear the freight of profound, multi-faceted theological concepts. In seventeenth-century English, the Holy Spirit is termed the *umpire*, that entity that mediates disputes and settles differences. Seventeenth-century French gives *relayeur* as a name for the Holy Spirit: one who creates relationships. These relationships are constructed through linguistic phenomena, a sort of spiritual semiotics. Significantly in this regard, the Jesuit Fathers often refuse to baptize the Native Americans until they are convinced that their pedagogy has been understood—this despite much criticism from Europe, who wanted to see numerical evidence of a successful mission. "How, then, could you possibly want them to maintain themselves in the faith and grace of God, if they have not first been well instructed, even twice more than others need to be? For we, who live in the ranks of the religious and under the care of so many pastors, are hardly able to do so, even though we are, so to speak naturalized Christians. How then should they prevail, newborns that they are, alone, without protection, unable to read, without institutions, without our customs? That's like saying it's good enough to have a child, without ever giving a thought to how that child will be reared and nourished and protected."[48] *Relation*—as relationship—requires a *relayeur* or translator, and translation is at the heart of the Jesuits' endeavor.

Translation in the *Relations* fulfils the role of, and may be symbolized by, the Holy Spirit, who not only opens his understanding, but also indwells and changes hearts. Not only the Native Americans are

---

planter avant que recueillir, et ne point tant estre ou avare ou impatient, qu'on veuille comme les usuriers, aussi-tost le profit que le prest."

48. *Relations*, I, x. "Comment est-ce donc que vous voulez qu'ils se puissent entretenir en la foy et grace de Dieu, s'ils ne sont bien instruits, et au double des autres? Car nous, qui vivons entre les troupes des Religieux et sous la garde de tant de Pasteurs . . . et à peine le pouvons-nous, qui sommes . . . pour le dire ainsi, naturalisés Chrestiens: comment le pourront-ils faire tout nouveaux qu'ils sont, seuls, sans garde, sans lettres, sans institution, sans coustume? Or de dire que c'est asses d'engendrer, sans penser comment on donnera l'entretien . . . "

changed—converted—by this encounter; the Jesuits, too, are challenged and transformed by their need to translate. They can no longer proceed hierarchically or exclusively didactically, but must now become one people of faith with those from whom they must first learn, like infants, to speak before they may proselytize.[49]

The cathedral of ice with which this essay opens freezes in time the moment of translation epiphany in which two alien cultures are able, however paradoxically, to communicate. It offers a model for theological translation, as the Jesuit Fathers import to the new world their cultural stock of imagery—cathedrals, castles, palaces—but begin to perceive them, through the eyes of their Native American converts, as natural phenomena. Yet they do not devalue or distrust this new perspective, but rather move through it, imbuing it with their own theological message. This is theological translation at its best.[50]

49. "Les *Relations* développent un recit dans une atmosphère vierge de toute interference, où les hommes, causes secondaires et instrumentales, ne sont que des outils dans les mains de la Providence." Lemire, *La vie littéraire*, 72. This essay takes up the issue of translation as a significant tool in proselytizing. It must be admitted that, if we know that text which has been transmitted to us, and we realize that to some extent the voice of the Native has been rendered and through that lens, nonetheless we do not always know what the "text of departure" was: what words were first spoken? heard? Yet, realizing that the animating force for the project of evangelizing comes from God, we may construe that original and primary text to be biblical. The word that the Jesuit Fathers impart, and that which the Natives eventually comprehend, devolves from the inspirational source of Scripture, God as author, ultimate translator and *relayeur*.

50. I want to recognize in this essay a modern-day Jesuit who does a wonderful job of translating the best of the Jesuit tradition to his colleagues, and providing inspiration for many of us, at Fordham University, Father Joseph McShane, S.J., President of Fordham University.

BIBLIOGRAPHY

For more reading on the Jesuits and the Jesuit Relations
Chapple, Christopher, ed. *The Jesuit Tradition in Education and Missions: A 450-Year Perspective*. Scranton, Penn.: University of Scranton Press, 1993.
McCoy, J. C. *Jesuit Relations* of Canada, 1632–1673. Paris: Rau, 1937.

For further information on individual Jesuits of the era
Feest, Christian. "Father Lafitau as Ethnographer of the Iroquois." *European Review of American Studies*, 15 (1001): 19–25.
Latourelle, René. *Etude sur les écrits de Saint Jean de Brébeuf*. 2 vols. Montréal: Les éditions de l'Immaculée-Conception, 1952.
Ouellet, Réal, ed. *Rhétorique et conquête missionaire: le Jésuite Paul Le Jeune*. Sillery: Septentrion, 1993.
Perron, Jean. "Isaac Jogues: From Martyrdom to Sainthood," in *Colonial Saints: Discovering the Holy in Americas, 1500–1800*. eds. Allan Greer and Jodi Bilinkoff. New York: Routledge, 2003.

For more reading on Ursulines or other Frenchwomen involved in the mission
Davis, Natalie Zemon. *Women on the Margins: Three Seventeenth-Century Lives*. Cambridge, Mass.: Harvard University Press, 1995.
Incarnation, Marie de l'. *Ecrits spirituels et historiques*. 4 vols. Paris: Desclée de Brouwer, 1929–1939, rpt. 1985.

Mères Ignace et Ste-Hélène. *Histoire de l'Hôtel-Dieu de Québec.* Montauban: Jérosme Legier, 1751.

Marshall, Joyce, ed. and trans. *Word from New France: The Selected Letters of Marie de l'Incarnation.* New York: Oxford University Press, 1967.

Oury, Dom Guy, ed. *Marie de l'Incarnation, Ursuline (1599–1672): Correspondance.* Solesmes: Abbaye Saint-Pierre, 1971.

Rapley, Elizabeth. *The Dévotes: Women and Church in Seventeenth-Century France.* Montréal: McGill–Queen's University Press, 1990.

For reading on Native American women of the era

Anderson, Karen. *Chain Her by One Foot: The Subjugation of Women in Seventeenth-Century New France.* London: Routledge, 1991.

Clermont, Normand. "Catherine Tekakwitha: 1656–1680." *Culture,* 7 (1987): 47–53.

Deroy-Pineau, Françoise. *Marie de l'Incarnation: Marie Guyart, femme d'affaires, mystique, mère de la Nouvelle-France, 1599–1672.* Paris: Editions Robert Laffont, 1989.

Greer, Allan. *Mohawk Saint: Catherine Tekakwitha and the Jesuits.* New York: Oxford University Press, 2005.

Holmes, Paula E. "The Narrative Repatriation of Blessed Kateri Tekakwitha." *Anthropologica,* 43 (2001): 87–101.

Niethammer, Carolyn. *Daughters of the Earth: The Lives and Legends of American Indian Women.* New York: Macmillan, 1977.

For more reading on Native American ethnography and interaction with Jesuits

Blackburn, Carole. *Harvest of Souls: The Jesuit Missions and Colonialism in North America, 1632–1650.* Montréal: McGill–Queen's University Press, 2000.

Campeau, Lucien. *La Mission des Jésuites chez les Hurons, 1634–1650.* Montréal: Bellarmin, 1987.

Dorsey, Peter. "Going to School with Savages: Authorship and Authority among the Jesuits of New France." *William and Mary Quarterly,* 3rd Series, 55 (1998): 399–420.

Galloway, Colin G. *The World Turned Upside Down: Indian Voices from Early America.* The Bedford Series in History and Culture, 2003.

Greer, Allan. *The Jesuit Relations*: Natives and Missionaries in Seventeenth-Century North America. The Bedford Series in History and Culture, 2000.

Jaene, Cornelius. *Friend and Foe: Aspects of French-American Cultural Contact in the Sixteenth and Seventeenth Centuries*. 1976.

Lafrenière, Denis. "L'Eloge de l'Indien dans les *Relations* des Jésuites." *Canadian Literature*, no. 131 (winter 1991): 26–35.

Mali, Anya. "Strange Encounters: Missionary Activity and Mystical Thought in Seventeenth Century New France." *History of European Ideas*, 22 (1996): 67–92.

Moore, James T. *Indian and Jesuit: A Seventeenth-Century Encounter*. Chicago: Loyola University Press, 1982.

Morrison, R. Bruce, and C. Roderick Wilson, eds. *Native Peoples: The Canadian Experience*. Toronto: McClelland and Stewart, 1986.

Pagden, Anthony. *European Encounters with the New World*. New Haven, Conn.: Yale University Press, 1993.

Parkman, Francis. *France and England in North America*. 2 vols. New York: Library of America, 1983.

Richter, Daniel. *Facing East from Indian Country: A Native History of Early America*. Cambridge, Mass.: Harvard University Press, 2001.

———. "Iroquois versus Iroquois: Jesuit Mission and Christianity in Village Politics, 1642–1686." *Ethnohistory*, 32 (1985): 1–16.

Seeman, Erik R. "Reading Indians, Deathbed Scenes: Ethnohistorical and Representational Approaches." *Journal of American History*, 88 (2001): 17–47.

Taylor, Monique. "'This Our Dwelling': The Landscape Experience of the Jesuit Mission to the Huron." *Journal of Canadian Studies*, 33 (1998): 85–96.

Thwaites, Reuben Gold, and Edna Kenton, eds. *The Jesuit Relations* and Allied Documents: Travels and Explorations oif the Jesuit Missionaries in North America 1610–1791. New York: Boni, 1925.

For analysis of the Jesuit Relations

Dainville, François. "L'évolution de l'enseignement de la rhétorique au dix-septième siècle," in *L'éducation des Jésuites xviie-xviiie siècles*. Paris: Minuit, 1978.

Doiron, Normand. "Rhétorique jésuite de l'éloquence sauvage du xviie siècle au xviiie siècle: Les *Relations* de Paul Le Jeune (1632–1642)." *Dix-septième siècle*, 43 (1991): 375–402.

Laflèche, Guy. "Les *Relations* des Jésuites de la Nouvelle-France, un document anthropologique majeur de l'Amérique français du xviie siècle." *Recherches Amérinidennes au Québec*, 29, no. 2 (1999): 77–87.

———. "L'analyse littéraire des *Relations* des Jésuites." *Recherches Amérindiennes au Québec*, 30 (2000), no. 1, 103–8; no. 2, 89–93; no. 3, 101–9.

Randall, Catharine. "Cathedrals of Ice: Translating the Jesuit Vocabulary of Conversion" in Special issue on Spirituality, Faith, Belief/Spiritualité, foi et croyance. *International Journal of Canadian Studies*, 23 (2001): 17–37.

For further reading on Ignatian spirituality

Loyola, Ignatius of. *The Spiritual Exercises*, trans. A. Mottola. New York: Doubleday, 1964.

Melloni, Javier. *The Exercises* of St. Ignatius of Loyola in the Western Tradition. Leonminster: Gracewing, 2000.

O'Malley, John. *The First Jesuits*. Cambridge, Mass.: Harvard University Press, 1993.

Wright, Jonathan. *God's Soldiers: Adventure, Politics, Intrigue and Power—A History of the Jesuits*. New York: Doubleday, 2004.